ON
THE
FRONT LINE
OF
LIFE

ON THE FRONT LINE OF LIFE

Stephen Leacock: Memories and Reflections, 1935 – 1944

Selected, Edited, and Introduced
by Alan Bowker

THE DUNDURN GROUP
TORONTO

Copy-Editor: Jennifer Bergeron
Design: Andrew Roberts
Printer: AGMV Marquis

Library and Archives Canada Cataloguing in Publication

Leacock, Stephen, 1869-1944.
    On the front line of life : Stephen Leacock : memories and reflections, 1935 – 1944 /
    Stephen Leacock ; selected, edited and introduced by Alan Bowker.

Includes bibliographical references.
ISBN 1-55002-521-X

    I. Bowker, Alan, 1943- II. Title.

PS8523.E15A16 2004   C814'.52   C2004-905472-4

1   2   3   4   5   08   07   06   05   04

Conseil des Arts du Canada   **Canada Council for the Arts**   Canada   ONTARIO ARTS COUNCIL CONSEIL DES ARTS DE L'ONTARIO

We acknowledge the support of the **Canada Council for the Arts** and the **Ontario Arts Council** for our publishing program. We also acknowledge the financial support of the **Government of Canada** through the **Book Publishing Industry Development Program** and **The Association for the Export of Canadian Books**, and the **Government of Ontario** through the **Ontario Book Publishers Tax Credit** program, and the **Ontario Media Development Corporation's Ontario Book Initiative**.

Care has been taken to trace the ownership of copyright material used in this book. The author and the publisher welcome any information enabling them to rectify any references or credits in subsequent editions.

J. Kirk Howard, President

Printed and bound in Canada
Printed on recycled paper

www.dundurn.com

Dundurn Press
8 Market Street
Suite 200
Toronto, Ontario, Canada
M5E 1M6

Gazelle Book Services Limited
White Cross Mills
Hightown, Lancaster, England
LA1 4X5

Dundurn Press
2250 Military Road
Tonawanda, NY
U.S.A. 14150

ON THE FRONT LINE OF LIFE

TABLE OF CONTENTS

Preface   9
Introduction   13
Chronology   43

Leacock's Essays

1. Life on the Old Farm (1944)   47
2. My Remarkable Uncle (1941)   75
3. The Struggle to Make Us Gentlemen (1941)   83
4. My Education and What I Think of It Now (1944)   89
5. Looking Back on College (1936)   97
6. On the Need for a Quiet College (1938)   101
7. Andrew Macphail (1938)   107
8. How Much Does Language Change? (1938)   113
9. From the Ridiculous to the Sublime (1935)   123
10. What Is Left of Adam Smith? (1935)   129
11. Through a Glass Darkly (1936)   143
12. So This Is Winnipeg (1937)   153
13. The Land of Dreams (1937)   165
14. I'll Stay in Canada (1936)   175
15. This International Stuff (1936)   181
16. Canada and the Monarchy (1939)   185
17. Bonds of Union (1940)   201
18. Paradise Lost (1936)   209
19. Looking Back from Retirement (1937)   213
20. Bass Fishing on Lake Simcoe with Jake Gaudaur (1939)   219
21. Common Sense and the Universe (1942)   229
22. Three Score and Ten (1940)   243
23. War-Time Santa Claus (1942)   249
24. To Every Child (1944)   253

Endnotes   255
Bibliographical Information   263

PREFACE

Stephen Leacock Jr. sat on the edge of his bed and began to read from his father's essay. It was the winter of 1970. As a graduate student I had been trying for some time to meet him. At last I got the opportunity through the courtesy of the family who had taken him in as he tried to regain his health and reclaim his life. I do not remember their names, but they were immensely kind and I would have liked to know them better. The place was Ardtrea, Ontario, on Lake Couchiching. Stephen Jr. was dressed in pyjamas and a dressing gown, recovering but fragile — in fact he died of a heart attack only a few years later. As a research exercise it was a disappointment. He was guarded and told me little I did not already know. The only piece of information I can recall after all these years was how devastated he had felt when he had asked his father what happened to people when they die, and his father had answered that nothing happens, they just cease to exist.

Then Stephen Jr. insisted on reading a passage of his father's work, one that obviously held deep meaning for him, perhaps in his own attempt to come to grips with the Leacock legacy. It was part of a lecture entitled "How Soon Can We Start the Next War," which Stephen Jr. had probably heard his father deliver many times when he accompanied him on a tour of Western Canada in 1936–7. Suddenly it seemed as though the son were conjuring from the past the voice and manner of Stephen Leacock as he warned isolationist North Americans about what another European war would mean:

> Do not think that we can escape it here. Do not think that we can shelter ourselves behind the ocean and look upon this wreckage as destined only to blot the continent of Europe and never to matter to America. If it comes it will spread like a plague, driving across the continents with all the evil winds of disaster behind it.

We are as much interested as they. "*Hodie mihi, cras tibi*," so wrote the medieval monks on the stone coffins of their dead. "Mine today, yours tomorrow." "Your fate will be mine and your salvation shall be mine."

So we must plead unceasingly for an earnest sympathy with Europe, wiping out all the angers of the past, wiping out all the questions of whose are the honour and whose the guilt of the late war, remembering not the brutality, but only the bright pages of the heroism, the golden pages that open in either direction, pages that open as well for our so-called enemies as for ourselves. [...]

I tell you this: if the world is to be saved, that is the path of salvation in Europe. They may take it; they may not. The sky is heavy with a lurid light threatening to break from the clouds. There is the cool fresh air blowing above. Which can conquer? We don't know. You and I and all of us if we live a few years will know of wonderful happenings in the world, for the path has got to be made straight or the path will lead over the abyss. The problem cannot wait. It has grown too acute. The world has no time for bungling, or muddling through. That was good enough for the older civilization, but not for us now.[1]

I had read all of Leacock's books, some many times. Why had this passage never caught my eye? Because it is buried in a lecture that contains mostly foolish stuff, warmed-over satire about European diplomacy, jokes, and funny stories — a lecture Leacock had used to entertain dozens of audiences and thousands of people. But now I could imagine the electric effect of this funnyman suddenly turning serious and delivering this heartfelt message.

A quarter-century later the memory of that evening at Ardtrea came back to me when I was asked to add a postscript to my introduction to Stephen Leacock's *Social Criticism*, which was being republished after twenty-two years. I had been long away from academe, pursuing another career. Now I found that new research and the passage of time had altered opinions about Leacock and his work. Some of what had once been thought funny and topical was now considered dated, as were many of his ideas and opinions. But as I took a fresh look at his essays written in the 1930s and 1940s, I saw again what Stephen Jr. had shown me: there was a great deal of fine writing here that deserved to be presented to modern readers.

Scholars had found much of Leacock's late work repetitive and of poor quality. They had attributed this to writing too quickly, for money. But this was only partly true. Leacock wrote "funny pieces" for money, but he was also very generous with his pen when he thought the cause worthy or the subject interesting. Sometimes Leacock seemed obsessed with the idea that he was writing against time in response to an urgent public need for what he had to say. He would have been puzzled by criticism of his self-plagiarism (whatever that means). He was a public figure whose views were frequently sought, and there was a steady demand for his humour. He gave the same lectures time after time, and no one complained about that. Why should he not rework good material when it was likely that his readers would not have previously encountered it? Surely what was important was that the material was good in the first place.

The 1930s marked a turning point in Leacock's life. In the 1920s he had settled into a comfortable career as humorist and campus "character." The Great Depression rekindled the passion for public controversy that had animated him before 1920. He believed that as a professor he had a responsibility to address the economic collapse that had occurred and the social catastrophe that threatened. He wanted his countrymen to know more about themselves, their history, and their heritage, and to have more faith in their future. His attempts to blend this new public role with his humour, his lecturing, and his popular writing proved unsuccessful. Instead, he gradually developed a new informal essay voice to address a wide audience and to confront the challenges of his own life with increasing frankness. The later Leacock you will encounter in this book is writing in a different way than he did in the essays in my earlier collection. He has many of the same ideas (though he has changed his mind on some things), but we are much more aware that beneath the brilliance and the wit there is a person — intelligent, committed, but increasingly vulnerable — talking to us as one human being to another.

The essays are representative of many more that could have been chosen. I have tried to encompass his main interests and have avoided taking too many from any one book. Where essays were published in book form, that is usually the version I have used (see page 263 for bibliographical information). I have edited lightly, correcting some obvious misprints, standardizing spelling, punctuation, and format but ignoring issues such as whether numbers are written out in some essays and numerals are used in others. Where elisions are mine they are marked thus […]; any other use of dots in punctuation is Leacock's. My introduction attempts to frame the essays within the history of the time as well as Leacock's life and thought. Beyond this, I have added explanatory footnotes only to provide information not familiar to today's readers that Leacock would have expected his readers to know. The book is aimed at the general reader, and if the essays stimulate readers to explore in more depth some of the people and ideas discussed, that will fulfill my purpose, and Leacock's.

For me this book is a gesture of atonement for writing off, as I did in 1973, the later Leacock as an irrelevant funnyman. It would have been impossible without the wise counsel of David Staines, the advice of His Honour James Bartleman, the assistance of Agathe Blier, and the confidence of Barry Jowett and the staff of Dundurn Press. I am grateful for the kindness of archivists and librarians, including the staff of the National Archives of Canada, the McGill University Library Rare Books and Special Collections Department, the McGill University Archives, and the Department of Culture and Heritage, Leacock Museum, Orillia (whose permission to use material in the Leacock collection is hereby acknowledged). Above all the patient help and encouragement of my wife, Carolyn, over the many years it has taken for this labour of love to evolve from dream to fruition.

INTRODUCTION

The Roaring Twenties gave way to the new and uncertain decade of the 1930s two days after Stephen Leacock's sixtieth birthday. Well might a man at such an age, and at such a time, see darker clouds on the horizon of his future than there had been in his past. Until 1925 he had been the most popular humorist in the English language. His lectures in the late 1920s were earning him $350 per appearance in the United States.[2] On his estate at Old Brewery Bay he spent the long summer days gardening, fishing, boating, and entertaining, but always writing in the early mornings while his guests were still asleep. Year after golden year this eccentric economics professor was a familiar figure on the McGill University campus, with his loose-fitting clothes, tattered gown, and coonskin coat, banging his heavy cane and filling the halls with his rich voice, holding court in the afternoons at the University Club — a popular teacher, a world-famous writer, commentator, and lecturer, a friend of influential people in Montreal and beyond.

But the dark clouds were gathering nonetheless, clearly and unmistakably. Leacock's wife had died in 1925. His son was beginning to experience the problems of being small in stature and the son of a famous, busy man. It had been years since Leacock had produced any scholarly work that could be called original, and his humour was becoming forced and stale. But it was characteristic of Leacock that his biggest concern was the economic collapse in the fall of 1929 that was beginning to deepen into the Great Depression. He could not have foreseen that by 1932 one in four Canadians would be out of work, that the GNP would fall by one-third in constant dollars by 1933, and that industrial activity would fall to 57 percent of the average figure for the boom years of the previous decade.[3] He would have been horrified if he had known then that the Depression would last a decade and would finally lift only with a second world war. But as an economist he was already profoundly shaken.

Leacock had never been a man much given to introspection. His response to challenge was hard work, to the point that the president of McGill, Sir Arthur Currie, scolded him for applying so little of the discipline of his work to looking after his own health.[4] If humour was running dry he would write popular biography, literary criticism, history, economics, books about humour, and even poetry. Nonetheless, by 1936 the crisis in his personal and professional life was coming to a head. His humorous collections in the early 1930s were the worst of his career. His income had been sharply reduced. His mother, who had been the pillar of his life, died in 1934. He was devastated by his forced retirement from McGill in 1936, and reacted with a bitterness that embarrassed even some of his friends.

Yet he still had many things going for him. His public audience was the largest of any Canadian popular writer of his day. He was a constant presence in leading newspapers and popular journals, with interviews, articles, and stories about him.[5] In 1936–7 he made a triumphal tour of the Canadian West "in a blaze of front-page publicity and broadcasts over every province," and the resulting book won the Governor General's Award for Non-Fiction.[6] Leacock's expertise and literary reputation opened lucrative opportunities for sponsored writing on subjects like banking, nickel, gold, asbestos, and oil. It was natural for Seagram's to ask him in 1941 to write *Canada: The Foundations of Its Future* — a book that was panned by historians but became one of the great publishing successes in Canadian history, with 165,000 free copies distributed by 1967.[7]

With this platform to work from, Leacock began creating a new public persona, that of sage, blending his humour with broad learning and ripened wisdom. By the time he retired from the lecture platform in 1937 he had refined a new essay style to address important subjects like humour, education, history, language, economics, world affairs, and life itself in an interesting way. These essays began to appear about 1936 in upscale popular magazines and were scattered through his annual collections and within longer works. This new essay style became the most effective "voice" of his later years.

Leacock had shown throughout his career an ability to use a variety of "voices."[8] Before fame came to him as a humorist in 1910, he had made a reputation as a scholar with the clear, straightforward prose of his 1906 textbook *Elements of Political Science* and his articles and historical books. He also made an early reputation as a public speaker with polemics such as his calls for imperial federation (which led to his Empire tour in 1907–8) and in political speeches in opposition to Reciprocity during the 1911 election. Then during the Great War Leacock perfected the humorous lecture "voice" for which he is best remembered, and for two decades he was a platform superstar. His confidence and delivery were superb, and he had a powerful voice with precise articulation; "I can talk to 1000 in a whisper,"[9] he once boasted. He was a master at varying his pace, content, rhythm, and mood to catch his audience, hold it, lift it emotionally, make it laugh, deliver punchlines, and leave a serious message.

But the "voice" Leacock worked hardest on during his early years was that of essayist. Almost immediately upon arriving at McGill in 1901, Leacock fell under the influence of (Sir) Andrew Macphail and was accepted into the brilliant circle of artists and writers who formed the Pen and Pencil Club[10] (beautifully evoked in the essay "Andrew Macphail," which is included in this collection). Macphail created the *University Magazine* in 1907 as a vehicle for sophisticated commentary for a wide audience, like the best of the great British magazines, and Leacock was one of its major contributors. For this and for British and American journals, as well as more popular Canadian journals, Leacock poured out a stream of brilliant articles on Canadian contemporary affairs, as well as religion, education, humour, women, prohibition, and other subjects.[11] The apogee of this early essay voice was *My Discovery of England* (1922), which contained the masterpiece "Oxford As I See It."

Leacock wrote few essays in the 1920s, and when he returned to the genre in the mid-1930s, his style had changed. In his earlier essays his sparkling wit, his deft turn of phrase, and his occasional whimsy had been moderated by a certain distance from the reader. Now Leacock increasingly used the greater freedom of the lecture, a more conversational style, and an increasing personal frankness to address the issues he cared about most. His later essays were informal, more chatty and folksy, often appearing to ramble but in fact very disciplined and focused, whimsical but with the humour growing out of and reinforcing the subject matter. Macphail recognized this development in 1935: "I admired even more your choice and use of words, as if you had a secret joy in them. There is a faint echo from the 17th, not the 18th century; here and there profound depths disclose themselves below the surface and behind the mask. You never laugh in the wrong place; where there is laughter, tears are not far away." He expressed the hope that "one day you will write a book of short 'essays', as the form practised by the great Essayists of the 18th century, with the humour so blended that no one will notice it, like the French Vermouth in a cocktail. Your writings are full of these little essays."[12] The culmination of Leacock's late essay style were the essays in My Remarkable Uncle (1942), Last Leaves (1945), and his autobiography, where (according to Robertson Davies) "he writes with the assurance of an old man and with self-knowledge he has never before chosen to reveal."[13]

The book you are reading is a belated answer to Macphail's wish. The essays presented here have been selected from books and articles spanning the last decade of Leacock's life. They show that in spite of his relentless industry and repetition, Leacock at his best was still capable of freshness and vigour. He had learned how to reminisce without being a bore, and how to convey his insights to a younger audience who would listen respectfully even if they did not always agree. Of course, greater freedom also sometimes allowed him to indulge crotchets and prejudices. Some of his ideas now seem dated, and some of his predictions were wrong. Modern readers will not like his patronizing references to Canadian Native peoples, immigrants, and the non-white peoples of the British Empire, and his attitude to women is, simply put, not politically correct. Leacock was a man of his time. But he also had flashes of insight that speak to us across the six or seven turbulent decades since they were written, perhaps in some ways more clearly than to his contemporaries, and he has much to teach us about the technique of essay-writing.

The essays in this collection are arranged by subject to follow the course of Leacock's life, rather than in the chronological order of their publication. In fact, we begin with a posthumously published chapter of autobiography describing his childhood as a boy brought from

England to a farm in Ontario. Following this is his memoir of his "remarkable uncle," E.P. Leacock, a formative figure in his early life. The next few essays explore his memories and thoughts on education, his training in language, his friendship with Macphail, his views on humour, and his disillusionment with political economy. The chapter on Winnipeg completes a circle by bringing together personal recollections of his boyhood with his sense of Canada's history and its future. This theme, as well as the British Empire, relations with the United States, and international affairs in a world drifting toward war, are covered in the next group of essays. Then Leacock explores retirement and old age and the tragedy of a second world war. His charming essay on bass fishing evokes his lifelong passion for Lake Simcoe, and "Common Sense and the Universe" discusses science, religion, and philosophy. The book closes with a succinct testament to future generations that sums up Leacock's view of life: only the human spirit can truly lead to social justice, peace, and progress. It is his need to reach that spirit that underlies Leacock's life and work as an educator, lecturer, economist, humorist, and essayist.

II

In one way or another Leacock wrote about himself all his life. His early writings, like the hilarious autobiographical preface to *Sunshine Sketches*, use humour to conceal more than they reveal. Only in his late essays did he begin to write seriously about his youth, but his story evolved as he recounted it in the four essays included in this book. In his 1936 essay "I'll Stay in Canada," Leacock described his father's and brothers' migration to the West, but he is wrong in almost every detail of the story. The following year in "So This Is Winnipeg" he first told the story of his uncle E.P. Leacock, who went to Winnipeg for the great boom of 1880–2 and drew Leacock's father and older brother after him. In his 1941 essay "My Remarkable Uncle," Leacock made E.P. into a lovable humbug who was fond of telling the children that "the Star of the Empire glitters in the West." Then Leacock exploited the success of this essay by writing a screenplay about a totally fictitious E.P. Only in the last year of his life, in the chapter of his autobiography entitled "Life on the Old Farm," did he seem able to provide anything like a straightforward account of his boyhood.

The picture that emerges is a life of poverty on an isolated farm, the incompetence of his father, Peter Leacock, his "remarkable uncle" E.P. (whose indomitable will he contrasted with his father's weakness), and his strong admiration and protective feelings for his mother. Agnes Butler Leacock was Victorian to the core, and under her guidance Leacock absorbed Victorian literature, world views, and values, which (except for her strict religion) stayed with him even as he became a sophisticated man of the world. Stephen was the brightest of the family, reading by candlelight and listening with open-mouthed awe as his mother read the children Walter Scott, *Robinson Crusoe*, and *Tom Sawyer*. Having failed in Winnipeg, his father returned to the farm in 1886, drank frequently, became increasingly tyrannical and abusive, and let the place go to ruin. After a particularly violent episode, seventeen-year-old Stephen is reported to have taken his father to the station in 1887 and threatened him with death if he ever returned. From then on he assumed the role of head of the family, since both his older brothers were now in the West. One can easily believe that this is the wound that some suggest the sensitive boy covered with humour and his carefully cultivated, sometimes domineering, persona.[14]

But Robertson Davies cautions us not to "judge Leacock as if he were upon oath every time he took up his pen."[15] Leacock is telling a painful story that has taken him many years to bring himself to relate. He is giving us *his* perception of events, late in his life. This is as important as any objective truth for our understanding of Leacock; but it is equally important that we compare his story to such external evidence as we do have.

We catch a different glimpse of Peter Leacock in Elsie Tolson's history of Bedford, Nova Scotia, where Peter settled on leaving the farm and for fifty-three years carried on a second life with a woman under the pseudonyms of Captain and Mrs. Lewis. Where she came from and what if anything he did for a living are unclear, but he seems to have had enough money to live comfortably until he died in 1940. He did not drink and was a gentle person who was kind to children and heartbroken at the loss of a son. Leacock never saw his father again, but his younger siblings may have kept in touch.[16] There is clearly more to this story than we will ever know. We must remember that Peter Leacock was barely nineteen when he secretly married Agnes, who had just turned twenty-three. The pair were packed off almost immediately to South Africa, where they predictably failed. Peter was twenty-seven when he was sent to Canada, thirty-two when he went to Manitoba, and thirty-nine when he finally left the farm and his eleven children. Even a stronger man might have buckled under lesser challenges for which he was so manifestly unprepared. Peter's frustration probably became acute only when he and Agnes were forced in 1886 to return to their now-worthless farm after having both been away for several years. And seventeen is not an age when a son cuts his father much slack.

As for Stephen's "remarkable uncle," E.P. Leacock's career in Manitoba has been documented in an excellent article by Wendy Owen as well as by some recollections by family members. The real E.P. was a charming, educated man who was neither dishonest nor a humbug. On arriving in Winnipeg he made a killing in a real estate flip, which he parlayed into a fortune. In his heyday he owned large houses and was renowned for his elegant style and lavish entertaining. When his wife, who was the granddaughter of Susannah Moodie, died suddenly, E.P.'s three children were sent to Toronto and remained close to Stephen, who paid for their education. E.P. was elected a municipal warden, was a justice of the peace, and served three terms as a member of the Manitoba legislature, where he was chairman of the Conservative caucus and a confidant of Premier Norquay. After the boom broke he secured work in government offices for Stephen's father and older brother Jim, the latter remembered years later as a witty young man-about-town with an interest in theatre.[17]

E.P. was involved with several companies, including the Hudson Bay Railway company — not a chimera but a potent symbol of western alienation, with substantial lands and sixty-four kilometres of track by 1887. He suffered financially with the collapse of the boom, and when Norquay's government fell in1887 and he lost his own seat the following year, his decline was assured. He campaigned for the Macdonald

Conservatives in Manitoba in 1891, but having fallen out with the local party, he failed to secure a patronage appointment. He left for England in 1894. Though there seems no reason to question Leacock's story that E.P. lived comfortably in a monastery after his return to England, a family member says that he also had inherited money.[18] The last we hear of him is an exchange of letters in 1926 with J.W. Dafoe, then at the height of his influence as editor of the *Manitoba Free Press*, who had known him as a young reporter. Delighted that Dafoe still remembers him, E.P. reminisces at length about the Hudson Bay Railway and concludes: "Forgive the garrulity of an old man whose heart is still in Western Canada."[19]

Without doubt, an Ontario farm in the 1870s was a hard place to grow up: backward, isolated, and mired in a decade of agricultural depression. Yet his mother's income of $80 a month was the salary of a high school teacher, and there were occasional remittances or inheritances from England. Though finances were always uncertain, there was money to hire a private tutor for the children and to pay the school fees at Upper Canada College, money for servants, money for a phaeton and mare, money for a cottage where Stephen began a lifelong love affair with Lake Simcoe, money to rent a house in Toronto in 1883.[20] Their isolation was at least partly self-imposed, since the family chose to mingle only with those of their own class, including the Sibbald gentry at Sibbald's Point. The real poverty of the farm was the sense of exile felt by Agnes Leacock, a latter-day Susannah Moodie raising an ever-growing family in the Canadian bush with a ne'er-do-well husband. Leacock repeatedly expresses resentment against his paternal grandfather for sending his son out to the "colonies." Agnes's heartbreak passed to her sensitive favourite son, producing a wound less sharp than the pain caused by his father, but perhaps also deeper and more lasting.

But the farm also made the Anglocentric Stephen into a North American, with a hatred of class and privilege, a sense of the value of the one-room school and the country "entertainment," and a tendency at times to pretend that he was just one of the "fellers." He wrote often about the virtues of being raised on a farm, the closeness to nature, the early rising, the physical labour. The farm was the great North

American equalizer, where all the important men were poor before they made good.[21] But you had to get off the farm. His family background and his fear of failure gave him an intense desire to succeed and an outsider's deep resentment of a society that did not respect education, coupled with an equally deep disdain for the unambitious who did not stay the course in pursuing their dreams. In his essay on Macphail, Leacock shares his friend's belief "that the real virtue of a nation is bred in the country, that the city is an unnatural product"; but he also admits this was "something of an affectation" between them (page 111). The country and Lake Simcoe were in Leacock's blood from his boyhood, but as a rich man he could have a big house in Montreal and play gentleman farmer at Old Brewery Bay. This was only one of many contradictions in Leacock's life and thought — contradictions that he sometimes recognized and sometimes didn't — that lie at the root of his humour and his view of life.

Perhaps Leacock exaggerated in his own mind the "wounds" of his early years, just as he exaggerated his "remarkable uncle" and the poverty of the farm, to objectify fears and doubts that ran deeper. All children, he writes in "War-Time Santa Claus," sooner or later discover that "Father, so to speak, is not Santa Claus — no longer the all-wonderful, all-powerful being that drew them in a little sleigh, and knew everything, and told them about it. Father seems different when children realize that the geography-class teacher knows more than he does, and that Father sometimes drinks a little too much, and quarrels with Mother." (See page 250.) Like all favoured children, Leacock suffered the more prosaic but nonetheless real trauma of simply growing up.

III

Education got Leacock off the farm, and he pursued it with passion, working long hours and reaping high academic rewards. Following his "splendid classical education" (page 89) at Upper Canada College (1882–7), Leacock studied modern languages at the University of Toronto, an honours course only recently introduced. All his life he was fluent in French and German, and one essay in this book, "How Much

Does Language Change," illustrates his strong interest in the working and evolution of language. He was characteristically ambivalent about the value of a classical education, with its gleeful ignorance of anything modern, whose product was too often the clergyman dozing over his Theocritus or the expatriate Englishman reciting fragments of Virgil in a bar. But languages did at least impose the discipline needed for lifelong learning. Leacock always believed that the best education was in the humanities, though he could see the value of science and mathematics. Engineering, medicine, and law should be taught at schools, not colleges, and schools of commerce were "admirable things in so far as they keep away from Commerce."[22]

Leacock idealized the "quiet college" and the otherworldly professor, "absorbed, ecstatic, and a little silly" (page 98) who lived for scholarship. Nothing must stand in the way of the professor's right to think and teach. He believed that business had no place in a university (the best trustees were rich but invisible, or dead) and that women distracted young men from the pursuit of knowledge. Modern education merely substituted "four years in college for one in a workshop."[23] The academic disciplines had lost their original purpose as broad fields of inquiry and now served only as "subjects" to be "taken" as tickets to a degree and to employment. Leacock denounced research that merely amassed facts or quoted dead opinions, and he regarded as valueless a PhD that only rewarded perseverance and industry. A scholar should be broad in his learning, concerned with character and moral issues, and have something to say to the intelligent public and not just to a small coterie of fellow specialists.

In fact Leacock never experienced such a "quiet college." He attended the University of Toronto full-time for only one year (1887–8) before financial stringency forced him to teach at a public high school. In 1889 he got a job at Upper Canada College, where he could combine teaching with occasional attendance at classes — essentially private study for his degree, which he received in 1891. Until he became a housemaster he lived in a succession of boarding houses, about which he wrote so memorably. He then taught himself political economy to a level that qualified him for doctoral work, which meant two years of courses at Chicago ("a raw place" with a huge new graduate school but no student common facilities)[24] followed by a rather thin thesis. In "Looking Back on College" Leacock wistfully notes that "only people who have had to study for themselves, as I had to, know how good lectures are, even the worst of them — how hard it is to work without set times and hours and set companionship." (See page 100.)

One point about which Leacock was unambiguous was his hatred of schoolteaching. In "Three Score and Ten," he wants to run the film of his life as a teacher "fast, a series of stills, any year is typical, I want to forget it" (page 244). He concedes that for those like his beloved tutor Mr. Park, for whom teaching is a vocation, it would be all right if it conferred the opportunity to live a comfortable and respectable life. But for him and most like him it threatened to be the graveyard of ambition. Leacock did not consider himself fortunate to teach at Upper Canada College even if it was the best school in the country, with a first-class staff and a principal (Sir George Parkin) who was well acquainted with men and affairs (he left in 1902 to become the organizing secretary of the Rhodes Scholarship Trust). Parkin's ambition was to elevate Upper Canada College to the level of the best British public schools. But Leacock's North American egalitarianism rebelled against Parkin's vision, and he could never accept that a teacher, at *any* school, was anything more than a servant to rich parents, an enforcer of tyrannical rules, a dispenser of a prescribed curriculum to inferior intellects. Parkin described Leacock as "clever, ready and versatile," an excellent teacher who inspired his students, and a loyal man who got along with everyone. But he did not consider him "exactly suited for being a school master, and especially a house master, as he was somewhat impatient of the infinite detail and routine necessary in a residential school," and he believed that "Professorial work was more completely in his line than housemastership."[25]

Leacock agreed, and in 1899 he resigned and borrowed money to pursue graduate studies. In 1901 he was hired as a sessional lecturer by McGill, and on completion of his doctorate in 1903 his appointment was made permanent. In 1908 he was named head of the Political Economy Department. Now, he instructs the imaginary projectionist of his life, "settle the film down to McGill University, and run it round and round as slowly as you like for thirty-six sessions — college calling in the Autumn, students and co-eds and Rah! Rah! all starting afresh, year after year." (See page 244.) Whatever he might have written about the frivolity of college life, the weaknesses of modern university education, and the evils of coeducation, he loved it, all of it. Why hate teaching with such a passion and love college unconditionally? Simple: "The one means the boy; the other means the book."[26] His intellect could range across many subjects, he could be eccentric, and he could even write humour! He might still resent the low value placed on learning by a society steeped in materialism and business values, but he could write essays and books and make speeches, teaching the public and satirizing the vulgar rich. He had a platform, he had status, he could mingle with the wealthy, learned, and famous, and he might even make money. He was free. He was somebody.

Whether as a professor, a humorist, an essayist, a commentator on public affairs, or a popular lecturer, Leacock was always an educator. He had a need to reach people, to enlighten them, to change them, to examine with them the ultimate questions of life. He prided himself on his knowledge and his ability to express complex ideas in a clear and entertaining way. His essays never talked down to his readers, whom he saw as intelligent people who shared his curiosity and would appreciate his knowledge. All the essays in this book, not just those on education, are the product of a lifelong vocation to teach.

IV

As a young teacher between 1894 and 1899, Leacock's first foray into literature was to write more than thirty humorous sketches for magazines in Canada and the United States. These bits, most of which later appeared in *Literary Lapses*, are some of his purest genius, reflecting the almost violent exuberance of youth, with extravagant nonsense and laughter that seems to leap off the page. But they are also marked by a strong element of pathos, which Peter McArthur saw as the sign of the sensitive boy. "Hoodoo McFiggin's Christmas" poignantly captures a minor tragedy that happens to nearly every child, including Leacock.

All his life Leacock was determined to demonstrate that humour had a social and literary value that "in its highest reach touches the sublime."[27] In 1907 (three years before *Literary Lapses*) Leacock wrote that humour reflects the incongruities of life, "the sad contrast of our aims and achievements," and provides a palliative to the ills that mankind cannot cure. Sadness was the origin of humour; "pathos keeps humour from breaking into guffaws and humour keeps pathos from subsiding into sobs."[28] Peter MacArthur thought that Leacock's skill in combining pathos with satire and irony made him "one of the truest interpreters of American and Canadian life that we have had" with an even greater potential as a "broad and sympathetic interpreter of life as a whole."[29] The most palpable sign of Leacock's decline as a humorist in the late 1920s was that his stories lacked pathos, subtlety, and irony.

Leacock believed that the best humour, like the best literature, reflected the progress of human civilization, culminating in the Victorian era. Thus humour rose "from the trivialities of the 'Ancients,' the indecencies of Chaucer, through the great Elizabethans and on past the smiles of Addison and the tears of Sterne and Goldsmith, through the crepitudinous mouthings of Smollett to the open sunlight of the nineteenth century."[30] This is merely silly, as is his frequent insistence that humour must be "kindly," even though much of it isn't, and certainly his best wasn't. Indeed, he frequently quotes from W.S. Gilbert's *Bab Ballads* and Harry Graham's *Ruthless Rhymes for Heartless Homes*, a book of brutal humour that challenged all Victorian ideas of decency.[31]

He is much closer to the mark in seeing humour as evolving from a primitive expression of triumph into a more complex awareness of ambiguities and ultimately a healing, uplifting art "from which all selfish exultation has been chastened by the realization of our common lot of sorrows."[32] Humour was "a leading factor in human progress" because it reflected "kindliness" (as opposed to being "kindly") — that is, our ability to feel sympathy for each other and support each other in our suffering.[33]

It is this sympathy that lies at the root of his humour. People suffer and the world is an unjust place. "Each of us in life is a prisoner," says Leacock in "From the Ridiculous to the Sublime." "We are set and bound in our confined lot. [...] Escape is barred." (See page 124–5.) History and humour can provide a consolation by softening the horrors of life, just as Punch (Pontius Pilate) and Judy (Judas Iscariot) convert a horrible chapter in human history into a puppet show with the passion and tragedy taken out of it.[34] What cannot be softened can be faced with the dark humour of a Gilbert or a Graham, and Leacock's occasional insensitivity — such as his fondness for a rhyme about a boy with skates who falls through the ice — reflects this darker side.

But it is not only society that imprisons us. Our lives themselves, and all our works, are "but as nothing, all that we do has in it a touch of the pathetic, and even our sins and wickedness and crime are pardoned in the realization of their futility." Outside is infinity, eternity, the emptiness of the cosmos. And so, in the end, all existence is humour, for there is no purpose to it, and it will end in nothingness "with one vast, silent, unappreciated joke." (See page 127–8.) This is heavy stuff, and suggests that, at least in his later life, Leacock's humorous impulse flowed from a far deeper despair than he was usually capable of acknowledging.

V

"Each of us in life is a prisoner." If the young teacher thought like that in the 1890s he was already coming to grips with what he called two decades later "The Unsolved Riddle of Social Justice." That riddle was very similar to the riddle of life that gave rise to humour. "The human mind," he wrote in 1919, "lost in a maze of inequalities that it cannot explain and evils that it cannot, singly, remedy, must adapt itself as best it can."[35] Humour might bring consolation. But if the young Leacock was not yet prepared to concede that we are "set and bound in our prescribed lot," he needed answers that languages could not offer. So he turned to political economy.

In Chicago at the turn of the century, Leacock absorbed the thinking of the leading political economists of the "progressive era," which he reflected in his *Elements of Political Science* (1906). He rejected both extreme individualism and state socialism and concluded instead that "the modern state" would curb plutocratic excesses, regulate business in the public interest, and provide welfare services, in order to protect the individual liberty that remained essential for economic progress and democratic government. But he was also deeply influenced by the maverick of the Chicago faculty, Thorstein Veblen.[36] Leacock was outraged by "the obvious and glaring fact of the money power, the shameless luxury of the rich, the crude, uncultivated and boorish mob of vulgar men and over-dressed women that masqueraded as high society."[37] Modern industrial capitalism, he wrote, had uprooted people, herding them into factories, "creating out of each man a poor miserable atom divorced from hereditary ties, with no rights, no duties, and no place in the world except what his wages contract may confer on him."[38] The values and institutions that would have mitigated these excesses were destroyed by capitalism. This was the world he mercilessly satirized in *Arcadian Adventures with the Idle Rich* (1914), where greedy plutocrats in the false pastoral setting of the Mausoleum Club scheme to get even richer, while education, religion, nature, links to the land, love, and the family are perverted to their materialist ends, politics is a corrupt grab for place and profit, and the poor suffer invisibly in the slums below the hill.

In *The Unsolved Riddle* Leacock took a more positive approach. This book was written in the atmosphere of idealism and unrest that followed the Great War. It expressed the hope that after a century of human progress it would now be possible to achieve "some part of all that has been dreamed in the age-long passion for social justice." "The government of every country," he concluded, "ought to supply work and pay for the unemployed, maintenance for the infirm and aged, and education and opportunity for the children."[39] But in calling for these reforms, Leacock again firmly rejected socialism. All his life he attacked social regulation, prohibition, and machine age capitalism, because they stifled humanity and freedom. Government intervention would succeed only if it were part of a moral and spiritual regeneration. People had to rediscover the older values of human decency, patriotism, self-sacrifice, public and private honesty, and empathy with the needs and suffering of others that the industrial and urban society had destroyed. "[D]emocracy," he wrote in 1917, "is valueless unless it can be inspired by the public virtue of the citizen that raises him to the level of the privileges that he enjoys. [...] We must manage to create as the first requisite of our commonwealth a different kind of spirit from that which has hitherto controlled us."[40]

This was a professor of political economy writing. Yet Leacock's critique was largely a moral one based not on economic principles or expertise but on humanistic values. He never believed that political economy alone could provide all the answers to the great social questions of the early twentieth century. Nor did he or most of his colleagues see it as unusual that Leacock chose to reach a wide audience rather than confine himself to academic journals. His conviction, that the professor's mission was not only to study and teach but to provide intellectual and moral leadership to society as a whole, was widely shared. It was, after all, the philosophy behind Macphail's *University Magazine*.

When the Great Depression struck, Leacock was staggered by the depth of the catastrophe, by the fact that it defied all the "laws" of conventional economics, and by the fact that he had not seen it coming. He felt his profession itself was under challenge. If political economy could not provide answers, or at least insight, what good was it? And if wise guidance were not forthcoming from professors, what would prevent a desperate society from abandoning reason and moderation in favour of irresponsible politics and demagoguery, government ownership, socialism, communism, or hare-brained ideas like Social Credit, which would only lead to worse misery? Civilization itself hung in the balance. "We are now in the last depression," he wrote in 1933, "or else in the last depression but one and that one final." Capitalism had not failed but rather had succeeded too well in increasing production without solving the problems of equitable distribution or ensuring that production was used for social benefit, and the war had accentuated this imbalance. The situation required drastic action but not revolution: "not a new game but a new set of rules."[41] There must be state intervention and regulation, higher wages, shorter hours, and social welfare, but not socialism, which would work only "in Heaven where they don't need it, or in Hell where they have it already." (See page 142.)

Leacock nailed his colours to the mast in the essay entitled "What Is Left of Adam Smith?" In 1934 Leacock and the head of the Political Economy Department at Toronto were invited to make keynote addresses to a conference to launch the new *Canadian Journal of Economics and Political Science*. "No one," says historian Brian McKillop, "could quite have anticipated the results."[42] Far from an academic article, Leacock mustered his most powerful prose to attack political economy by lumping it with philosophy as outmoded and irrelevant, hiding its bankruptcy by citing dead opinions and taking refuge in statistics and pseudo-scientific theories. With philosophy this did not matter, but the economic collapse and the threat to the social order made it imperative that political economy find answers. Classical economics had not predicted the Depression, could not explain it, and had no viable solutions to offer. "Who could dare to suggest," he cried, "that we could find our salvation in the legislative *laissez-faire* of Adam Smith and his school; that we could dare to leave to entire 'liberty' and free competition the wages of the workers, the conditions of employment, the lot of the children, the profits of monopoly, the gain of combinations? To turn our industrial world loose and empty to the unrestrained forces of 'liberty' and 'free competition' would be like turning out people into the fierce blizzard that sweeps our winter landscape." The answer, declared Leacock, was not *laissez-faire* but "'*faire-faire*'; not let things happen but 'make things happen'." (See page 141.) When we could not know what would work and what would not, we had to act, to experiment, to get things moving, not sit on our hands because classical economics said that what was happening was all for the best. But again he warned of the danger of socialism, for the one truth that remained from Adam Smith was that "economic man" would work only for his own betterment.

Between 1930 and 1937 Leacock put forward a variety of proposals to address the Depression. He published hastily written books for the Imperial Conferences of 1930 and 1932 advocating imperial tariffs, regulated trade, financial coordination, cancellation of war debts, an interchangeable currency based on gold, and assisted colonization schemes. In 1933 he published a pamphlet entitled *Stephen Leacock's Plan to Relieve the Depression in 6 Days, To Remove it in Six Months, to*

Eradicate it in Six Years, which advocated the pseudo-Keynesian solution of allowing temporary and controlled inflation by reducing the amount of gold backing the dollar. This would be followed by a massive reconstruction program, international agreements for trade, exchange, and investment, and after recovery the return to a sound gold standard. In *My Discovery of the West* in 1937, Leacock advocated consolidating and capping the debt of prairie farmers, providing free meals to all, building the St. Lawrence Seaway, and increasing rather than cutting back production of all commodities; and he pointed out that such projects would cost less than was being spent on relief. "If there is anything in the old economics," he wrote, "it is that money *wisely and properly* spent on public development, must in the end bring a return: and if there is anything in the new economics it is that the secret of economic activity is to 'start something' so the coagulated wealth of the rich, clotted into the ore, called investment, is smashed into the small coin of 'purchasing power' in the hands of the many."[43] He attacked Social Credit but explained it as an understandable response to the economic crisis. It would, in the end, "be a people's party of radical reform, having about as much to do with social credit as the Liberal party has to do with liberalism, or the Conservative party with conservatism."[44]

Leacock strongly believed that the most important requirement for getting the economy moving was a renewal of confidence and optimism. We were, he wrote in 1937, "greatly adding to the burden of our world by our new mentality of distress. Anxiety is becoming a habit."[45] He saw his humour as a means of lifting the mental depression that seemed to accompany economic depression and encouraging people to hope again. For the same reason he supported the Roosevelt New Deal, even though he believed that in the long run many of its experiments would fail. It was a way to overcome fear and paralysis, to "start something," and it might make possible similar measures in Canada. In "So This Is Winnipeg" he drew on the experience of his father and uncle in the Winnipeg boom, which he portrayed not as "a sort of economic fever" but as "a burst of economic health." "It was not because the buying and selling stopped that the boom broke," he insisted, "but because the hammerers stopped clattering on Main Street, our navvies stopped digging on the prairies. We 'called it a day' too soon." (See page 163)

These good times could come again if the kind of energy unleashed in the boom could once more be let loose and this time kept going.

Leacock could always get publicity, and although his ideas had some appeal in the business community and the Conservative Party, there is little evidence that they had widespread influence. Radicals wanted concrete action and social planning, not appeals to the spirit or vague exhortations to "start something." On the other hand, his views were too bold for an increasingly reactionary business elite.[46] The Orillia Board of Trade circulated one thousand copies of Leacock's 1930 book *Economic Prosperity in the British Empire* in Britain and Canada; but although his imperialist arguments appealed to people such as Lord Beaverbrook, John Maynard Keynes described the book as "extraordinarily commonplace." Macmillans of England refused to publish it — the first rejection of a Leacock book since his academic publisher turned down *Literary Lapses* in 1910.[47] Although five thousand copies of *Stephen Leacock's Plan* were distributed (including to President Roosevelt and Prime Minister Bennett), the pamphlet was "a spectacular flop" as a publishing venture. A 1936 book, *The Gathering Financial Crisis in Canada*, did no better.[48] Leacock hoped that R.B. Bennett would lead the Conservative Party in a progressive direction and he strongly supported the "Bennett New Deal."[49] But Bennett fumbled the chance to get meaningful imperial preferences at the Ottawa Conference of 1932 and gave only tepid support to his own "New Deal" prior to his crushing defeat in 1935. Nonetheless, Leacock remained a staunch Conservative and campaigned for Bennett, as he later did for George Drew in Ontario.

Like his friend Macphail, Leacock sometimes did not seem to know what he believed and what he didn't. He could advocate bold and radical solutions. Some were pipe dreams, such as his ideas about imperial tariff unity and assisted settlement. Some, like his proposals for public works, a devalued currency, debt relief, feeding the hungry, clearing slums, and social welfare programs, were more progressive and realistic, but they were not developed in depth or with any precision. Fundamentally, Leacock drew back from any proposals that might really threaten the social order. He could write with conviction that "there must be bread and work for all; and that ought to mean mighty little work and lots of bread,"[50] but what did that really mean? He could advocate rebuilding cities but concluded that we couldn't start "until we first rebuild ourselves."[51] He could staunchly defend the academic freedom of left-wing academics, including within his own department,[52] but he could also savagely satirize the CCF and support vicious anti-socialist campaigns.[53] Like Macphail, Leacock "would have made a fine radical if he hadn't hated radicalism." (See page 112.)

In any case Leacock's attacks on the older economics sealed his fate as a scholar. Times had changed. A professor was now expected to be an "expert" with *gravitas*, accurate information, scientific methods, and, above all, a prescription, not broad general culture, moralistic appeals, and a breezy style. Ironically, Leacock's style resembled that of the popular writers on economics that had sprung up in the Depression, the peddlers of nostrums he so desperately wanted to warn against. The acerbic Frank Underhill made the unkind if not very original gibe: "Professor Stephen Leacock still remains our leading humorist when it comes to writing serious books about Canadian social problems."[54] Fresh from the Regina Manifesto and the creation of the CCF, Underhill attacked Leacock's exhortation to "*faire-faire*" as "Fascist mysticism, shouting loudly à la Carlyle for leaders who will act and not talk, their action apparently to need no guidance from trained scientific intellects but to be decided by pure intuition."[55] Younger academics believed that it was possible to achieve prosperity and justice through social planning, and by the 1940s a remarkable group of intellectuals, politicians, and public servants (including several of his students) were creating a central bank with a managed currency, a welfare system, a modern government, and financial management along Keynesian lines.[56] They regarded Leacock's diatribes against socialism and his defence of the CPR (he was a close friend of its president, Sir Edward Beatty) as the prejudices of an outdated conservative.[57]

Still, Leacock had a point, which is best expressed in the essay "Through a Glass Darkly," included here. He was not wrong in arguing that the solution to economic depression lay in broad enquiry, bold action, and changing people's behaviour and outlook rather than relying only on statistics and theories, social engineering and planning. His quarrel was with academics, but his message was no longer directed to them. He needed to appeal to the spirit, to the common sense of the educated ordinary person. He could no longer be both a serious scholar and a popular writer. What he chose after his retirement was the role of sage, still proud to be called "professor" but increasingly determined to reach the public through essays, lectures, newspaper interviews, and commentary — to explain complex issues, to build confidence, to "start something," but above all to guard against extremes.

VI

Leacock's concern about the Depression was intertwined with his concern for Canada, its future, its place within the British Empire, and its partnership with the United States. His love for his country and his faith in its future ran deep. But his apprehensions deepened as the Depression dragged on and the sounds from Europe became increasingly ominous.

All his life Leacock was fascinated by Canada's history and optimistic about its future. Before the Great War, Leacock had boasted of the "coming Canada" that would rise to its destiny within a united empire as "heirs to the greatest legacy in the history of mankind, owners of half a continent, trustees, under God Almighty, for the fertile solitudes of the west," with 100 million people by the end of the century.[58] The materialism he deplored had its positive side in the magnificent visions of "railways in the wilderness, of a grain flotilla on the Hudson's Bay, and of the valley of the Peace broken under the ploughshare. The attraction of the great unknown hinterland that called to it the *voyageurs* and the *coureurs des bois* still holds the soul of the Canadian people."[59]

On his western tour in 1936–7, Leacock's constant refrain was that developing Canada's vast wealth was the way out of the economic and psychological depression in which the country was mired. Exploring the Canadian wilderness had been a saga of human courage and endurance, but it was great dreams, massive projects, machines, and technology that had finally conquered nature. Above all the country needed people: "immigrants — not thousands, millions — not gradually, but in a mass";

and children, "imported and homegrown, in cradlefuls."[60] Leacock's credo was expressed in the last sentence of his 1941 history of Canada: "Our day is to-morrow."[61]

But as always, Leacock's enthusiasm was tempered by doubts. He wondered whether business leaders would have the enterprise and courage to seize the dream. Politicians lacked the competence and vision needed to address the difficult problems and respond to the urgent need for state intervention and services. Unless the people chose their leaders wisely and in the right spirit, modern democracy would turn into demagoguery, dictatorship, or party anarchy.[62] He worried about the corruption, patronage, and debt that could go with vast public works. He was ambivalent about cities and industrialism. The far North was "the only place where Nature still can claim to rule, the only place as yet but little vexed by man"; but given time we "will spoil that too." (See page 167.) As for immigration, by the late 1930s he knew that his colonization schemes would not work, if for no other reason than that settlers in the twentieth century would not tolerate conditions he had found unbearable in the nineteenth.[63]

He particularly deplored the centrifugal forces he feared were tearing Canada apart. "The country is being rapidly 'Balkanized' in the economic sense," he wrote a friend. "The Dominion is committing hari-kari. Soon it will become only a weather bureau."[64] Provincial premiers were "Great Kings" in their narrow domains. Though sympathetic to the "French fact," Leacock was disturbed by the romantic nationalist writings of some younger Quebec intellectuals. But his big fear was the growing chasm between East and West, and he saw his western lecture tour as an opportunity to explain western grievances and radicalism to the East while convincing westerners that their attacks on banks and industrial capitalists were misguided.

Nonetheless, Leacock remained firm in his vision of Canada, a vision best expressed in his 1936 essay "I'll Stay in Canada," written in response to a suggestion from an English editor that after his retirement he might come "home." In the last sixty years, he said, Canada had been filled in "like a huge picture lying in a frame from the frozen seas to the American line, from Nova Scotia to the

Pacific" (page 178), and it was a proud feeling to have played some part in that. The vast distances, the immense resources, and the boundless energy of Canada — "shovelling up mountains, floating in the sky to look for gold, and finding still the Star of Empire in the West" — had an attraction that older civilizations could never offer. "Thank you, Mother England," he concluded, "I don't think I'll 'come home'. I'm 'home' now." (See page 179.)

Though Canada was home, Leacock's vision of Canada was firmly British. He believed that the British and "northern" peoples were best suited to colonize the temperate regions and govern the world, because of their experience — bred in the bone over two thousand years — of liberty, good government, and the impulse to exploration and adventure. Other races and peoples would develop, but only over a long time. "Learning English and living under the British flag," he wrote in 1930, "may make a British subject in the legal sense, but not in the real sense, in the light of national history and continuity."[65] Thus his colonization schemes called for settlers from British countries. During his western tour he was pleasantly surprised at how well people from other countries had adapted to Canada, and was usually willing after that to acknowledge the contribution of non-British immigrants to Canada. His writing is not marred by the anti-Semitic sentiments so common in his era. But he remained adamantly opposed to Chinese, Japanese, and Indian immigration because these cultures were alien to Canadian and British traditions and because their cheap labour could be exploited and could lower Canadian standards.[66] His belief, common in the early twentieth century, that races and peoples represented different stages of social and cultural evolution, predisposed him to regard the Native peoples who encountered the first white settlers as "savages," along with other "natives" in the Empire. Even for those much higher on the scale, like India, there could be no question of immediate self-government. Leacock's views, founded on "scientific" beliefs widespread in his younger days, all too easily shaded over into prejudice and stereotype.

Canada was fortunate to be part of the British Empire, which was the greatest institution the world had seen because it stood for progress and liberty. It combined freedom for the developed Dominions with the strength and resolve to keep the peace, and it held a sacred trust to rule subject peoples justly and wisely. Leacock detested imperialism based on conquest, greed, and oppression. He hoped, long after this was a lost cause, that the Empire would draw closer together or at least stop drifting apart. By the late 1930s, however, he had come to accept that he had been wrong about imperial federation and that the process of political independence and economic separatism in the Empire could not be reversed. But as he argued in "Canada and the Monarchy" (one of five articles he was asked to write for the 1939 visit of King George VI and Queen Elizabeth[67]), the Empire was more strongly united than ever by bonds of common purpose and sentiment, loyalty to the crown, democratic government, love of liberty, hatred of tyranny, and a desire for a peaceful and stable world. Only such an institution, hopefully in partnership with the United States, and not a weak League of Nations, could guarantee peace and freedom in a troubled world.

Silver Donald Cameron says that for Leacock the Empire was "a sort of limited internationalism."[68] Equally important was the close friendship between Canada and the United States. Leacock had been anti-American in his imperial federationist days and had campaigned against Reciprocity in 1911. By the 1930s, however, he regarded the undefended border as the linchpin connecting the Anglo-Saxon peoples. "If Canada is being Americanized," he wrote in 1937, "then what England needs is to be Frenchified, and what France needs is to be Anglicized — and both of them to be Germanized. [...] [T]he best hope for the European countries is to get into the kind of mutual relationship now fortunately held between the United States and Canada."[69] The final chapter of his wartime book on the British Empire, reprinted here, cavalierly brushes aside past disputes with the United States (including the 1911 election, in which he had played a part) in order to stress the common heritage and values of the Anglo-Saxon peoples.

Outside the Empire and North America, Leacock's internationalism became more and more limited. His 1936 essay "This International Stuff" urged an American audience to look past nationalism and prejudice, remember that we are all gardeners or farmers or family people, and realize that ordinary people can make a more peaceful world through tolerance and understanding. But his Mark Twainish innocence — like his frequent satires of the exotic peoples, the endless conflicts, the aristocratic machinations, the arcane diplomacy of old Europe — was as much a pose as was his folksy manner (the article was written for the *Rotarian*). He knew that treaties, fear, and force could not prevent war: "in the long run nothing conquers but ideas, nothing governs but the spirit." (See page 184.) He had no illusions that peace would come through reason and goodwill alone, but he did hope that after the terrible experience of the Great War all decent people would do everything they could to prevent it from happening again. Leacock at times appeared to hope that the monstrous tyrannies of Europe could be tamed by sympathetic understanding and forgiveness, just as in his writings on humour he argued that the softened retrospect of time could pardon all crimes and reconcile all hatreds. "I wish I could take Hitler or Mussolini out bass fishing on Lake Simcoe," he wrote in 1938. "They'd come back better men — or they'd never some back." (See page 179.)

For Canada there was comfort in the security of North America. "East and west are the two oceans far away; we are backed up against the ice cap of the pole; our feet rest on the fender of the American border, warm with a hundred years of friendship. The noise and tumult of Europe we scarcely hear — not for us the angers of the Balkans, the weeping of Vienna and the tumults of Berlin." (See page xx.) But North America could not be isolated in a world of modern communications and advanced weaponry. If war came, it would "spread like a plague, driving across the continents with all the evil winds of disaster behind it."[70] Leacock was as conflicted in this as in other elements of his thinking, alternately hoping for better things and despairing that humanity would ever change. But if there was a war, the Empire would be part of it and Canada would not be neutral. There was no question about that.

VII

With old age came retirement, sadness, disillusionment, and another war. Leacock behaved badly about his retirement, bitterly attacking and satirizing the administration of McGill, using his humour as a weapon, not a salve. He could deliver the graceful retirement speech

"Paradise Lost," reprinted here, but he could not adjust to retirement. In one essay he compared it to a bleak landscape at the onset of winter — you hadn't noticed how cold it had become or how the trees had lost their leaves and the sun had set, until you found yourself facing a bitter wind and a bleak future.[71] His essay "Looking Back on Retirement" observes wryly the illusions people have that they will complete some lifelong dream. His depiction of the tiresome old man "just old enough to be getting a nice shake on him even when he stood upright" (page 215), who can't stop talking, fears everything, predicts a dire future, and dies a week later, is darkly funny and certainly not kindly, but it is an honest expression of the fear and anger of a man who recognizes that he has lost paradise and that the end is approaching.

His pronouncements about how humour reconciles us to life's mysteries and disillusionments took on a new importance for him. Old age couldn't be "laughed off." It needed humour "in its highest form," that "no longer excites our laughter, no longer appeals to our comic sense, no longer depends upon the aid of wit" (page 123) — the humour of the essayist. Many of Leacock's best late essays address this struggle of an old man to accept his fate and to find meaning in his life. He recalled the people and moments he valued most, like the fishing, which he describes in "Bass Fishing on Lake Simcoe with Jake Gaudaur." He thought more deeply about religion and about the nature of life and the cosmos. "Common Sense and the Universe" is a remarkable essay, not only explaining to the ordinary reader the knowledge of his day about matter and the universe, but also posing the question he could never answer through conventional religion: what does it all mean? In the end, science and philosophy could not explain man's place in the universe any more than statistics and theories could explain the Depression. One had to have some kind of faith.[72] Far worse than doubt, he says in "War-Time Santa Claus," is the "impotent despair of those whose life has wearied to its end, disillusioned, and those who die turning their faces to the wall, still silent." "After all," Leacock quotes an Anglican cleric, "there must be a kind of something. That's just exactly how I feel about it." (See page 251.)

As he faced his own crisis there came the terrible disillusionment of a new world war. "The War is just a heart break here," he wrote a friend in 1939, "all these young boys around us to go to *that*." For those who had hoped and believed it could never come there was no point blaming Baldwin and Chamberlain, Leacock confessed, as "we were all to blame"; but, he added, "one almost wishes that the Black Death had destroyed Central Europe."[73] Now, as he had done before, he took consolation in fishing on Lake Simcoe, where "all around is peace & plenty and quiet, all the beauty & goodwill of Canadian Summer."[74] Nonetheless, he soon exhibited all the gritty patriotism he had showed in the Great War. He called for the total defeat of Germany and its allies and a settlement that would remove from them all means of ever again disrupting the peace of the world. He wrote essays, playlets, and stories extolling British courage and the need to see it through. He pressed Mariposa into service in sketches designed to sell war bonds. He made frequent comments on the war and on the world after the war, and he tried to use his humour to sweep away for a few moments the black clouds and to find the courage to carry on.

Leacock believed that his best contribution would be to explain to Canadians, Americans, and Britons what they were fighting for and why they had to work together. His pamphlet "All Right Mr. Roosevelt," which received wide circulation in the United States, was a heartfelt plea that, whatever happened in Europe, and despite America's refusal to enter the war, Canadians and Americans would preserve their friendship, their mutual assistance, and the flow of investment and people back and forth across an undefended border — a far cry from his vicious attacks on American neutrality during the Great War. He wrote history books on Canada, Montreal, and Canada and the sea. *Our Heritage of Liberty* traced in simple language the evolution of democracy. In 1939–40 he wrote a book about the British Empire, "at high speed under a great strain," which he believed would be "more important in the United States than at home" since it might "call sinners to repentance or at least keep converts from sin."[75] In fact, the book did not sell well in America, but in Britain it was "judged in certain quarters to be of use in helping national spirit" and was widely circulated.[76]

With war raging abroad, all his values under attack, and increasingly feeling the effects of age and illness,[77] Leacock began to look back on his life. In his brilliant essay "Three Score and Ten" he could finally confront what old age means in the context of his own life as death took his dearest friends. "Old age is the 'Front Line' of life," he wrote, evoking the powerful image from a previous war of soldiers moving forward into the mists of No Man's Land, dropping one by one (page 243). He could finally face the disillusionment that is at the centre of humour. He used his own life to illustrate the dilemmas of a world that had moved in a generation from backwoods isolation and certitude to "this present shrunken earth, its every corner known, its old-time mystery gone with the magic of the sea, to make place for this new demoniac confine, loud with voices out of emptiness and tense with the universal threat of death." This, he adds with devastating honesty, is "not mystery but horror. The waves of the magic sea called out in the sunlight: 'There must be a God.' The demoniac radio answers in the dark: 'There can't be.'" (See page 244.) In "War-Time Santa Claus" he invokes the spirit of Christmas, with its belief in goodness and the hope that we could have another chance at a more just and peaceful world. In the posthumously published "To Every Child" the humorist delivers straight talk in lean prose. We must, once and for all, create the prosperity and social justice without which the world will face an endless legacy of misery and war. "Older people," he says, "are battered out of shape, or were never battered into it. Faces all wrinkled and furrowed with care cannot be altered now. But to every child we must give the chance to live, to learn, to love." (See page 254.)

In spite of failing health Leacock drove himself hard with many projects. In late 1943 he was diagnosed with throat cancer, and by early 1944 he knew the end was near. Two years previously he had begun his autobiography, but in spite of the urging of his American publisher he had postponed the project until after the war. Now he returned to it, but only in time to complete four chapters. Like his publisher we can only wish that he had got further along. Instead, he focused on completing his "case against social catastrophe," which he hoped would have "wide national influence."[78] (It did not.) He was looking forward to writing a history of the Morgan Company of Montreal. He gathered essays and sketches to be published by his niece after his death. He died on March 28, 1944, and was buried at St. George's Church at Sibbald's Point, the church where he had first encountered Lake Simcoe as a boy.

VIII

When you read these essays you will know who Stephen Leacock was and why he was a great Canadian and a great writer. Throughout his writings runs the conviction that only a right spirit within each person could ensure that government, society, and business would produce social justice. At times he even invoked the idea of an inspiring Spirit, like the divine Grace of a religion in which he had ceased to believe. But what he really meant was the goodness and virtue that lies deep within us all, our innate consciousness of right and truth, set free and called forth to produce better people and a better world. As he told a Vancouver audience, "human love and human kindness are of far more importance in the world than all the talks and the works of the politicians. Instead of all the academic talk about social plans and social justice, let us cultivate those qualities that are as old as human nature and without which none can get along."[79] Humour, lectures, teaching, and essays — but especially his late, informal essays — could tell these truths and reach this spirit at the deepest level.

Leacock knew his views would find little resonance with academics or "serious" politicians and business people. An anonymous reader of *Our British Empire* told his British publisher that Leacock's vigorous style "does not accommodate the qualifying phrase which strict accuracy requires to be added to almost any historical generalization."[80] Leacock wanted to reach the many thousands of ordinary, thoughtful people who read his articles, bought his books, attended his lectures, and shared his conservative values and desire for action, even if they disagreed on specifics. These were his audience for his message of hope, of avoiding extremes, of recognizing the good in each other, of caring for each other, of facing life not only with fortitude but also with humour, and of never giving up the idea that the world could be a better place. When a pedantic editor said that his introduction to *Our Heritage of Liberty* read too much like a Rotary Club speech, Leacock responded: "after all, the world is a Rotary Club."[81]

Though they were very different men with very different talents, Leacock does in some ways remind us of Winston Churchill. They were men of great intelligence, range, and curiosity, strong and often dog-matic opinions, devoted to their country and empire and to the cause of liberty. They were considered outmoded in the 1930s, as in some ways they both were; they were certainly capable of espousing eccentric ideas and prejudices; and they were sometimes spectacularly wrong. But they were also capable of astonishing insight, great humanity, and the right instincts when these were most needed.

With all his limitations, his conflicts, and his contradictions, Leacock was fundamentally right about his public, his vision, and his faith. Liberal capitalism did survive the Depression, reinforced and modified by social programs and government intervention. We did attract massive immigration, develop our resources, and become a pros-perous, diverse, and tolerant society — a far cry from the British society he hoped for, but at a deeper level fully justifying the ideals he believed the British Empire stood for. We have learned that in confronting our problems, many of which have changed little since Leacock's day, we are most successful when we invoke the spirit of enterprise, compro-mise, and understanding. We have also discovered that one of the great strengths of Canada is our ability not only to live with contradiction and ambiguity but also to exploit the creative tension thus produced. "The ability to assume complexity," says John Ralston Saul, "is a great strength. You could call it the ability to deal with reality."[82] You could also call it the ability to create and appreciate great humour. It is no accident that humour is now considered a leading Canadian export.

In developing his late essay voice, Leacock not only disciplined his writing and honed his craft but also increasingly lowered his guard, confronted his past and his fears, and revealed his deepest feelings and his fondest hopes. Few who read these essays will not learn something new, be entertained, be frustrated, be angry, be moved, but in any case know that this is a man who has something to say, someone whose company they would enjoy. "*Non omnis moriar,*" he assures us, "I shall not altogether die." With that confidence and with the strength and wisdom revealed in these essays, he confronts his doubts and prepares for his walk into the unknown. "Give me my stick," he growls. "I'm going out on to No Man's Land. I'll face it." (See page 248.)

CHRONOLOGY

1869   Leacock is born in Śwanmore, Hants, England, the third child of Peter Leacock and Agnes Butler Leacock. They have recently failed at farming in South Africa.

1876   He is brought to a farm near Sutton, Ontario, where his father is making his third try at farming.

1878   Uncle E.P. Leacock arrives in Ontario; he reaches Manitoba in June 1879.

1881   Peter Leacock and Stephen's oldest brother depart for Manitoba; a second brother follows later.

1882   Stephen enters Upper Canada College.

1886   Peter returns from Winnipeg. Both older brothers remain in the west.

1887   Leacock graduates as Head Boy from UCC.
        Peter leaves his family, moves to Nova Scotia, lives under the pseudonym of Captain Lewis.
        Leacock enters the University of Toronto to study Modern Languages.

1888   Forced by financial circumstances to abandon his university study, Leacock attends Strathroy Collegiate Institute.

1889   Teaches at Uxbridge High School.
        Hired as junior modern languages master at Upper Canada College.
        Returns to the University of Toronto.

1891   Graduates with high honours from the University of Toronto in Modern Languages.

1894   Has his first humorous story published in a Canadian magazine; by 1899 he has published more than thirty stories in Canadian and American magazines.

1895   Begins privately to study Political Economy.

1899   Resigns from Upper Canada College; goes to the University of Chicago to take a PhD in Political Economy.
Marries Beatrix Hamilton, granddaughter of Sir Henry Pellatt.

1901   Hired by McGill University as sessional lecturer in Political Economy.
Joins Pen and Pencil Club.

1903   PhD conferred by Chicago.
Given permanent appointment by McGill.

1906   *Elements of Political Science*, his first and single best-selling book, is published.

1907   *University Magazine* begins under editorship of Andrew Macphail.
Leacock embarks on a tour of the British Empire as a "missionary" for imperial unity.

1908   Returns from world tour.
Appointed Head of the Department of Political Economy.
Purchases property at Old Brewery Bay, near Orillia.

1910   *Literary Lapses* makes Leacock instantly famous as a humorist.

1911   Fame confirmed with *Nonsense Novels*.
Leacock campaigns for the Conservatives, and against Reciprocity, in the general election.

1912   *Sunshine Sketches of a Little Town* is published.

1914   *Arcadian Adventures with the Idle Rich* is published.
The Great War begins.

1915   First humorous lecture tour for the Belgian Relief Fund.
Stephen Jr. is born.

1918   The Great War ends.

1919   *The Unsolved Riddle of Social Justice* is published in serial form
and in book form the following year.

1921   Lecture tour of England; *My Discovery of England* is published
the following year.

1925   Beatrix dies.

1928   New summer home at Old Brewery Bay is built (now the
Stephen Leacock Museum).

1929   The Great Depression begins.

1930   *Economic Prosperity in The British Empire* is published.

1932   *Back to Prosperity* is published.

1933   *Stephen Leacock's Plan* is published.

1934   Leacock's mother dies.
"What Is Left of Adam Smith" is read in Toronto and published
the following year.

1935   *Humour: Its Theory and Technique* is published.

1936   "Through a Glass Darkly" is published in the *Atlantic Monthly*.
Leacock retires from McGill.
Funny Pieces is published.
Leacock begins his western tour.

1937   My *Discovery of the West* is published.
        Here Are My Lectures and Stories is published.

1938   "Andrew Macphail" is published in *Queen's Quarterly*.
        Model Memoirs is published.

1939   *Too Much College* is published.
        "Canada and the Monarchy" is published in the *Atlantic Monthly*.
        Royal Tour of Canada by King George VI and Queen Elizabeth.
        World War II begins.

1940   *The British Empire* is published.
        Peter Leacock dies.

1941   *Canada: The Foundations of its Future* for Seagram's is published.

1942   *My Remarkable Uncle and Other Sketches* is published.
        Our Heritage of Liberty is published.
        Montreal, Seaport and City is published.
        "Common Sense and the Universe" is published in *Atlantic Monthly*.

1943   *Happy Stories* is published.

1943–4 Leacock completes four chapters of his autobiography.

1944   Leacock dies of throat cancer in Montreal.

1945   *Last Leaves* is published.

1946   *The Boy I Left Behind Me* is published.

1

LIFE ON THE OLD FARM

I enjoy the distinction, until very recently a sort of recognized title of nobility in Canada and the United States, of having been "raised on the old farm." Till recently, I say, this was the acknowledged path towards future greatness, the only way to begin. The biographies of virtually all our great men for three or four generations show them as coming from the farm. The location of the "old home farm" was anywhere from Nova Scotia to out beyond Iowa, but in its essence and idea it was always the same place. I once described it in a book of verse which I wrote as a farewell to economics,[83] which was so clever that no one could read it and which I may therefore quote with novelty now.

> The Homestead Farm, way back upon the Wabash,
> Or on the Yockikenny,
> Or somewhere up near Albany — the Charm
> Was not confined to one, for there were many.
> There when the earliest Streak of Sunrise ran,
> The Farmer dragged the Horses from their Dream
> With "Get up, Daisy" and "Gol darn yer, Fan,"
> Had scarcely snapped the Tugs and Britching than
> The furious Hayrack roared behind the team.
> All day the Hay
> Was drawn that way
> Hurled in the Mow
> Up high — and how!
> Till when the ending Twilight came, the loaded
> Wain
> With its last, greatest Load turned Home again.

The Picture of it rises to his Eye
Sitting beside his Father, near the Sky.

I admit that within the last generation or so, in softer times of multi-
plying luxury, men of eminence have been raised in a sickly sort of way
in the cities themselves, have got their strength from high-school
athletics, instead of at the woodpile and behind the harrows, and their
mental culture by reading a hundred books once instead of one book
a hundred times. But I am talking of an earlier day.

It was a condition, of course, that one must be raised on the old
farm and then succeed in getting off it. Those who stayed on it turned
into rustics, into "hicks", and "rubes", into those upstate characters
which are the delight of the comic stage. You had your choice! Stay
there and turn into a hick; get out and be a great man. But the strange
thing is that they all come back. They leave the old farm as boys so
gladly, so happy to get away from its dull routine, its meaningless sunrise and sunset, its empty fresh winds over its fields, the silence of the
bush — to get away into the clatter and effort of life, into the crowd.
Then, as the years go by, they come to realize that at a city desk and in
a city apartment they never see the sunrise and the sunset, have forgotten what the sky looks like at night and where the Great Dipper is,
and find nothing in the angry gusts of wind or the stifling heat of the
city streets that corresponds to the wind over the empty fields ... so
they go back, or they think they do, back to the old farm. Only they
rebuild it, but not with an axe but with an architect. They make it a
great country mansion with flagstoned piazzas and festooned pergolas
— and it isn't the old farm any more. You can't have it both ways.

But as I say, I had my qualifying share, six years of the old farm — after
I came out as a child of six from England — in an isolation which in
these days of radio and transport is unknown upon the globe.

[...] I was brought out by my mother from England to Canada as
the third of her six children in 1876 on the steamship *Sarmatian*,
Liverpool to Montreal, to join my father who had gone ahead and
taken up a farm. The *Sarmatian* was one, was practically the last one,

of those grand old vessels of the Allan Line which combined steam with the towering masts, the cloud of canvas, the maze of ropes and rigging of a full-rigged three-masted ship. She was in her day a queen of the ocean, that last word which always runs on to another sentence. She had been built in 1871, had had the honour of serving the Queen as a troopship for the Ashanti war and the further honour of carrying the Queen's daughter to Canada as the wife of the Marquis of Lorne, the Governor-General. No wonder that in my recollection of her the *Sarmatian* seemed grand beyond belief and carried a wealth of memories of the voyage of which I have already spoken. For years I used to feel as if I would "give anything" to see the *Sarmatian* again. "Give anything" at that stage of my finance meant, say, anything up to five dollars — anyway, a whole lot. And then it happened years and years after, when I had gone to Montreal to teach at McGill (it was in 1902), that I saw in the papers that the *Sarmatian* was in port; in fact I found that she still came in regularly all season and would be back again before navigation closed. So I never saw her. I meant to but I never did. When I read a little later that the old ship had been broken up I felt that I would have "given anything" (ten dollars then) to have seen her.

In those days most people still came up, as we did in 1876, by river steamer from Montreal to Toronto. At Kingston we saw the place all decked with flags and were told that it was the "Twenty-fourth of May." We asked what that meant, because in those days they didn't keep "Queen's Birthday" as a holiday in England. They kept Coronation Day with a great ringing of bells, but whether there was any more holiday to it than bell-ringing I don't remember. But, as we were presently to learn, the "Twenty-fourth" was at that time the great Upper Canada summer holiday of the year; Dominion Day was still too new to have got set. There wasn't any Labour Day or any Civic Holiday.

From Toronto we took a train north to Newmarket; a funny train, it seemed to us, all open and quite unlike the little English carriages, cut into compartments that set the fields spinning round when you looked out of the window. Newmarket in 1876 was a well-established country town — in fact, as they said, "quite a place." It still is. It was at that time the place from which people went by the country roads to the south side of Lake Simcoe, the township of Georgina, to which at that time there was no railway connection. From Newmarket my father and his hired man were to drive us the remaining thirty miles to reach the old farm. They had for it two wagons, a lumber wagon and a "light" wagon. A light wagon was lighter than a lumber wagon, but that's all you could say about it — it is like those histories which professors call "short" histories. They might have been longer. So away we went along the zigzag roads, sometimes along a good stretch that would allow the horses to break into a heavy attempt at a trot, at other times ploughing through sand, tugging uphill, or hauling over corduroy roads of logs through thick swamps where the willow and alder bushes almost met overhead and where there was "no room to pass." On the lift of the hills we could see about us a fine rolling country, all woods, broken with farms, and here and there in the distance on the north horizon great flecks of water that were Lake Simcoe. And so on, at a pace of four or five miles an hour, till as the day closed in we went over a tumbled bridge with a roaring milldam and beyond it a village, the village of Sutton — two mills, two churches, and quite a main street, with three taverns. My father told us that this was our own village, a gift very lightly received by us children after memories of Porchester and Liverpool and the *Sarmatian*. My mother told me years afterwards that to her it was a heartbreak. Beyond the village, my father told us, we were on our home road — another dubious gift, for it was as heavy as ever, with a great cedar swamp a mile through in the centre, all corduroy and willows and marsh and water; beyond that up a great hill with more farmhouses, and so across some fields, to a wind-swept hill space with a jumble of frame buildings and log barns and outhouses, and there we were at the old farm, on a six-year unbroken sentence.

The country round our farm was new in the sense that forty years before it was unbroken wilderness and old in the sense that farm settlers, when they began to come, had come in quickly. Surveyors had marked out roads. The part of the bush that was easy to clear was cleared off in one generation, log houses built, and one or two frame ones, so that in that sense the country in its outline was just as it is now: only at that time it was more bush than farms, now more farms than the shrunken remnant of bush. And of course in 1876 a lot of old primeval trees, towering hemlocks and birch, were still standing. The last of the great bush fires that burned them out was in the summer when we came, the bush all burning, the big trees falling in masses of spark and flame, the sky all bright, and the people gathered from all round to beat out the shower of sparks that fell in the stubble fields....

This country around Lake Simcoe (we were four miles to the south of it and out of the sight of it), beautiful and fertile as it is, had never been settled in the old colonial days. The French set up missions there among the Hurons (northwest of the lake), but they were wiped out in the great Iroquois massacre of 1649 in the martyrdom of Fathers Lalement and Brébeuf. The tourist of to-day sees from his flying car the road signs of "Martyr's Shrine" intermingled with the "Hot Dogs" and "Joe's Garage." After the massacre the French never came back. The Iroquois danger kept the country empty, as it did all western Ontario. Nor did the United Empire Loyalists come here. They settled along the St. Lawrence and the Bay of Quinte and Niagara and Lake Erie, but the Lake Simcoe country remained till that century closed, as empty as it is beautiful.

Settlement came after the "Great War" ended with Waterloo and world peace, and a flock of British emigrants went out to the newer countries. Among them were many disbanded soldiers and sailors and officers with generous grants of land. These were what were called in England "good" people, meaning people of the "better" class but not good enough to stay at home, which takes money. With them came adherents and servants and immigrants at large, but all good people in the decent sense of the word, as were all the people round our old farm no matter how poor they were. The entry of these people to the Lake Simcoe country was made possible by Governor Simcoe's opening of Yonge Street, north from Toronto to the Holland River. It was at first just a horse track through the bush, presently a rough roadway connecting Toronto (York) with the Holland River, and then, by cutting the corner of Lake Simcoe with the Georgian Bay and thus westward to the Upper Lakes, a line of communication safe from American invasion. It was part of Governor Simcoe's preoccupation over the defence of Upper Canada, which bore such good fruit in its unforeseen results of new settlement.

So the settlers, once over the waters of Lake Simcoe, found their way along its shore, picked out the likely places, the fine high ground, the points overlooking the lake. Here within a generation arose comfortable lake-shore homes, built by people with a certain amount of money, aided by people with no money but glad to work for wages for a time, till they could do better. From the first the settlement was cast in an aristocratic mould such as had been Governor Simcoe's dream for all his infant colony. Simcoe was long since gone by this time. He left Canada in 1796 and died in England in 1806. But the mark that he set on Upper Canada wore faint only with time and is not yet obliterated. Simcoe planned a constitution and a colony to be an "image and transcript" of England itself. An established church and an aristocracy must be the basis of it. To Simcoe a democrat was a dangerous Jacobin and a dissenter a snivelling hypocrite. He despised people who would sit down to eat with their own servants, as even "good" people began to do in Upper Canada; "Fellows of one table," he called them, and he wanted nothing to do with them in his government. Others shared his views, and hence that queer touch of make-believe, or real aristocracy, that was then characteristic of Simcoe's York (Toronto) and that helped to foster the Canadian rebellion of 1837.

So after the first "aristocracy" houses were built on the lake shore of Georgina Township settlers began to move up to the higher ground behind it, better land and cheaper. For the lake, for being on the water, most of them cared nothing. They wanted to get away from it. The lake shore was cold. It is strange to think that now you can buy all of that farmland you want at about thirty or forty dollars an acre, but an acre down at the lake shore is worth, say, a couple of thousand, and you can't get it anyway.

Our own farm with its buildings was, I will say, the damnedest place I ever saw. The site was all right, for the slow slope of the hillside west and south gave a view over miles of country and a view of the sunset only appreciated when lost. But the house! Someone had built a cedar log house and then covered it round with clapboard, and then someone else had added three rooms stuck along the front with more clapboard, effectually keeping all the sunlight out. Even towards the sunset there were no windows, only the half glass top of a side door. A cookhouse and a woodshed were stuck on behind. Across a grass yard were the stable, cedar logs plastered up, and the barns, cedar logs loose and open, and a cart shed and a henhouse, and pigsties and all that goes with a farm. To me as a child the farm part seemed just one big stink. It does still: the phew! of the stable — not so bad as the rest; the unspeakable cowshed, sunk in the dark below a barn, beyond all question of light or ventilation, like a medieval oubliette; the henhouse, never cleaned and looking like a guano-deposit island off the coast of Chile, in which the hens lived if they could and froze dead if they couldn't; the pigsties, on the simple Upper Canada fashion of a log pen and a shelter behind, about three feet high. Guano had nothing on them.

We presently completed our farmhouse to match the growing family by adding a new section on the far side of it, built of frame lumber only, with lath and plaster and no logs, thin as cardboard and cold as a refrigerator. Everything froze when the thermometer did. We took for granted that the water would freeze in the pitchers every night and the windowpanes cover up with frost. Not that the old farm was not heated. It had had originally a big stone fireplace in the original log house, but as with all the fireplaces built of stone out of the fields without firebrick, as the mortar began to dry out the fireplace would set the house on fire. That meant getting up on the roof (it wasn't far) with buckets of water and putting it out. My father and the hired man got so tired putting out the house on fire that we stopped using the fireplace and had only stoves, box stoves that burnt hemlock, red hot in ten minutes with the dampers open. You could be as warm as you liked, according to distance, but the place was never the same two hours running. There were, I think, nine stoves in all; cutting wood was endless. I quote again from my forgotten book.

Winter stopped not the Work; it never could.
Behold the Furious Farmer splitting Wood.
The groaning Hemlock creaks at every Blow
"Hit her again, Dad, she's just got to go."
     And up he picks
     The Hemlock sticks
     Out of the snow.

For light we had three or four coal-oil lamps, but being just from England, where they were unknown, we were afraid of them. We used candles made on the farm from tallow poured into a mould, guttering damn things, to be snuffed all the time and apt to droop over in the middle. It is hardly credible to me now, but I know it is a fact that when my brother and I sat round a table doing our lessons or drawing and painting pictures, all the light we had was one tallow candle in the middle of the table. It should have ruined our eyesight, but it didn't. I don't think any of us under fifty wore spectacles; just as the ill-cooked food of the farm, the heavy doughy bread, the awful pork and pickles should have ruined our digestions but couldn't. Boys on the farm who go after the cattle at six in the morning are in the class of the iron dogs beside a city step.

My father's farm — one hundred acres, the standard pattern — was based on what is called mixed farming — that is, wheat and other grains, hay, pasture, cattle, a few sheep and pigs and hens, roots for winter, garden for summer and wood to cut in the bush. The only thing to sell was wheat, the false hope of the Ontario farmer of the seventies, always lower in the yield than what one calculated (if you calculated low it went lower) and always (except once in a happy year) lower than what it had to be to make it pay. The other odd grains we had to sell brought nothing much, nor the cattle, poor lean things of the pre-breeding days that survived their awful cowshed. My father knew nothing about farming, and the hired man, "Old Tommy," a Yorkshireman who had tried a bush farm of his own and failed, still less. My father alternated furious industry with idleness and drinking, and in spite of my mother having a small income of her own from England, the farm drifted onto the rocks and the family into debt. Presently there was a mortgage, the interest on which being like a chain around my father's neck, and later on mine. Indeed, these years of the late 1870s were the hard times of Ontario farming, with mortgages falling due like snowflakes.

Farming in Ontario, in any case, was then and still is an alternating series of mortgages and prosperity following on like the waves of the sea. Anyone of my experience could drive you through the present farm country and show you (except that it would bore you to sleep) the mark of the successive waves like geological strata. Here on our right is the remains of what was the original log house of a settler: you can tell it from the remains of a barn, because if you look close you can see that it had a top story, or part of one, like the loft where Abraham Lincoln slept. You will see, too, a section of its outline that was once a window. Elsewhere, perhaps on the same farm, but still standing, is an old frame house that was built by mortgaging the log house. This one may perhaps be boarded up and out of use because it was discarded when wheat went to two dollars and fifty cents a bushel in the Crimean War and the farmer, suddenly enriched, was able to add another mortgage and built a brick house — those real brick houses that give the motorist the impression that all farmers are rich. So they were — during the Crimean War. Later on, and reflecting the boom years of the closing nineties and the opening century, are the tall hip-roofed barns with stone and cement basements below for cattle and silos at the side, which give the impression that all farmers are scientists — only they aren't; it's just more mortgages.

Such has been the background of Ontario farming for one hundred years.

Our routine on the farm, as children, was to stay on it. We were too little to wander, and even the nearest neighbours were half a mile away. So we went nowhere except now and then, as a treat, into Sutton village, and on Sunday to the church on the lake shore. Practically, except for school, we stayed at home all the time — years and years.

There was, a mile away, a school (School Section No. 3, Township of Georgina) of the familiar type of the "little red schoolhouse" that has helped to make America. It was a plain frame building, decently lighted, with a yard and a pump and a woodpile, in fact all the accessories that went with the academic life of School Section No. 3. The boys and girls who went there were the children of decent people (there were no others in the township), poor, but not exactly aware of it. In summer the boys went barefoot. We didn't — a question of caste and thistles. You have to begin it at three years old to get the feel for it.

There were two teachers, a man teacher and a lady teacher, and it was all plain and decent and respectable, and the education first class, away ahead of the dame-school stuff in England. All of the education was right to the point — reading, spelling, writing, arithmetic, geography — with no fancy, silly subjects such as disfigure our present education even at its beginning and run riot in the college at the top. Things about the school that were unsanitary were things then so customary that even we children from England found nothing wrong. We spit on our slates to clean them with the side of our hand. We all drank out of the same tin mug in the schoolyard. The boys and girls were together in classes, never outside.

The only weak spot in the system of the little red schoolhouse was that the teachers were not permanent, not men engaged in teaching making it their lifework, like the Scottish "dominie" who set his mark upon Scotland. You can never have a proper system of national education without teachers who make teaching their lifework, take a pride in it as a chosen profession, and are so circumstanced as to be as good as any-body — I mean as anything around. In the lack of this lies the great fault in our Canadian secondary education, all the way up to college.

So it was with the country schools of 1876. The teachers were young men who came and went, themselves engaged in the long stern struggle of putting themselves through college, for which their teaching was only a steppingstone. An arduous struggle it was. A schoolteacher (they were practically all men; the girl teachers were just appendages to the picture) got a salary of three hundred dollars to four hundred dollars a year. Call it four hundred dollars. During his ten months a year of teaching he paid ten dollars a month for his board and washing. I don't suppose that his clothes cost him more than fifty dollars a year, and all his other extras of every kind certainly not more than another fifty. For in those days, after necessaries were paid for, there was nothing to spend money on. The teacher never drank. Not that he didn't want to, but every drink cost money, five cents, and he hadn't got it. If a teacher did begin to drink and did start to loaf around the taverns, it undermined the sternness of his life's purpose as a slow leak undermines a dam. It became easier to drink than to save money; he felt rich instead of poor, and presently, as the years went by, he drank himself out of this purpose altogether, quit schoolteaching, went north to the lumber shanties, or worked in a sawmill — living life downhill, marked out still, by the wreck of his education, as a man who had once been a teacher and still quoted poetry when he was tight.

But most, practically all, stuck right at it, saving, say, two hundred dollars a year towards college. And this is what college cost, college being the University of Toronto. The fees were forty dollars a year (say sixty dollars in medicine), and board and lodging in the mean drab houses of the side streets where the poorer students lived cost three dollars a week and washing, I think, twenty-five cents a week. They washed anything then for five cents, even a full-dress shirt, and anyway the student hadn't got a full-dress shirt. College books in those days cost about ten dollars a year. There were no college activities that cost money, nothing to join that wanted five dollars for joining it, no cafeterias to spend money in, since a student ate three times a day at his boardinghouse and that was the end of it. There was no money to be spent on college girls, because at that time there were no college girls to spend money on. Homer says that the beauty of Helen of Troy launched a thousand ships (meaning made that much trouble). The attraction of the college girl was to launch about a thousand dollars — added to college expenses.

But all that was far, far away in 1876, and a student's college budget for the eight months of the session, including his clothes and his travel expenses and such extras as even the humblest and sternest must incur, would work out at about three hundred dollars for each college year. That meant that what he could save in a year and a half of teaching would give him one year at college. Added to this was the fact that in the vacation — the two months of a teacher's vacation or the four months of a college vacation — he could work on a farm for his board and twenty dollars a month and save almost the whole of the twenty dollars. I have known at least one teacher, later on a leader of the medical profession of Alberta, who put in seven years of this life of teaching to get his college course. But in most cases there would be some extra source of supply: an uncle who owned a sawmill and could lend two or three hundred dollars, or an uncle over in the States, or an older brother who came down from the "shanties" in the spring with more money than he knew what to do with. For what could he do with it, except drink or go to college?

So in the end adversity was conquered, and the teachers passed through college and into law or medicine, with perhaps politics and public life, and added one more name to the roll of honour of men who "began as teachers." Some failed on the last lap, graduated, and then got married, tired of waiting for life to begin, and thus sank back again on teaching — as a high-school teacher, a better lot but still not good enough.

But the system was, and is, all wrong. Our teacher, with his thirty dollars a month, didn't get as much as our Old Tommy, the hired man, for he and his wife had twenty dollars a month and a cottage with it and a garden, milk and eggs and vegetables and meat to the extent of his end (I forget which) of any pig that was killed. A teacher situated like that could be a married man, as snug and respected as a Scottish dominie with his cottage and his kailyard, his trout rod and his half dozen Latin books bound in vellum — "as good as anybody", which is one of the things that a man has got to be in life if he is to live at all. The teachers weren't. I never was, and never felt I was, in the ten years I was a teacher. That is why later on I spent so many words in decrying schoolteaching as a profession, not seeing that schoolteaching is all right for those who are all right for it. The thing wrong is the setting we fail to give it.

Such was our school at School Section No. 3, Township of Georgina, County of York. It had also its amenities as well as its work. Now and again there were school "entertainments." I can't remember if the people paid to come. I rather think not, because in that case they wouldn't come. For an entertainment the school was lit with extra lamps. The teacher was chairman. The trustees made speeches or shook their heads and didn't. The trustees were among the old people who had come out from the "old country" with some part of another environment, something of an older world, still clinging to them. Some, especially Scotsmen like old Archie Riddell, would rise to the occasion and made a speech with quite a ring and a thrill to it, all about Marmion and Bruce and footprints on the sands of time. Then the teachers would say that we'd hear from Mr. Brown, and Mr. Brown, sitting in a sunken lump in a half-light, would be seen to shake his head, to assure us that we wouldn't. After which came violin music by local fiddlers, announced grandiloquently by the chairman as "Messrs. Park and Ego," although we knew that really they were just Henry Park and Angus Ego. Perhaps also some lawyer or such person from the village four miles away would drive up for the entertainment and give a reading or a recitation. It was under those circumstances that I first heard W. S. Gilbert's *Yarn of the "Nancy Bell."* It seemed to me wonderful beyond words, and the Sutton lawyer, a man out of wonderland.

But going to the country school just didn't work out. It was too far for us, and in rough weather and storm impossible, and it was out of the question for a younger section of the family (the ones in between the baby and ex-baby and the "big boys"). Moreover, my mother was haunted with the idea that if we kept on at the school we might sideslip and cease to be gentlemen. Already we were losing our Hampshire accent, as heard in *Twinkle, Twinkle, Little Star* — not "stah," and not "star," but something in between. I can still catch it if I am dead tired or delirious. We were beginning also to say "them there" and "these here" and "who all" and "most always," in short, phrases that no one can use and grow up a gentleman.

So my mother decided that she would teach us herself and with characteristic courage set herself at it, in the midst of all her other work with the baby and the little children and the kitchen and the servants and the house. Servants, of course, we always had: at least one maid — I beg pardon, I'm losing my language — I mean one "hired girl" and a "little girl" and generally an "old woman." Top wages were eight dollars a month; a little girl got five dollars. There was a certain queer gentility to it all. The hired man never sat down to eat with us, nor did the hired girl. Her status, in fact, as I see it in retrospect, was as low and humble as even an English Earl could wish it. She just didn't count.

My mother had had in England a fine education of the Victorian finishing-school type and added to it a love and appreciation of literature that never left her all her life, not even at ninety years of age. So she got out a set of her old English schoolbooks that had come with us in a box from England — Colenso's *Arithmetic*, and Slater's *Chronology*, and Peter Parley's *Greece and Rome*, and Oldendorf's *New Method of French* — and gathered us around her each morning for school, opened with prayers, and needing them. But it was no good; we wouldn't pay attention, we knew it was only Mother. The books didn't work either — most of them were those English manuals of history and such, specially designed for ladies' schools and for ladies who had to teach their own children out in the "colonies." They were designed to get a maximum of effect for a minimum of effort, and hence they consisted mostly of questions and answers, the questions being what lawyers call leading questions, ones that suggest their own answers. Thus they reduced Roman history to something like this:

> Q. Did not Julius Caesar invade Britain?
> A. He did.
> Q. Was it not in the year 55 B.C.?
> A. It was.
> Q. Was he not later on assassinated in Rome?
> A. He was.
> Q. Did not his friend Brutus take a part in assassinating him?
> A. He did.

In this way one could take a birdlike flight over ancient history. I think we hit up about two hundred years every morning, and for ancient Egypt over one thousand years. I had such a phenomenal memory that it was all right for me, as I remembered the question and answer both. But my elder brothers Dick and Jim were of heavier academic clay, and so they just — as the politicians say — took it as read.

The *Arithmetic* of Bishop Colenso of Natal was heavier going. After multiplication and division it ran slap-bang into the Rule of Three, and Mother herself had never understood what the Rule of Three was, and if you went on beyond it all you found was Practice and Aliquot Parts. I know now that all this is rule-of-thumb arithmetic, meant for people who can't reason it out, and brought straight down from the Middle Ages to Colenso. The glory of the unitary method, whereby if one man needs ten cigarettes a day then two men need twenty, and so on for as many men and as many cigarettes and as long a time as you like — this had not dawned on the British mind. I think it was presently imported from America.

So my mother's unhappy lessons broke down, and we were just about to be sent back to the red schoolhouse when by good luck we managed to secure a family tutor, from whom we received, for the next three or four years, teaching better than I have ever had since and better than any I ever gave in ten years as a schoolteacher. Our tutor was a young man off a nearby farm, stranded halfway through college by not having taught long enough and compelled to go back to teaching. So my grandfather from England put up the money (for fear, of course, that we might come back home on him), and there we were with a tutor and a schoolroom, inkwells, scribblers, slates — in fact, a whole academic outfit. Our tutor was known as "Harry Park" to his farm associates, but to us, at once and always, as "Mr. Park," and he ranked with Aristotle in dignity and width of learning. Never have I known anyone who better dignified his office, made more of it, so that our little schoolroom was as formal as Plato in his Academy could have wished it. Mr. Park rechristened my brother Jim as "James," to give him class, and Dick reappeared as "Arthur". The hours were as regular as the clock itself, in fact more so, since Mr. Park's watch soon took precedence over the kitchen clock, as the "classes" (made up of us four boys and my little sister, just qualified) were as neatly divided as in a normal school. I had to be Class I, but my brothers didn't care, as they freely admitted that

I was the "cleverest" — they looked on it as no great asset. For certain purposes, poetry and history, we were all together.

For us "Mr. Park" knew everything, and I rather think that he thought this himself. Ask him anything and we got the answer. "Mr. Park, what were the Egyptians like?" He knew it and he told it, in measured formal language.

Under "Mr. Park's" teaching my brothers at least learned all that could be put into them, and I personally went forward like an arrow. At eleven years of age I could spell practically anything, knew all there was to know of simple grammar (syntax, parsing, analysis) beyond which there is nothing worth while anyway, knew Collier's *British History* and *History of English Literature*, all the geography of all the countries including Canada (the provinces of Canada which had not been in Mother's book), and in arithmetic had grasped the unitary system and all that goes with it and learned how to juggle with vulgar fractions even when piled up like a Chinese pagoda, and with decimals let them repeat as they would.

After Mr. Park came to us as tutor and the little red schoolhouse of School Section No. 3, Township of Georgina, was cut out, our isolation was all the more complete. We practically stayed on the farm. But of course a part of the old farm, to children of eight to twelve years old, newly out from England, was a land of adventure; all the main part of it, as it sloped away to the south and west, was clear fields of the seven-acre pattern with snake fences all round it, piles of stones that had been cleared off the fields lying in the fence corners, raspberry bushes choking up the corners, but here and there an old elm tree springing up in an angle of the fence as a survival of the cleared forests. Elm trees have the peculiarity that they can do well alone, as no storm can break them, whereas hemlocks isolated by themselves are doomed. Hence the odd elm trees scattered all through this part of Central Ontario, as if someone had set them on purpose to serve as shade trees or landscape decoration. Heaven knows no one did. For the earlier settlers, trees, to a great extent, were the enemy. The Upper Canada forest was slaughtered by the lumber companies without regard for the future, which in any case they could neither foresee nor control. In the early days the export of lumber was only in the form of square timber — great sticks of wood from twelve to eighteen inches each way, not cut up into the boards and deals and staves of the later lumber trade. Hence the trees were squared as they fell in the falling forest, and about one-third of the main tree and all its branches burned up as litter to get rid of it. That was the early settlers' idea of the bush: get rid of it where he could, and where it lay too low, too sunken, too marshy, to clear it. Then cut out the big trees and haul them out, leave the rest of the bushes there, and let farm clearings and roads get round it as best they could. As to planting any new trees to conserve the old ones, the farmers would have thought it a madman's dream. The only trees planted were the straight, fast-growing Lombardy poplars, still seen in their old age, set out in single or in little rows in front of the early Ontario houses. These owe their origin to the legend or the fact that they act as lightning conductors, a part of Benjamin Franklin's legacy to North America, along with the box stove and much else.

I am saying then that our old farm at its north end fell slap away down a steep hillside at the foot of which began the bush that spread off sideways in both directions as far as one could see, and directly in front it rose again in a slope that blotted out all view of Lake Simcoe four miles away. Along the fringes of it were still some of the giant hemlocks that had escaped the full fury of the last bush fire, dead, charred and still standing, but falling one by one. The bush, as one tried to penetrate it, grew denser and denser, mostly underbrush with tangled roots and second growth sprung up after the fires. It was so dense that for us it was impenetrable, and we ventured our way further and further in, carrying hatchets and alert for wildcats, which I am practically certain were not there, and for bears, which had left years and years ago.

We had hardly any social life, as we were prevented, partly by "class" and mainly by distance, from going over to the other farms after dark. To one farm where lived a family of English children of something the same mixed antecedents as ourselves we sometimes went over for tea, and at times all the way to the village or to the lake-shore houses. But such treks meant staying overnight.

So mostly we stayed at home, and in the evenings we did our lessons, if we had lessons to do, and my mother read to us Walter Scott and carried us away to so deep an impression of the tournaments and battle-fields of the Crusade and of the warring forests of Norman-Saxon England that any later "moving picture" of such things is but a mere blur of the surface. We cannot have it both ways. Intensity of mental impression and frequency of mental impression cannot go together. Robinson Crusoe's discovery of Friday's footprints on the sand — read aloud thus by candlelight to wondering children — has a dramatic "horror" to it (horror means making one's hair stand up) that no modern cinema or stage can emulate. Similarly I recall the reading aloud of *Tom Sawyer*, then of course, still a new book, and the dramatic intensity of the disclosure that Indian Joe is sealed up in the great cave.

Our news from the outside world came solely in the form of the *Illustrated London News* sent out by my grandmother from England. In it we saw the pictures of the Zulu War and the (second) Afghan War and of Majuba Hill. With it we kept alive the British tradition that all Victorian children were brought up in, never doubting that of course the Zulus were wrong and the Afghans mistaken and the Boers entirely at fault. This especially, as mother had lived in South Africa and said so.

On one point, however, of British Victorian orthodox faith I sideslipped at eight years old and have never entirely got back, and that too the greatest point in all British history. I refer to the question of George Washington and George the Third and whether the Americans had the right to set up a republic. It so happened that there came to our farm for a winter visit an English cousin of my father's who had become (I do not know how, for it must have been a rare thing in the seventies) a female doctor in Boston. She used to tell me, while Jim and Dick were mucking out the chores in the barnyard, which was their high privilege, about the United States and the Revolution, and when she saw how interested I was she sent to Boston and got a copy of Colonel Thomas Wentworth Higginson's *Young Folk's (or People's) History of the United States*. There it was, pictures and all — General Gage and the Boston Boys (very neat boys and a very neat General), Washington crossing the Delaware (hard going), Washington taking command at Cambridge. "Cousin Sophy" used to read it out loud to us — a needed rest for Walter

Scott — and we were all fascinated with it, Jim and Dick with the pictures and the soldiers, but I chiefly from the new sense of the burning injustice of tyranny, a thing I had never got from history before.

Forthwith the theory of a republic, and the theory of equality, and the condemnation of hereditary rights seemed obvious and self-evident truths, as clear to me as they were to Thomas Jefferson. I stopped short at the Queen partly, I suppose, because one touched there on heaven and hell and the church service and on ground which I didn't propose to tread. But for me, from then on, a hereditary lord didn't have a leg to stand on. In the sixty years (nearly seventy) since elapsed I have often tried to stand up hereditary peers again (I mean as members of a legislature), but they won't really stay up for me. I have studied it all, and lectured on it all, and written about it all. I know all about the British idea that if a thing had existed for a long time, and if most people like it and if it seems to work well and if it brings no sharp edge of cruelty and barbarity such as the world has learned again, then it is silly to break away from established institution on the ground of a purely theoretical fault. But I can't get by with the arguments. I broke with the House of Lords, with its hereditary peers and its bishops voting because they are bishops in 1879 — or whenever it was — and the breach has never been really healed. People from India have told me that no matter how scientific an education you may smear over an Indian doctor or scientist, put him in any emergency or danger and back he comes to his first beliefs: away goes medicine in favour of incantation and charms, and science abandons its instruments and its metric measurement and harks back a thousand years to astrology and mysticism.

I'm like that with my underlying Jeffersonian republicanism: back I slip to such crazy ideas as that all men are equal, and that hereditary rights (still saving out the British monarch) are hereditary wrongs.

Occasional treats broke the routine of our isolation on the farm, such as going into Sutton village for the "Twenty-Fourth" (of May), the great annual holiday, or to see cricket matches between Sutton and other places, such as Newmarket, within cricket reach. For up to that time cricket still remained the game of the Upper Canada countryside, the game living on strong as against the competition of Yankee baseball and dying hard. At present cricket has shrunken in on Toronto and a few larger cities and school centres. But in the seventies and eighties it was everywhere. The wonder is, though, that it could survive at all — it makes such heavy demands — a decent "pitch" of prepared ground, without which the game is worthless, an outfield not too rough, and even for decent practice a certain minimum of players; while cricket "at the nets" is poor stuff without a good pitch and good bowling, especially if you haven't any nets. Nor can you have a real "match" at cricket without a real side of eleven or something close to it. Baseball, on the other hand, is quick and easy and universal. It can be played in a cow pasture or behind the barnyard or in the village street; two people can "knock out flies" and three can play at "rolling over the bat", and if you can't get nine for a game, a pitcher, catcher, and baseball will do — what's more, the game can be played out in an afternoon, an hour, or a minute. The wonder is that the British settlers in Upper Canada kept doggedly on with their British cricket as against the facile Yankee baseball and the indigenous lacrosse. I am quite sure that in the township of Georgina no one had ever seen the latter game in 1880.

Rarest and most striking of all treats was to be taken on a trip to Toronto on the new railway, which reached Lake Simcoe from the south by a branch line of the Toronto and Lake Nipissing Railway extended from Stouffville to Sutton and Jackson's Point Wharf (on the lake). It was part of that variegated network of little railways — of varied gauges and plans, all crooked as country roads, all afraid of a hill, and all trying to keep close to a steamer dock, each under different ownerships — which represents the shortsighted railway building of Ontario. Shortsighted? And yet I suppose it was hard to see ahead at all, in a community that stumbled and fell with every new onslaught of bad times and fought stubbornly against its forests and its torrents — half-strangled in its own opportunity.

The completion of the railway and the arrival of the first train was a great event, much ringing of bells and blowing of whistles; then the train itself arrived by the sash factory and the gristmill. It made a great difference, too, with commodities, such as coal and oranges, seen in

Sutton for the first time. But, as with most town and village advances of that date, it just went so far and then stopped. Sutton fell asleep again and woke only to the sound of the motor horn and the advent of the tourist, in another world years later.

But for us children a trip on the train to Toronto, a treat that was accorded to each of us about twice in the next three years, was a trip into wonderland — England had grown dim. Toronto […] was marvellous beyond all description.

But the most real of our standing treats and holidays came to us on contact with Lake Simcoe. This grew out of our going every Sunday in summer to the Lake Shore Church four miles away. To our farm equipment there had been added a "phaeton" for Mother to drive and the kind of horse that is driven in a phaeton, that is born quiet, never grows old, and lives on into eternity. The ease and comfort of a phaeton can be appreciated by riding once in a buckboard (just once is all you need), a vehicle that means a set of slats on axles, with a seat on the slats. Its motion is similar to that of the new "seasickness medicine." A phaeton with steel springs, low entrance, and two seats can carry a capacity load and attain a speed, on the level, of six miles an hour. Even at that we walked in turns.

The parish church of Georgina stood on the high bank dotted with cedar trees overlooking Lake Simcoe, and oh! what a paradise the view presented. I have often and often and often written of Lake Simcoe. I know, with a few odd miles left out here and there, its every stick and stone, its island and points, and I claim that there is in all the world no more beautiful body of water. Writing it up years ago in a Canadian Geographical Journal,[84] I said:

> The islands of the Aegean Sea have been regarded for centuries as a scene of great beauty; I know, from having seen them, that the Mediterranean coast of France and the valleys of the Pyrenees are a charm to the enchanted country; and I believe that for those who like that kind of thing there is wild grandeur in

the Highlands of Scotland, and a majestic solitude where the midnight sun flashes upon the ice peaks of Alaska. But to my thinking none of those will stand comparison with the smiling beauty of the waters, shores, and bays of Lake Simcoe and its sister lake, Couchiching. Here the blue of the deeper water rivals that of the Aegean; the sunlight flashes back in lighter colour from the sand bar on the shoals; the passing clouds of summer throw moving shadows as over a ripening field, and the mimic gales that play over the surface send curling caps of foam as white as ever broke under the bow of the Aegean galley.

The Aegean is old. Its islands carry the crumbling temples of Homer's times. But everywhere its vegetation has been cut and trimmed and gardened by the hand of man. Simcoe is far older. Its forest outline is still what Champlain saw, even then unchanged for uncounted centuries. Look down through the clear water at the sunken trees that lie in the bay south-east of Sibbald's Point. They sank, as others sank before them, a hundred years ago; no hand of man has ever moved or touched them. The unquarried ledges of Georgina Island stood as they stand now when the Greeks hewed stone from the Pentelicus to build the Parthenon.

The whole point of our going to Church on the lake shore on summer mornings was that we were allowed, by a special dispensation from the awful Sunday rules we were brought up on, to go in for a swim and to stick around beside the lake for an hour or so. The spot was one of great beauty. The earliest settlers had built a wooden church among the cedar trees, and in the very years of which I speak it was being replaced by the Lake Shore Church of cut stone that is one of the notable landmarks of the scenery of the district. It was built by the members of the Sibbald family, one of the chief families of the district, whose sons had gone abroad for service in the British

Army and Navy and in India and, returning (in our day) as old men enriched in fortune and experience, built the stone church still standing as a memorial to their mother. A Latin motto (which outclassed me at nine years old) cut in a memorial stone on the face of the tower commemorates the fact. The church was built during two of our summers of churchgoing and swimming. The masons were not there on Sundays, but we could follow its progress every Sunday, in the stones new drilled for blasting, in the fresh-cut completed stones, and then in the rising layers of the walls, the upsweep of the tall roof (one Sunday to the next), the glass, the slates, and then — all of a sudden, as it were — we were singing in it.

Better still was it when my mother, a year or two later, 1880, was able to take a "summer cottage" near the church for a holiday of a month or so. "Summer cottage" is a courtesy title. It was an old log building built as a "parsonage," which in time proved unfit for habitation even by the meekest parson. But for a summer habitation it did well enough, and with it went the glory of the lake and of the return to the water, which we lost since Porchester. We were like Viking children back to the sea! So will you find any British children, used to sight and sound of the sea, shut from the water a brief space in some inland or prairie town but exulting to get back to their agelong heritage. So were we with Lake Simcoe: making rafts of logs and boards before we had a boat, blown out to sea on our rafts and rescued, and thus learning what an offshore wind means — a thing that even today few Lake Ontario summer visitors understand. After rafts a flat-bottomed boat, liberally plugged up with hot pitch, then an attempt at making a sail and discovering that a flat-bottomed boat is no good — and so on, repeating the life of man on the ocean as the human race repeats in the individual its every stage of evolution.

In my case Lake Simcoe was a more interesting field of navigation then than now, more real. It is strange how our inland lakes have deteriorated from the navigation of reality to the navigation of luxury. What do you see now? Motorboats! Powerboats! Speed — sailing dinghies built like dishes and used for water aquations but with no connection with sailing in the real sense. And all this in any case only a fringe that fills the lakeshore resorts, crowds round luxury hotels, and leaves the open water of Simcoe and such lakes emptier than when La Salle crossed them.

Not so in the 1880s. Navigation filled the lake. Far out on its waters a long ribbon of smoke indicated a tug with a tow of logs heading for the mills at Jackson's Point. Sailing vessels, lumpy, heavy and ungainly, and nearly as broad as long, carried quarry stone and heavy stuff from the top of Lake Couchiching to the railway pier at Belle Ewart. The *Emily May* steamer circulated the Lake all day and all night (in her prime days), with double crew, half of it awake and half asleep — two captains, two mates, two stewardesses and two bartenders. The railways bit off her job point by point and place by place, the railway to Sutton and Jackson's Point being the last straw that broke her back. Yet for years after the passenger boats in the real sense had gone the excursion lived on. *Ho! for Beaverton!* read its placards on the boardside fence, *Ho! for Jackson's Point* — and then it was a summer morning carrying its sons of England, or its Knights of Ireland, its brass band, its improvised bar, its ladies' cabin as tight shut and as uncomfortable as being at home — all that went with Ho! for a day on the water in 1880. And so for years. Then came the motorcar and killed all that was left of navigation.

And all this time, although we didn't know, for my mother kept it hidden from us, at intervals my father drank, drove away to the village in the evening to return late at night after we were in bed, or lay round the farm too tired to work, and we thought it was the sun. And the more he drank, the more the farm slid sideways and downhill, and the more the cloud of debt, of unpaid bills, shadowed it over, and the deeper the shadow fell, the more he drank. My mother, I say, hid it all from us for years with a devotion that never faltered. My father, as he drank more, changed towards us from a superman and hero to a tyrant, from easy and kind to fits of brutality. I was small enough to escape from doing much of the farm chores and farm work. But I carry still the recollection of it — more, no doubt, than Jim or Dick ever did. In fact, the sight and memory of what domestic tyranny in an isolated, lonely home, beyond human help, can mean helped to set me all the more firmly in the doctrine of the rights of man and Jefferson's liberty.

By the end of the year 1881 the "old farm" as a going concern had pretty well come to a full stop. Bad farming had filled the fields with weeds; wild oats, a new curse of Ontario farming spread by the threshing machines, broke out in patches in the grain; low prices cut out all profit; apples rotted on the ground; potatoes hardly paid the digging. There was the interest of the mortgage of two hundred and fifty dollars a year, wages not paid, store bills not paid — just a welter of debt and confusion. So my father was led to give it all up and go away to Manitoba, the new land of promise that all the people on the farms were beginning to talk about. The opening of the Northwest by the Dominion taking it over had revealed the secret, so carefully guarded for two hundred years, that what had been thought of as a buffalo pasture and a fox range, a land for the trapper to share with the aurora borealis, was in reality a vast bed of deep alluvial soil, black mould two or three feet deep, the gift of the ages, the legacy of the grass and the flowers that had blossomed and withered unseen for centuries. You had but to scratch and throw in the wheat, and with that, such crops would grow as older Canada had never seen! But with that no clearing of the land to do, no stubborn fight against the stumps still all around us on the Ontario farms — empty country and land for the asking, one hundred and sixty acres free under the new homestead law and more if you wanted it "for a song." No phrase ever appealed to the farmer's heart like that of getting land for a song! In the glory of the vision he forgets that he can't sing, and starts off looking for it.

To this was added the fact that there was rail connection now (1878) all the way to Manitoba by Chicago and St. Paul and the Red River route, and that it was known that the new government — which carried the election of 1878 under John A. Macdonald — was pledged to build a Canadian Pacific Railway clear across the plains and over the Rockies to the ocean. And with that was set up a sort of suction that began to draw people to Manitoba from all the Ontario farms, and presently beyond that from the old country itself, and in particular to Winnipeg, a place that had been a sort of straggled-out settlement of the Hudson's Bay Company, Fort Garry, and now broke on the horizon as a town whose geographical site in the bottleneck entrance of the West marked it as a future metropolis. Hence the "Winnipeg boom" and the noise of hammers and saws, and the shouts of the real-estate agents, selling real estate all day and all night, and selling it so far out on the prairie that no one ever found it again.

My father was to go to Manitoba not on his own initiative — he hadn't any — but at the call of a younger brother who had gone on ahead and was already riding on the crest of the wave. This was "my remarkable uncle", to whose memory I have devoted many sketches and even the scenario of a moving picture which I hope will one day move. He had come out to Canada, to our farm, in 1878, had captivated the countryside with his brilliant and unusual personality, taken a conspicuous part in the election of 1878, and passed on to a larger local notoriety in Toronto. He scented Winnipeg from afar, was one of the first in, and at the time of which I speak was piling up a fortune on paper, was elected to the New Manitoba legislature, and heaven knows what.

In my sketches I referred to my father and uncle as going away together, which is an error in the record. My father, and presently my brother Jim followed.

So we had a sale at the farm at which, as I have said elsewhere, the lean cattle and the broken machinery fetched only about enough in notes of hand (nobody had cash) to pay for the whisky consumed at the sale.

So my father left for the West, and my mother was left on the farm with the younger children and Old Tommy, and my elder brothers and I were sent away to school at Upper Canada College. That was for me practically the end of the old farm, though the rotten place hung round our family neck for years, unsalable. For the time being it was rented to the neighboring farmer for two hundred and fifty dollars a year, the same amount as my mother had to pay on the mortgage. The farmer didn't pay the rent and Mother didn't pay the mortgage; all debts in those days dragged along like that. But the year after that my mother moved into Toronto on the strength of a casual legacy from England that should have been hoarded as capital but was burned up as income. Then my father came back (broke) from the Northwest in 1886, and that meant another move back from Toronto to the old farm, but I was not in it, being a boarder at Upper Canada College. Things went worse than ever for my father on his return to the farm — a shadowed, tragic family life into which I need not enter. I always feel that it is out of place in an autobiography to go into such details. The situation ended by my father leaving home again in 1887. No doubt he meant to come back, but he never did. I never saw him again. My mother lived on at the old farm, because it was unsalable, for four more years, with eight children to look after as best she could on about eighty dollars a month and with Old Tommy and his wife as bodyguard. Tommy's wages had not been paid for so long that he couldn't leave, but anyway he didn't want to. In his old-fashioned Yorkshire mind wages due from the aristocracy were like shares in the National Debt. My elder brothers Jim and Dick had both left home for good, both to the West, Dick into the Northwest Mounted Police and Jim in the wake of my remarkable uncle. That made me — my father being gone — the head of the family at seventeen. But since I was away at school and college and then teaching school, I was only at the farm on holidays and odd times. I at last got rid of the rotten old place on my mother's behalf simply by moving Mother off it and letting it go to the devil — mortgages, creditors and all. I don't know who finally got it. But for me the old farm life ended with my going to Upper Canada College in the beginning of the year 1882.

2

My Remarkable Uncle
A Personal Document

The most remarkable man I have ever known in my life was my uncle Edward Philip Leacock — known to ever so many people in Winnipeg fifty or sixty years ago as E. P. His character was so exceptional that it needs nothing but plain narration. It was so exaggerated already that you couldn't exaggerate it.

When I was a boy of six, my father brought us, a family flock, to settle on an Ontario farm. We lived in an isolation unknown, in these days of radio, anywhere in the world. We were thirty-five miles from a railway. There were no newspapers. Nobody came and went. There was nowhere to come and go. In the solitude of the dark winter nights the stillness was that of eternity.

Into this isolation there broke, two years later, my dynamic Uncle Edward, my father's younger brother. He had just come from a year's travel around the Mediterranean. He must have been about twenty-eight, but seemed a more than adult man, bronzed and self-confident, with a square beard like a Plantagenet King. His talk was of Algiers, of the African slave market; of the Golden Horn and the Pyramids. To us it sounded like the *Arabian Nights*. When we asked, "Uncle Edward, do you know the Prince of Wales?" he answered, "Quite intimately" — with no further explanation. It was an impressive trick he had.

In that year, 1878, there was a general election in Canada. E. P. was in it up to the neck in less than no time. He picked up the history and politics of Upper Canada in a day, and in a week knew everybody in the countryside. He spoke at every meeting, but his strong point was the personal contact of electioneering, of bar-room treats. This gave full scope for his marvelous talent for flattery and make-believe.

"Why, let me see" — he would say to some tattered country specimen beside him glass in hand — "surely, if your name is Framley, you must be a relation of my dear old friend General Sir Charles Framley of the Horse Artillery?" "Mebbe," the flattered specimen would answer. "I guess, mebbe; I ain't kept track very good of my folks in the old country." "Dear me! I must tell Sir Charles that I've seen you. He'll be so pleased." ... In this way in a fortnight E. P. had conferred honours and distinctions on half the township of Georgina. They lived in a recaptured atmosphere of generals, admirals and earls. Vote? How else could they vote than conservative, men of family like them?

It goes without saying that in politics, then and always, E. P. was on the conservative, the *aristocratic* side, but along with that was hail-fellow-well-met with the humblest. This was instinct. A democrat can't condescend. He's down already. But when a conservative stoops, he conquers.

The election, of course, was a walk-over. E. P. might have stayed to reap the fruits. But he knew better. Ontario at that day was too small a horizon. For these were the days of the hard times of Ontario farming, when mortgages fell like snowflakes, and farmers were sold up, or sold out, or went "to the States," or faded humbly underground.

But all the talk was of Manitoba now opening up. Nothing would do E. P. but that he and my father must go west. So we had a sale of our farm, with refreshments, old-time fashion, for the buyers. The poor, lean cattle and the broken machines fetched less than the price of the whisky. But E. P. laughed it all off, quoted that the star of the Empire glittered in the west, and off to the West they went, leaving us children behind at school.*

They hit Winnipeg just on the rise of the boom, and E. P. came at once into his own and rode on the crest of the wave. There is something of

---

*The version of events given in "Life on the Old Farm" is the correct one — E.P. went in 1879 and Peter Leacock in 1881. —ED

magic appeal in the rush and movement of a "boom" town — a Winnipeg of the 80's, a Carson City of the 60's.... Life comes to a focus; it is all here and now, all *present*, no past and no outside — just a clatter of hammers and saws, rounds of drinks and rolls of money. In such an atmosphere every man seems a remarkable fellow, a man of exception; individuality separates out and character blossoms like a rose.

E. P. came into his own. In less than no time he was in everything and knew everybody, conferring titles and honours up and down Portage Avenue. In six months he had a great fortune, on paper; took a trip east and brought back a charming wife from Toronto; built a large house beside the river; filled it with pictures that he said were his ancestors, and carried on in it a roaring hospitality that never stopped.

His activities were wide. He was president of a bank (that never opened), head of a brewery (for brewing the Red River) and, above all, secretary-treasurer of the Winnipeg Hudson Bay and Arctic Ocean Railway that had a charter authorizing it to build a road to the Arctic Ocean, when it got ready. They had no track, but they printed stationery and passes, and in return E. P. received passes all over North America.

But naturally his main hold was politics. He was elected right away into the Manitoba Legislature. They would have made him Prime Minister but for the existence of the grand old man of the province, John Norquay. But even at that in a very short time Norquay ate out of E. P.'s hand, and E. P. led him on a string. I remember how they came down to Toronto, when I was a schoolboy, with an adherent group of "Westerners," all in heavy buffalo coats and bearded like Assyrians. E. P. paraded them on King Street like a returned explorer with savages.

Naturally E. P.'s politics remained conservative. But he pitched the note higher. Even the ancestors weren't good enough. He invented a Portuguese Dukedom (some one of our family once worked in Portugal*)

---

*Stephen's great-grandfather made a fortune in the Madeira wine trade; that was the basis of the family fortune. Leacock's is still an important name in Madeira. —ED

— and he conferred it, by some kind of reversion, on my elder brother Jim who had gone to Winnipeg to work in E. P.'s office. This enabled him to say to visitors in his big house, after looking at the ancestors — to say in a half-whisper behind his hand, "Strange to think that two deaths would make that boy a Portuguese Duke." But Jim never knew which two Portuguese to kill.

To aristocracy E. P. also added a touch of peculiar prestige by always being apparently just about to be called away — imperially. If some one said, "Will you be in Winnipeg all winter, Mr. Leacock?" he answered, "It will depend a good deal on what happens in West Africa." Just that; West Africa beat them.

Then came the crash of the Manitoba boom. Simple people, like my father, were wiped out in a day. Not so E. P. The crash just gave him a lift as the smash of a big wave lifts a strong swimmer. He just went right on. I believe that in reality he was left utterly bankrupt. But it made no difference. He used credit instead of cash. He still had his imaginary bank, and his railway to the Arctic Ocean. Hospitality still roared and the tradesmen still paid for it. Any one who called about a bill was told that E. P.'s movements were uncertain and would depend a good deal on what happened in Johannesburg. That held them another six months.

It was during this period that I used to see him when he made his periodic trips "east," to impress his creditors in the West. He floated, at first very easily, on hotel credit, borrowed loans and unpaid bills. A banker, especially a country town banker, was his natural mark and victim. He would tremble as E. P. came in, like a stockdove that sees a hawk. E. P.'s method was so simple; it was like showing a farmer peas under thimbles. As he entered the banker's side-office he would say: "I say. Do you fish? Surely that's a greenhart casting-rod on the wall?" (E.P. knew the names of everything.) In a few minutes the banker, flushed and pleased, was exhibiting the rod, and showing flies in a box out of a drawer. When E. P. went out he carried a hundred dollars with him. There was no security. The transaction was all over.

He dealt similarly with credit, with hotels, livery stables and bills in shops. They all fell for his method. He bought with lavish generosity, never asking a price. He never suggested pay till just as an afterthought, just as he was going out. And then: "By the way, please let me have the account promptly. I may be going away," and, in an aside to me, as if not meant for the shop, "Sir Henry Loch has cabled again from West Africa." And so out; they had never seen him before; nor since.

The proceeding with a hotel was different. A country hotel was, of course, easy, in fact too easy. E. P. would sometimes pay such a bill in cash, just as a sportsman won't shoot a sitting partridge. But a large hotel was another thing. E. P., on leaving — that is, when all ready to leave, coat, bag and all — would call for his bill at the desk. At the sight of it he would break out into enthusiasm at the reasonableness of it. "Just think!" he would say in his "aside" to me, "compare that with the Hotel Crillon in Paris!" The hotel proprietor had no way of doing this; he just felt that he ran a cheap hotel. Then another "aside," "Do remind me to mention to Sir John how admirably we've been treated; he's coming here next week." "Sir John" was our Prime Minister and the hotel keeper hadn't known he was coming — and he wasn't.... Then came the final touch — "Now, let me see ... seventy-six dollars ... seventy-six.... You give me" — and E. P. fixed his eye firmly on the hotel man — "give me twenty-four dollars, and then I can remember to send an even hundred." The man's hand trembled. But he gave it.

This does not mean that E. P. was in any sense a crook, in any degree dishonest. His bills to him were just "deferred pay," like the British debts to the United States. He never did, never contemplated, a crooked deal in his life. All his grand schemes were as open as sunlight — and as empty.

In all his interviews E. P. could fashion his talk to his audience. On one of his appearances I introduced him to a group of college friends, young men near to degrees, to whom degrees mean everything. In casual conversation E. P. turned to me and said, "Oh, by the way you'll be glad to know that I've just received my honorary degree from the Vatican — at last!" The "at last" was a knock-out — a degree from the Pope, and overdue at that!

Of course it could not last. Gradually credit crumbles. Faith weakens. Creditors grow hard, and friends turn their faces away. Gradually E. P. sank down. The death of his wife had left him a widower, a shuffling, half-shabby figure, familiar on the street, that would have been pathetic but for his indomitable self-belief, the illumination of his mind. Even at that, times grew hard with him. At length even the simple credit of the bar-rooms broke under him. I have been told by my brother Jim — the Portuguese Duke — of E. P. being put out of a Winnipeg bar, by an angry bar-tender who at last broke the mesmerism. E. P. had brought in a little group, spread up the fingers of one hand and said, "Mr. Leacock, five!" . . . The bar-tender broke into oaths. E. P. hooked a friend by the arm. "Come away," he said. "I'm afraid the poor fellow's crazy! But I hate to report him."

Presently even his power to travel came to an end. The railways found out at last that there wasn't any Arctic Ocean, and anyway the printer wouldn't print.

Just once again he managed to "come east." It was in June of 1891. I met him forging along King Street in Toronto — a trifle shabby but with a plug hat with a big band of crape round it. "Poor Sir John," he said. "I felt I simply must come down for his funeral." Then I remembered that the Prime Minister was dead, and realized that kindly sentiment had meant free transportation.

That was the last I ever saw of E. P. A little after that some one paid his fare back to England. He received, from some family trust, a little income of perhaps two pounds a week. On that he lived, with such dignity as might be, in a lost village in Worcestershire. He told the people of the village — so I learned later — that his stay was uncertain; it would depend a good deal on what happened in China. But nothing happened in China; there he stayed, years and years. There he might have finished out, but for a strange chance of fortune, a sort of poetic justice, that gave to E. P. an evening in the sunset.

It happened that in the part of England where our family belonged there was an ancient religious brotherhood, with a monastery and dilapidated estates that went back for centuries. E. P. descended on them, the brothers seeming to him an easy mark, as brothers indeed are. In the course of his pious "retreat," E. P. took a look into the brothers' finances, and his quick intelligence discovered an old claim against the British Government, large in amount and valid beyond a doubt.

In less than no time E. P. was at Westminster, representing the brothers. He knew exactly how to handle British officials; they were easier even than Ontario hotel keepers. All that is needed is hints of marvellous investment overseas. They never go there but they remember how they just missed Johannesburg or were just late on Persian oil. All E. P. needed was his Arctic Railway. "When you come out, I must take you over our railway. I really think that as soon as we reach the Coppermine River we must put the shares on here; it's too big for New York...."

So E. P. got what he wanted. The British Government are so used to old claims that it would as soon pay as not. There are plenty left.

The brothers got a whole lot of money. In gratitude they invited E. P. to be their permanent manager; so there he was, lifted into ease and affluence. The years went easily by, among gardens, orchards, and fishponds old as the Crusades.

When I was lecturing in London in 1921 he wrote to me: "Do come down; I am too old now to travel; but any day you like I will send a chauffeur with a car and two lay-brothers to bring you down." I thought the "lay-brothers" a fine touch — just like E. P.

I couldn't go. I never saw him again. He ended out his days at the monastery, no cable calling him to West Africa. Years ago I used to think of E. P. as a sort of humbug, a source of humour. Looking back now I realize better the unbeatable quality of his spirit, the mark, we like to think just now, of the British race.

If there is a paradise, I am sure he will get in. He will say at the gate — "Peter? Then surely you must be a relative of Lord Peter of Tichfield?"

But if he fails, then, as the Spaniards say so fittingly, "May the earth lie light upon him."

3

THE STRUGGLE TO MAKE US GENTLEMEN
A Memory of My Old School

I mentioned above that I had gone away from the farm where I lived as a child to a boarding-school — the old Upper Canada College that stood half a century ago on King Street in Toronto. It has all been knocked down since. I look back at it now with that peculiar affection that every one feels for his old school after it has been knocked down and all the masters dead long ago.

But certain things that I was reading the other day, in the English papers, brought the old school back vividly to my mind. What I was reading belonged in the present English discussion, which the war has so much accentuated, about social classes, and whether "gentlemen" can go on finding a place. For it seems there is a good deal of alarm now in England over the idea that "gentlemen" may be dying out. In an old civilization things come and go. Knighthood came and went; it was in the flower, then in the pod and then all went to seed. Now it seems to be gentlemen that are going. It appears that the upper classes are being so depressed and the lower classes so pushed up, and both shifting sideways so fast, that you simply can't distinguish an upper birth from a lower. In fact it is hard to make up their births at all.

I wasn't meaning to write on that topic. The thing is too big. Every one admits that if gentlemen go, then Heaven only knows what will happen to England. But then Heaven only ever did. But the point here is that the question has got mixed up with the fate of the public schools; I mean of course public in the English sense, the ones the public can't get into. The best solution — it is generally admitted — in fact a solution "definitely in sight" is in the idea that if you throw the big board schools into the public schools and then throw the small private schools into both of them, then you so mix up your gentlemen with your others that they all turn into gentlemen. Of course you can't face this all at once; a whole nation of gentlemen is a goal rather than — well, I mean to say it takes time. Meantime, if it is "definitely in sight," that's the place where the genius of England likes to leave it. It can roost there and go fast asleep along with Dominion Status for India and the Disestablishment of the Church.

So, as I say, this talk of "gentlemen" in England turned me back to our old Upper Canada College on King Street sixty years ago, and the desperate struggle there to make us gentlemen. We didn't understand for a while just what they were trying to do to us. But gradually we began to catch on to it, and feel that it was no good. There was a kindly and oratorical principal, whom I will not name but whom the affection of Old Boys will easily recall — a kindly principal, I say, with a beautiful and sonorous voice that used to echo through the Prayer Hall in exaltation of the topic. "This school, I insist," he would declaim, "must be a school of *gentlemen*." We used to sit as juniors and think: "Gee! This is going to be a tight shave! I'll never make it." But presently we learned to take it more easily. We noticed that the gentlemen question broke out after a theft of school-books, or the disappearance of small change foolishly left in reach. Not being yet gentlemen, we made a distinction between "stealing" a thing and "hooking" it. A gentleman, you see, classes both together. He'd just as soon steal a thing as hook it.

But, bit by bit and gradually, we were led towards the ideal. We were often told, by oratorical visitors, that Upper Canada College was founded as a "school for gentlemen." When I entered the school there were still a few old, very old, boys around, who belonged to the early generations of the foundation. We felt that the school had been fooled in some of them. They seemed just like us.

Personally, however, I got by on a side issue. In those days there was none of the elaborate registration, the card index stuff, that all schools have now. Any information that they wanted about us they got *viva voce* on the spot by calling us up in front of the class and asking for it. So there came a day soon after I entered when the principal called me up to be questioned and a junior master wrote down the answers. "What," he asked, "is your father's occupation?" I hesitated quite a while and then I said, "He doesn't do anything." The principal bent over towards the junior master who was writing and said in an impressive voice, "A gentleman." A sort of awe spread round the room at my high status. But really why I had hesitated was because I didn't know what to say. You see, I knew that my father, when in Toronto, was probably to be found along on King Street having a Tom-and-Jerry in the Dog and Duck, or at Clancey's — but whether to call that his occupation was a nice question.

Slowly we learned the qualifications of a gentleman and saw that the thing was hopeless. A gentleman it seemed would take a bath (once a week on bath night) and never try to dodge it. A gentleman would not chew gum in St. George's Church, nor imitate the voice of an Anglican Bishop. A gentleman, it seemed, couldn't tell a lie — not wouldn't, just couldn't. Limitations like these cut such a swath through our numbers that in time we simply gave up. There was no use in it. Mind, don't misunderstand me. Of course we could behave like gentlemen — oh, certainly — act like gentlemen. At first sight you'd mistake us for it. But we knew all the time that we weren't.

So, like the other boys, I left school still puzzled about the gentlemen business, and as the years have gone by the perplexity has only gone deeper. What is, or was, a gentleman, anyway? I remember that a little after I left school, while I was at college, there was a famous Canadian murder case that attracted wide attention because the murderer, who was presently hanged, was a gentleman. He was a young Englishman who enticed another young Englishman into a dismal swamp and for the sake of his money shot him in a brutal and cowardly way from behind. I met and knew afterwards several of the lawyers and people on the case and they all agreed that the murderer was a gentleman; in fact several of them said, "a thorough gentleman." Others said, "a perfect gentleman." Some of them had the idea that his victim was perhaps "not quite a gentleman" — but you'd hardly kill a man for that.

This shows, if any demonstration is needed, that a "gentleman" is not a *moral* term. As a matter of fact, all attempts to make it so break down hopelessly. People have often tried to sort out a class of people whom they call "nature's gentlemen." These are supposed to have it all — the honour, the candour (you can see it in their candid faces), all except the little touches of good manners and good English and the things that lie, or seem to lie, on the surface. They may be. But gentlemen don't mix with them.

Hence you can't qualify for being a gentleman by being good, or being honest, or being religious. A gentleman may be those things, but if he is, he never talks about them. In fact a gentleman never speaks of himself and never preaches. All good people do; and so they are not gentlemen. See how perplexing it gets? No wonder it worried us at school. For example can a clergyman be a gentleman? Certainly, if he keeps off religion. Or, for example, would a gentleman steal? He would and he wouldn't. If you left a handful of money right on a table near him, with no one in sight, no one to find out, he wouldn't steal it. Of course not; it's not the kind of thing a gentleman does. But if you left it in a bank account, he might have a go at it; but, of course, that's not exactly stealing; that's embezzlement. Gentleman embezzle but don't steal.

And, of course, it goes without saying that being a gentleman isn't just a matter of wearing good clothes. You can't make yourself a gentleman by going to a good tailor. There is all the difference in the world between a man dressed like a gentleman and a tailor's dummy. No gentleman ever lets a tailor have his way with him. After the tailor has a suit measured to what he thinks an exact fit, a gentleman always has it let out six inches behind. You can tell him by that; and just when the tailor has the waistcoat what he calls "snug," the gentleman has it eased out across the stomach. You see, if you give a tailor his way he carries everything too far; his profession becomes a mania. All professions do. Give a barber his own way and he'll roll a man's hair into little ringlets, like a baby's coqueluche. That's why foreigners, as seen by a gentleman, are never well dressed and well shaved. They are too submissive to their tailor and their coiffeur. Hence instead of being well dressed and clean shaven, they are all overdressed and parboiled. This is what a gentleman means by a "French Johnny."

So one understands that a gentleman may dress as he likes.

I noticed an excellent example of this as related in a recent fascinating book of Australian travel. The scene was in that vast Australian empty country that you are not allowed to call desert. They speak of it as the "never-never country," or the "walla-boo" or the "willa-walla" — things like that. Out there — or in there — I don't know which you call it — there is nothing but sand and cactus and spinnifex, and black fellows, with occasional excellent shooting at great flocks of cockatoos, and an odd shot at a partridge or a pastoralist.

It was away off in this country that the travellers in the book I speak of came across a queer lost specimen of humanity, who had been living there twenty or thirty years — "a hairy, bushy-whiskered, unkempt individual. Grey hair grew on every part of his face. The only place where there was no hair was the part of the head where hair usually grows. That part was as bald as an egg. He had elastic-side boots but no socks. He had trousers but neither braces nor belt. The trousers were loose about the waist-band, and whilst he talked, when standing, he spent most of the time grabbing them and hitching them up just as they were on the point of falling down. It was constant competition between himself and the trousers — the trousers wanting to fall down and he wanting them to keep up."

But the odd thing is that when they came to talk to this man, there is no mistaking from their narrative that he was a gentleman. It was not only his contempt of a tailor that showed it. He had been to a public school, in the proper English sense as above. He still talked like a gentleman and, like a gentleman, had no word of complaint against a little thing like twenty years of sand.

When we say that this man "talked like a gentleman," how then does a gentleman talk? It is not so much a matter of how he talks but how he doesn't talk. No gentleman cares to talk about himself; no gentleman talks about money, or about his family, or about his illness, about the inside of his body or about his soul. Does a gentleman swear? Oh certainly; but remember, no gentleman would ever swear at a servant

— only at his own friends. In point of language a gentleman is not called upon to have any particular choice of words. But he must, absolutely must, have a trained avoidance of them. Any one who says "them there," and "which is yourn" and "them ain't his'n," is not a gentlemen. There are no two ways about it; he may be "nature's gentle-man"; but that's as far as you can get.

The more I look at this problem of the gentlemen the more I realize how difficult it is, and yet, in spite of everything, there seems to be something in it. One recalls the story of how Galileo was bullied and threatened by the Inquisition till he took back and denied his theory that the earth went round the sun. Yet as he came out from the tribunal he muttered to himself, "But it does really." So with the gentleman. There's something in it. This quiet man who never breaks his word and never eats with his knife; never complains of hard luck and wears his pants as he wants them; deferential to those below, independent to those above; the soul of honour, except in embezzlement; and when down and out goes away and looks for a wallaboo and enough sand and cactus to die in —

It's a fine thing. I'm sorry they failed at my school. I must have another go at it.

4

MY EDUCATION AND WHAT
I THINK OF IT NOW

[…] I look back to the education I received in those years and I find in it plenty to think about. It was what is, or was, called a splendid classical education, as it was for a couple of hundred years, in England and America, looked on as the mainstay of national culture, the keystone in the arch of civilization; and before that in England it was the only kind of education and it was embedded deep in theology and so intimately connected with the Church that it was inseparable from it. Any form of education not connected with the Church was held to belong to the devil, as witness the education for which Oxford in its infant years imprisoned or secluded Roger Bacon for ten years. There was the Church's education and the devil's education. In the long run the devil's education has won out. Any nation whose leaders are not trained in it will no longer survive; any nation whose life is not based on it, whose people are not equipped with it, cannot last a generation. In other words, the "survival quality" that was attributed to the old classical education has passed away, or is visibly passing away, with the generation of the present leaders.

People who admit they know nothing of the history of education among English-speaking peoples may tolerate a few words of explanation. All through the Middle Ages the only education (we are speaking broadly) was that of the Church. It was carried on in Latin. When the modern age began, say about A.D. 1500, and printing multiplied books, education widened and included a lot of what had been the education of the Greeks and Romans, such as the philosophy of Aristotle, which in no way contradicts the teaching of the Church and could be read side by side with it, and the great poems and plays of the Greeks, of Homer and the tragedians, and those of Rome, such as Virgil's account of how Aeneas escaped from the fall of Troy and founded the Roman nation, and the great histories, Thucydides' *History of Greece,* and the works of Livy and Tacitus and Julius Caesar in Latin, of Demosthenes and of Cicero. All this made such an imposing body of literature, especially when set off in the new glory of print on vellum, that there was in vernacular English, or indeed in any vernacular, nothing like it at all. It was so to speak the world's literature, containing all the wisdom of the world. Even when people in England such as Shakespeare began to write things that were better no one knew it or admitted it. Many people still don't. A Greek professor, especially if growing old and apt to sit under a tree and fall asleep over Theocritus, will tell you, of course, that Greek literature is unsurpassed. Nor can you contradict him, since you don't know it, except by telling him that the Chinese classics are better still.

So here then was the education that went into the rising glory of England and with the earliest beginnings of the United States. Oddly enough it carried with it a fringe, which kept growing and expanding, of mathematics and physics that had not been part of the education of the Greeks at large. The Greeks abhorred anything practical (just as Oxford one hundred years ago tried to ignore "stinks," meaning chemistry), and they never had any decent system of calculation by numbers on paper, so that Greek mathematics was queer, odd, ingenious stuff, as if one worked out puzzles for puzzles' sake. It was complicated and difficult enough, as when they speculated on the kind of curves made by slicing through a cone (conic sections), an enquiry carried on "just for fun" in their time. Only one part of their Greek mathematics, the art of field measurement, or geometry, was especially developed into a complete and rounded form, particularly in Egypt, in the great Greek centre of learning in Alexandria. This was because in Egypt, with each annual flood of the Nile, land measurement by sight lines had a special importance. Hence the treatise of Euclid came into our education intact and stayed there till into the present century.

To what the Greeks had of mathematics, the new English classical education, as it got consolidated after, say, A.D. 1500, added all that went with the wonderful system of calculating by giving figures a "place value" (so that, for example, the figure two may mean two, or twenty, or two hundred, and so on). We are so accustomed to this that we take it for granted and no longer see how wonderful it is. The Greeks and Romans and all the ancient nations fooled round with it and got even as close to it as the method of counting of beads on strings, et cetera, but they never learned how to put it on paper and so make the figures add and subtract and multiply in our present marvellous and simple method of columns and places. It was the Hindus who worked this out, but the Arabs put the cap on it by inventing the use of the figure zero, the round O for nothing that means everything.

Luckily for English education, mathematics developed side by side with classical education not as an equal partner but as an adjacent. This was partly by the genius of the nation which tends to produce men of exception as seen in Napier, who invented logarithms, Isaac Newton, who invented calculus and went, in an effortless way, beyond all known boundaries, and Halley, who invented Isaac Newton by keeping him at work. Nor could even Halley keep him at it for good. It is odd that Newton, who lived to a great old age, was all done with science relatively early in life, pursued no more discoveries, and felt proud to be in Royal Service as the Master of the Mint.

But what made mathematics for England was its connection with navigation. When the era of colonial expansion brought England on to the seven seas, navigation by means of mathematical astronomy became the peculiar privilege and pursuit of the British. The Portuguese and the Spanish had known only the beginnings of it. Columbus was really, in spite of some tall talk on his part, quite ignorant. He merely threw a chunk of wood overboard to see how fast the ship was going. The English forged ahead. The Elizabethans "took the sun." Isaac Newton himself explained that longitude at sea could be accurately known each day at noon as soon as someone could invent a clock to keep time at sea. Even at that the Admiralty prize of ten thousand pounds went begging till late in the eighteenth century. But with the use of chronometrics and sextants and the compilations of astronomical tables worked out on shore and applied at sea, and ingenious mathematical tables of logarithms to apply them with, British navigators led the world. It was the British government that sent out astronomers with captains to observe the transit of Venus in the South Pacific in 1769. After which the use of mathematics got mixed up with the glory of Old England and Britannia ruling the waves, and no scheme of English education was complete without it. Not that the English schools took to it gladly. We are told (in the *Memoirs* of General Lyttelton) that even at Eton the study of mathematics was tolerated rather than appreciated as late as the sixties of the last century.

In all this I am not wandering from the point. I am explaining where I got my Upper Canada College education from; well, that's where it came from, from the theologians and the classical scholars and Isaac Newton and the *Nautical Almanac*.

But the thing that especially consolidated the position of the classical education in England, as it presently did also in America, was the discovery, by experience, that it was a great training for leadership. This applied particularly to a nation which had grown not democratic, but parliamentary, a nation where oratory in the legislature counted for more and more, and where forensic oratory in free and open courts was one of the great highways to success and political preferment.

To this was added presently the power of the press, the value of the written word and the persuading paragraph, things for which the classical education had, and still retains when most else is gone, a commanding eminence.

Side by side with classical education, in a position that has slowly grown from the lowest to the highest, grew up medicine and medical education: from its earliest beginnings, in black art and barbers' surgery with its red-and-white rags, out of the mists of astrology and the incantations of superstition, out of empirical remedies and old wives' tales, till with the age of science it began to build on definite organized truth and on knowledge gathered from the facts of dissection and the observations of anatomy. But medicine was no part of the education of a cultivated man, and till far down the nineteenth century the social status of a doctor, other than a court physician, was dubious and humiliating.

Science remained for the few, for the investigators, for the Royal Society founded under Charles II, a factor in the national advance of England second only to the Royal Navy for people who, like Benjamin Franklin, with electricity, wanted to know. The list of the great names in science — Priestley, Faraday, Lyell, Darwin — lies outside of the orbit of academic education.

Such was the classical education. It is my opinion that the world moved it on just in time and that England especially was saved in the nineteenth century from degenerating into intellectual stagnation only by the fact that other forces in the nation, clear outside of its scholars and all that they stood for, pursued science for science's sake; promoted invention, applied it to industry and transport, and presently — by the dead weight of circumstance and opinion — thrust it into the schools and colleges.

A chief trouble with the classical scholarship was its infernal conceit. The typical classical scholar developed under encouragement into a sort of pundit. He knew it all — not part of it, all of it. What he didn't know wasn't college. The phrase was used long after by Benjamin Jowett, Master of Balliol, but it might have been used by any of them from the days of Dr. Busby of Westminster, in the days of Charles II, down to their last octogenarian successors of yesterday. They knew it all. That is to say, they knew nothing whatever of medicine and would have roared with laughter over their own ignorance of it, with a neat Latin quotation to cap it. They knew nothing whatever of the geographical and geological globe about them, replacing it with an intimate knowledge of the Aegean Sea as of 500 B.C. They knew nothing of modern languages, regarding them as a thing for couriers or dragomen. They knew nothing of the investigations of natural science, had no vision as to where it was leading, nothing of its application to industry, nothing of industry itself, nothing of finance — in fact, looked at in a proper focus, all that they did know was nothing as compared with the vast portentous knowledge that was rising on the horizon of a changing world.

Even for literature and the drama, all that goes with the republic of letters, their point of view was turning hopelessly astray by their persistent tradition that of course Latin and Greek literature was far superior to that of our own day. To say this in A.D. 1500 was to state a plain truth. To say it in A.D. 1900 was to say pure unadulterated nonsense.

The old classical education had at least the advantage that it was hard and difficult with no royal road. It was as hard as ever a teacher liked to make it. For witness call in anyone who has studied Greek moods and tenses or tried to translate the Greek dramatists into something intelligible. In all this it was miles above a great deal of the slush and mush, which has in part replaced it, the effortless, pretentious study of things that can't be studied at all, the vague fermentations that tend to replace stern disciplinary work when education is all paid for and free for all and popular and universal, provided that it is not made difficult.

The classical curriculum had also the advantage, to be rightly or wrongly used, that it lent itself admirably to competitive study, to examinations, to marks, to prizes, to going up and down in class. It was from that aspect that I made my Upper Canada College education even less beneficial than it need have been, accentuated its faults by utilizing its weakness. We had at Upper Canada College the system whereby each day's class consisted mainly of questions and answers, that is, either questions on homework done the night before or on something done at sight in class. The boys sat all along one side or all across the front of the room. If the master asked a boy a question and he couldn't answer it, then it was passed on, "Next! Next!" till somebody did answer. The boy who thus answered correctly moved up above the ones who had failed to answer. Theoretically, but very rarely in practice, a question might be asked of a boy at the top of the class and be passed on, "Next! Next!" with increasing excitement all the way to the bottom boy of the class, who might answer correctly and "Go up ahead" in one swoop. Hence the system had in it a certain element of sport, something of the attraction of a horse race. At least it kept the class from going to sleep and it made the class do the work and not the teacher. It always seems to me that in a lot of the revised education of today, which quite rightly undertook to modify the severities, the rigour, the physical punishment, and the needless difficulties of the older teaching, the mistake is made in the contrary direction. Everything is made too easy. The teacher has to "sell" the subject to the class, and in trying to make everything clear and simple it is forgotten that there are some things that can't be made clear and simple because they are by nature difficult and complex.

For me the old-fashioned system of going up and down and trying to move up to the head of the class and stay there proved altogether too congenial and attractive and helped to give a false bias to my education. In the junior form, the first and second, I took my studies easily, didn't bother whether I went up or down, and got a very good place without trying for it. But from the third form on, I got more and more drawn into study and overstudy till presently I filled all my time outside of school as well as in. After the third form, by this continuous industry, I ranked first in everything except mathematics, and after the fourth form first in everything by learning by heart in mathematics every possible thing that would let itself be learned by heart.

Study by this pattern knocked all the reality out of certain subjects. History for me just turned into an underlined book of which I knew by heart all the underlined tags, headings and dates. I knew them then and I still know all the clauses of the Treaty of Utrecht of 1713, and all sorts of dates and lists, and all kinds of headings. The reality of history gradually was lost from sight behind this apparatus of preparation for examinations.

The very thoroughness of the old classical system made it still worse suited for modern education.

5

Looking Back on College

During all my thirty-five years of college teaching I always felt that there was no profession in the world for which I would have exchanged my own. I have never had any envy of business men, no matter how rich, who work all the week and all the year, no matter how easy and simple their work may be as compared with Greek verbs and simultaneous equations.

College teachers enjoy a spacious feeling toward the flight of time that no business man can know. They have time to *think*. Very often they *don't* think but at least they have time to. Their fixed engagements are few, their open time — they don't like to call it a *vacation:* they resent that — is vast and alluring as an empty wood. In a well-ordered college — its finances unchangeable, its trustees mute as ancestral portraits, its departments feudalized into little kingdoms, with nothing of the bossy and brutal interference from above that begins to disfigure so many colleges — a professor's life in its outlook touches as close to eternity as any form of existence still with us. In the past there was the medieval scriptorium, with a stained-glass window under the light of which a scholar copied upon vellum a volume of Polybius: or there was, shall we say, an Elizabethan rectory where a pious Hooker penning his *Ecclesiastical Polity* looked out over the clipped lawns and the immemorial trees, and beyond that to the distant sea, and the clouds and the sunset. This timeless age our hurrying world destroyed. The professor still keeps a little bit of it: and it elevates his life to a plane that outsiders never can know — fortunately, or they would scramble for our places.

I am not decrying outside work. It is necessary. The world cannot go on without it. But we do not realize its artificial and unnatural character.

Our race has been schooled by long ages of compulsion, tied to our tasks like galley slaves, till we have been bred and evolved to the "work-habit" and take it now for granted. We are surprised when we see a real man — like a Portuguese West African — who won't work. We do not understand that what the business man does, except that it is necessary, is quite inexplicable. We can understand a man hunting deer, or fishing, or playing golf or chess — these are real things. But why should a man spend his busy days in trying to sell things — which he hasn't got — and make things which he never sees? At times he gets absorbed in it — and it becomes self-explanatory. But mostly it is just for the reward, the money and things it will buy. Partly, too, animal habit.

But with the professor it is all different. He has no *work* in that sense, not if he is a real professor. His class? — you can't keep him out of it. Preparing his lectures? — that's no more work than a lion getting up his appetite. People who do not live in colleges cannot understand the unworldly absorption of the professor's task. Poets talk of the joy of the springtime — of the month of May breaking the hills into green and filling all the air with rapture. The "merry month of May," says the poet. I know a merrier. Give me the murky month of February, with the snow blowing on the window pane of the class-room, the early darkness falling already and the gas-light bright in the class-room; that and a blackboard, and a theorem, and a professor — the right kind, absorbed, ecstatic, and a little silly. Give me that and the month of May may keep its fronds and toadstools as it will.

One would imagine that anyone who looks back, as I do, over nearly fifty years of college life, would know a great deal about the problems of education. Indeed I made a remark to that effect at a banquet given to me by my past students in exultation over my leaving McGill. I said, I think, that the setting sun, breaking out from under the clouds that had obscured the day, illuminated the landscape with a wider and softer light than that of noontide.* But that was just oratory, or gratitude for a good dinner. As a matter of fact the great problems

---

*See "Paradise Lost," page 210. —ED

of education seem to be just about as unsolved now as they were half a century ago.

When I entered college there was much talk of co-education, half a dozen dangerous-looking girls having just slipped into the classes. The question was, would women ruin college education, or would they endow it with newer, nobler and higher life? Or, more simply, were they a curse or a blessing, a nuisance or a charm? I still don't know. You can argue it either way according to how you are feeling. Certainly college is not what it was; but neither is anything. Old people live, and always have, in a world hurrying to ruin, young people in a world bright with the colours of the morning.

We talked, too, of the classics, very much to the fore fifty years ago, but even then having to bear the first onslaught of the rival studies of science and commerce. It was asked whether the study of the classics was the only real approach to the higher cultivation of the mind or whether they were a mere historical survival, a remnant of a rude, illiterate but reviving age, when any book in Latin seemed a treasure, and any play in Greek a masterpiece. Are the classics really great literature? I don't know. They don't sound like it, but that may be my fault. Can a man really be a gentleman without studying the Greek moods and tenses; perhaps he can, but can he be the best kind of a gentleman? I don't know. Greek has been pushed overboard by the sheer pressure of the crowd on deck. Is it a loss? I don't know.

And what about science? Is a person as totally ignorant of chemistry as I am, as almost totally ignorant of physics, biology, geology as I am, any the worse for it? He must be. And yet if you do learn by heart, and then forget, the names of the palaeozoic, mesozoic, and kainozoic ages, are you any better off than the Greek student who knows what they are anyway and can't forget it. Is a smattering of *science* anything more than a list of words; or does it unlock for us the vast general store-house of the world's wisdom on which alone a reasonable outlook can be based? I think so. Which? Both.

Then, as to method of education. I hear students nowadays say that *lectures* are no good, that you don't learn anything by hearing a professor read out notes. We used to say that, too, fifty years ago. It is claimed now that you can get it all out of a book. So it was then. So you can.

But will you? The student's mind, so it is said, must work for itself, assimilate its own material; so it must, of course, but how do you do it? Plato and Aristotle were giving lectures 2000 years ago: and men very like them will be giving lectures, the same lectures, 2000 years from now. Only people who have had to study for themselves, as I had to, know how good lectures are, even the worst of them — how hard it is to work without set times and hours and set companionship. Let the lecturers keep on lecturing, and if some of the lectures are worthless, the rest will seem all the snappier. After all it is not the *words* that the teacher reads or recites or quotes; it's the teacher himself — the peculiar element of personal magnetism or whatever one calls it — that "gets over" to the class.

So it would seem that the college is always new and yet always old: living its own life on its own vital energy. The problems of education are just the shifting of the sunlight on the surface of a moving current.

6

On the Need for a Quiet College

If somebody would give me about two dozen very old elm trees and about fifty acres of wooded ground and lawn — not too near anywhere and not too far from everywhere — I think I could set up a college that would put all the big universities of today in the shade. I am not saying that it would be better. But it would be different.

I would need a few buildings, but it doesn't take many — stone, if possible — and a belfry and a clock. The clock wouldn't need to go; it might be better if it didn't. I would want some books — a few thousand would do — and some apparatus. But it's amazing how little apparatus is needed for scientific work of the highest quality: in fact "the higher the fewer."

Most of all, I should need a set of professors. I would need only a dozen of them — but they'd have to be real ones — disinterested men of learning, who didn't even know they were disinterested. And, mind you, these professors of mine wouldn't sit in "offices" dictating letters on "cases" to stenographers, and only leaving their offices to go to "committees" and "conferences." There would be no "offices" in my college and no "committees," and my professors would have no time for conferences, because the job they would be on would need all eternity and would never be finished.

My professors would never be findable at any fixed place except when they were actually giving lectures. Men of thought have no business in an office. Learning runs away from "committees." There would be no "check up" on the time of the professors: there would be no "hire and fire" or "judge by results" or "standards" or "norms" of work for them: or any fixed number of hours.

But, on the other hand, they would, if I got the ones I want, be well worth their apparent irresponsibility: and when they lectured each one would be, though he wouldn't know it, a magician — with such an interest and absorption that those who listened would catch the infection of it, and hurry from the lecture to the library, still warm with thought.

It must be understood that the work of professors is peculiar. Few professors, real ones, ever complete their work: what they give to the world is fragments. The rest remains. Their contributions must be added up, not measured singly. Every professor has his "life work" and sometimes does it, and sometimes dies first.

I can recall — I say it by way of digression — one such who was working on Machiavelli. When I first met him he had worked fourteen years. He worked in a large room covered a foot deep with Machiavelli — notes, pamphlets, remains. I asked him — it seemed a simple question — what he thought of Machiavelli. He shook his head. He said it was too soon to form an opinion. Later, ten years later, he published his book, *Machiavelli*. One of the great continental reviews — one of the really great ones (you and I never hear of them: they have a circulation of about 300) said his work was based on premature judgments. He was hurt, but he felt it was true. He had rushed into print too soon.

Another such devoted himself — he began years ago — to the history of the tariff. He began in a quiet lull of tariff changes when for three or four years public attention was elsewhere. He brought his work up to within a year or so of actual up-to-date completeness. Then the tariff began to move: two years later he was three years behind it. Presently, though he worked hard, he was five years behind it.

He has never caught it. His only hope now is that the tariff will move back towards free trade, and meet him.

Not that I mean to imply that my professors would be a pack of nuts or freaks. Not at all: their manners might be dreamy and their clothes untidy but they'd be — they'd have to be — the most eminent men in their subjects. To get them would be the main effort of the college: to coax them, buy them, if need be, to kidnap them. Nothing counts beside that. A college is made of men, not by the size of buildings, number of students and football records. But trustees don't know this, or, at best, catch only a glimmer of it and lose it. Within a generation all the greatest books on the humanities would come from my college.

The professors bring the students. The students bring, unsought, the benefactions. The thing feeds itself like a flame in straw. But it's the men that count. A college doesn't need students: it's the students who need the college.

After twenty years my college would stand all alone. There are little colleges now but they ape bigness. There are quiet colleges but they try to be noisy. There are colleges without big games but they boom little ones. Mine would seem the only one, because the chance is there, wide open, and no one takes it. After twenty years people would drive in motor cars to see my college: and wouldn't be let in.

Round such a college there must be no thought of money. Money ruins life: I mean, to have to think of it, to take account of it, to know that it is there. Men apart from money, men in an army, men on an expedition of exploration, emerge to a new life. Money is gone. At times and places whole classes thus lift up, or partly: as in older countries like England the class called "gentry" that once was. These people lived on land and money from the past — stolen, perhaps, five hundred years ago — and so thought no more of it. They couldn't earn more; they didn't know how. They kept what they had, or dropped out, fell through a trestle bridge of social structure and were gone in the stream. This class, in America, we never had. They grow rare everywhere. Perhaps we don't want them. But they had the good luck that, in their lives, money in the sense here meant, didn't enter. Certain money limits circumscribed their life, but from day to day they never thought of it. A cow in a pasture, a fairly generous pasture, doesn't know it's in. It thinks it's outside. So did they.

So I would have it in my college. Students not rich and not poor — or not using their wealth and not feeling their poverty — an equality as unconscious as that where Evangeline lived.

Nor would their studies lead to, or aim at, or connect with wealth. The so-called practical studies are all astray. Real study, real learning must, for the individual, be quite valueless or it loses its value. The proper studies for my college are history and literature and philosophy and thought and poetry and speculation, in the pursuit of which each shall repeat the eager search, the unending quest, of the past. Looking for one thing he shall find another. Looking for ultimate truth, which is unfindable, they will learn at least to repudiate all that is false.

I leave out at one sweep great masses of stuff usually taught: all that goes under such a name as a university faculty of Commerce. There is no such thing. The faculty of Commerce is down at the docks, at Wall Street, in the steel mills. A "degree" in Commerce is a salary of ten thousand a year. Those who fail to pass go to Atlanta — and stay there.* Certain things in Commerce are teachable: accountancy, corporate organization and the principles of embezzlement. But that's not a university.

Out goes economics, except as speculation: not a thing to teach in instalments and propositions like geometry. You *can't* teach it. No one knows it. It's the riddle of the Sphinx. My graduates will be just nicely fitted to think about it when they come out. A first-year girl studying economics is as wide of the mark as an old man studying cosmetics. The philosophical speculative analysis of our economic life is the highest study of all, next to the riddle of our existence. But to cut it into classes and credits is a parody. Out it goes.

Out — but to come back in again — goes medicine. Medicine is a great reality: it belongs in a *school*, not a college. My college fits people to study medicine, study it in crowded cities among gas-lights and ambulances and hospitals and human suffering, and keep their souls alive while they do it. Then later, as trained men in the noblest profession in the world, the atmosphere of the college, which they imbibed among my elm trees, grows about them again. The last word in cultivation is, and always has been, the cultivated "medicine man."

The engineers? — that's different. Theirs is the most "manly" of all the professions — among water power and gold mines and throwing bridges half a mile at a throw. But it's a *school* that trains them, not a college. They go to my college but they don't like it. They say it's too damn dreamy. So they kick out of it into engineering. For a time they remember the Latin third declension. Presently they forget it. Doctors grow cultivated as they grow older. Engineers get rougher and rougher.

---

*Atlanta was a U.S. federal prison best known when this essay was written as the place where Al Capone was incarcerated.—ED

What I mean is that our studies have drifted away, away from the single-minded absorption of learning. Our students of today live in a whirl and clatter of "student activities." They have, in any large college, at least a hundred organizations and societies. They are "all up!" for this today and "all out!" for that tomorrow. Life is a continuous rally! a rah, rah! a parade! They play no games: they use teams for that. But exercise, and air, is their life. They *root*, in an organized hysteria, a code of signals telling them what to feel. They root, they rush, they organize, they play politics, run newspapers — and when they step from college into life, they fit it absolutely, having lived already.

No one is denying here what fine men and women college makes, physically fine and mentally alert. Any one of them could run an elevator the day he steps out of college.

But there's something wanting: do they *think*? Or is there anything after all to think about? And yet, surely, in the long run the world has lived on its speculative minds. Or hasn't it?

Some who think of course there must be. You can't submerge humanity in two generations. But mostly, I believe, the little poets fade out on their first-year benches, and the wistful intelligence learns to say "*Rah! Rah!*" and is lost.

Not so in my college. There will be no newspaper, except a last week's paper from the back counties of New England. There will be no politics because there will be no offices to run for. My students will control nothing. The whole movement of student control is a mistake. They're so busy controlling that they're not students.

They shall play games all they want to, but as games, not as a profession, not as college advertising — and no gate receipts. Till only a few years ago the country that taught the world its games, played them as apart from money — as far apart as sheer necessity allowed. If Waterloo was won on the playing fields of Eton (it wasn't, really: it was won in Belgium), there was at least no stadium at two dollars a seat.

One asks, perhaps, about the endowments, about the benefactors of my ideal college. The benefactors are all dead: or at least they must act as if they were. Years ago on the prairies many authorities claimed that the only good Indian was a dead Indian. It may not have been true. But it is certainly true that the best college benefactor is a dead one. After all, the reward in the long run is his, those sculptured letters graven in the stone, "To the greater glory of God and in memory of Johannes Smith." That, in a college among elm trees — that's worth a lifetime of gifts, given and given gladly. Such things should best be graven in Latin. In my college they will be; Latin and lots of it, all over the place, with the mystic conspiracy of pretence, the wholesome humbug, that those who see it know what it means. Latin lasts. English seems to alter every thousand years or so. It's like the tariff that I named above — too mobile for academic use.

As with the benefactors, so with the managing trustees who look after the money and never lose it. Not dead, these, but very silent: solid men who don't need to talk and don't, but who can invest a million dollars over three depressions, and there it still is, like gold in a pot in the Pyramids. You find them chiefly in New England, at least I seem to have seen them there, more than anywhere else. They are at the head of huge investment businesses, so big that you never hear of them. Mostly, if they don't talk, it means that they are thinking where to place fifty million dollars. You see, they hate to break it.

And women? The arrangements in my college for the women students, and the women's dormitories? Oh, no — no, thank you. There aren't any women. Coeducation is a wonderful thing for women: college girls under coeducation leave college more fit to leave college than any others. College girls are better companions, better wives (as your own or as someone else's) than any others. It's the women who have made our college life the bright, happy thing it is — too bright, too happy.

But men can't *study* when women are around. And it's not only the students. If I let the women in, they'd get round some of my dusty old professors, and marry them — and good-bye to Machiavelli, and the higher thought.

7

ANDREW MACPHAIL

I am not attempting to write here a biography of Andrew Macphail. That must be left for other and worthier hands, inscribing a larger page. I am not qualified for the task. I never knew him during the earlier and more strenuous days in which his career was made; I never knew him in his home on "the Island," the environment most congenial to his temper; and I never had the honour of that war service which illustrated his middle age and earned him his fitting knighthood. It will remain for someone intimate with these phases of his career to write for us presently a full and worthy biography of Sir Andrew Macphail, undoubtedly one of the most outstanding and distinctive personalities that our country has known.

But till such a task is undertaken it is fitting that those of us who enjoyed his long friendship and companionship should record our tributes to his memory.

I first knew Andrew Macphail nearly forty years ago when I came to McGill, as nothing and nobody in particular, in the unstable equilibrium of a "sessional lecturer." On the strength of a few random excursions into the kingdom of letters I was honourably admitted to membership in the old Pen and Pencil Club, and there I first knew Andrew. He was my senior by some five years, and already an established and recognized man, the first arduous period of his career gone by, his life enlarged and tempered by marriage and fatherhood, and shadowed already by that premature bereavement that lay large across it.

From the first Andrew Macphail seemed to me, as he still does, one of the most distinctive personalities I have ever known. In his outward semblance he wore, then as always, an air of gloom and deliberation, carried not as a pose, but as the native expression of a mind always heavy with thought that did not of necessity break to the surface in voluble expression. It was as a shadowed pond with shifting shades but no ripples. What Andrew really thought of life in general I didn't know, and never knew, and I doubt if he did. He carried with him from his hereditary background and his upbringing, a stern, set frame of beliefs and traditions from which he was unwilling to depart: he always hated idle scoffing, cheap rationalism, one might almost say, reason and logic itself, and he always loved the sterner ideas of conduct that went with the illumination of older beliefs. If there had been no Westminster Catechism, Andrew would have invented it for himself.

The old Pen and Pencil Club of forty years ago, in which I first knew Andrew, used to meet every other Saturday night in Edouard Dyonnet's studio, under the Fraser Institute on Dorchester Street. It was made up as a sort of half and half of painters — who certainly could paint, as later recognition has shown — and of writers who were at least challenged to prove themselves by reading something they had written not less than once in six weeks. On the roll of the artists were such well-known names as those of Robert Harris, William Brymner, Maurice Cullen — to name only those now gone. The writers included dear old "Uncle" George Murray, whose memory is still carried as a garland by generations of Montreal High School boys; Paul Lafleur, chivalrous as knighthood and touchy as a sensitive plant; Jack McCrae of "Flanders Fields," admitted just when I was, whose works being poetry, had the signal merit of brevity.

It was the routine of the Club that the artists should first show to us their latest work. We, of the "pen" class, like George the Third with the British Constitution, admired where we couldn't understand, and took a more than equal vengeance by reading aloud our current writings. Our poets, Jack McCrae and John Logan (a tear to his rugged memory), made but a small demand. A very little poetry goes a long way. But Andrew and I were the chief sinners. I can still call up a vision of the kindly club, drawn up in a horseshoe of armchairs, the room darkened, and apparently getting darker all the time, listening to the measured tones of an essay-writer reading his essay, with the full consciousness that even when he had finished another essay writer would pick up the torch. Somnolence gained them; they tied themselves in knots in their chairs; or broke from the ranks to dive behind the curtains where the whisky and soda was.

This fellowship in evil brought Andrew and me together. It was characteristic of him that the more the listeners suffered the better he liked it. His attitude was that no one should show him pictures without his striking back. He was fond of saying — he loved an epigram — that a really good essay always put people to sleep. Those who remember Andrew Macphail will bear me out as to how characteristic such a saying was. You couldn't tell whether Andrew really meant it, or just said it. I don't think he knew. He just coined these things out of his lower consciousness and palmed them off on his upper. Again and again I have heard Andrew get off such judgments to plain business men, to the man in the next seat at a dinner, or a casual visitor at the club — to the great perplexity of the listener.

Witness this example. Speaking of the latest sermon at his church, Andrew said (to a casual friend we were with): "Edgar Hill gave us a great sermon on the poor this morning." "Is that so?" said the listener, making conversation, "what did he say about them?" Andrew answered, "He gave them hell!" — then uttered a deep sigh and no further information. I knew, but of course the man didn't, that underneath in Andrew's mind were deep thoughts about the merits and defects of the poor, which he didn't propose to bring to the surface. He let it go at that. He loved mystification. Most people, most writers, are terribly touchy if their meaning is mistaken. Not so Andrew. Much of his humour was of that truly Scottish kind which is best when least shared.

This love of epigram, of shaded meaning, trained Andrew in the course of years to an exquisite exactness of words. He never wrote careless English. The last essay that I know of from his pen, his appreciation of the most recent Life of General Lee,* is fascinating, not as reflecting General Lee or his biographer, but as reflecting Andrew Macphail. You feel as you read it that it is the writer, not the topic, that fascinates. This literary interest he often brought to an intense focus in single sentences, terse and final. Consider the opening of his essay on General Wilson. "The Irish have always had a sure instinct in murder."

---

*[In original] *Queen's Quarterly*, Spring, 1938.

Who wouldn't go on, after reading that? The plain man feels like saying — "An instinct in murder, eh? Have they really? — you don't say so! — tell me more about that." Such sudden beams of illumination are among the best part of Andrew's literary work. There is neither space nor occasion here to catalogue the long and interesting list of all he wrote. Much of it was spent on topics of mere ephemeral interest, as the rise and fall of Conservatives and Liberals, or at best of an interest that time must soon dim, but all of it was illuminated with this peculiar quality of salient phrase and pointed epigram.

It is naturally in connection with the bygone *University Magazine* of 1907 onwards, that one chiefly recalls Macphail's literary career. Full justice has still to be done to the great service which he here performed for Canadian letters. The magazine was a transformed resurrection of an older college publication, that had died from sheer bulk, the kind of literary dropsy that attacks the writing of professors. It was proposed — no doubt Principal Peterson fostered the idea — to found a magazine as learned as its predecessor but more susceptible to common sense in the length of the topics and the "availability" of its articles. The magazine was to be conducted by some sort of board — I think perhaps I was on it — I don't remember. But it didn't matter, for the "board" was virtually swept aside by Andrew, as you brush away the chess pieces of a finished game. Historians recall to us the first meeting of General Bonaparte in 1799 with the Abbé Siéyès and the others who were to be the joint government of France under the new "consulate." As they came out the Abbé remarked to a colleague, "Nous avons un maître" — and with that the "joint-stuff" ended. So it was with Andrew. After a meeting or two, the magazine became and remained Andrew Macphail. Like all competent men who can do a job and who know it, he had no use for co-operation. We, his colleagues, were invited occasionally to have Scotch whisky in Andrew's queer little library and then some more Scotch whisky with cold beef in his beautiful big dining-room. That was all the co-operation he wanted: and in this we met him (I am sure I did) more than half-way.

On this frail support, with a diligence such as only a man bred to hard work can maintain, with a taste found only in a scholar but mated to the discrimination of a journalist — thus, and with one hand ever in his generous pocket, Andrew Macphail carried the *University Magazine* to a place second to nothing of its type. Only those of us who knew him well could tell what unremitting work this labour of love entailed.

But it was not only by his literary work that Andrew Macphail, in the fuller years of his career, obtained the high consideration which fell to his lot. He had his part and place, as much as he could ask, in everything that was social, public or ceremonial. Andrew seemed so different from other men that his presence seemed to lift an occasion out of the commonplace. Introduced to strangers, he made an instant impression. Those of us who had to entertain, in public or in private, a visiting celebrity at once sent for Andrew: just as one sends for the doctor; and no celebrity could "celebrity" him. He treated them as a man used to horses treats a new one. It always seemed amazing to me that he could handle them so easily. Rudyard Kipling came to Montreal. Andrew had him tamed in half an hour, took him over to his house and then put him upstairs to write a speech. "Has Kipling come?" asked a next-entering visitor, in the awestruck tones we used for celebrities in the days before the Great War gave us our own. "He's upstairs," Andrew said. "I told him he ought to *write* his speech for McGill; he's writing it." From this beginning, incidentally, dated the long friendship, the mutual service and the mutual esteem of these two men.

I am not qualified, as I have said, to talk of Andrew's boyhood in the country, his early years of school and farm life, in the days when rural Canada offered little more than a pioneer life with few alleviations. The Canadian countryside in those days was dark and solitary, and life there had little converse and less amenity. Yet it bred, unconsciously, a love of the open air, of early hours, of the remembered stillness of the woods and the unceasing breaking of the sea. This, to people lucky enough to get out of it, as both Andrew and I had been, was coloured with the mellow hues of retrospect. Adversity that has long since gone by, leaves a sweet memory for luxury to linger on. And for people like Andrew and myself our country upbringing became a source of pride and a bond of sympathy and, as the years drew on, something of an affectation. It is hard in such cases to know where reality ends and attitude, or at least self-deception, begins. Andrew at any rate could push reality hard, much harder than I ever could. He could speak of buttermilk (over a glass of whisky and soda) with wistful relish, and talk of long drinks of maple sap out of its wooden trough — a beverage little better in reality than a solution of sawdust and dead flies. It became with Andrew a sort of whimsical make-believe that everything in the country was right, and everything in the city wrong. The only real boots were made by country cobblers: home-spun clothes fitted better than the tailored product of the city: and so forth, till the thing verged on burlesque and Andrew himself would start to laugh at it. In all this, as in so much else, I am certain that he never quite knew what he believed and what he didn't; but underneath it was a deep-seated feeling that the real virtue of a nation is bred in the country, that the city is an unnatural product. From this point of view Andrew, though frequenting the rich in his daily walk of life, was never quite satisfied of their right to be. Toward plutocrats, bankers, manufac-turers and such, he felt a little bit as a rough country dog feels towards a city cat. He didn't quite accept them. Andrew would have made a fine radical if he hadn't hated radicalism.

Andrew Macphail's death came to those of us who were his friends with a shock as of something that could not be. It had not seemed that he could die. Always he had kept his sorrows and his ailments to him-self. In the thirty-seven years I knew him I never heard him once refer to what I know had been the greatest sorrow of his life. His damaged sight he faced with equanimity and dismissed with scorn. He never complained because he hated complaint. Those of us of weaker temper carried our troubles to Andrew but never were asked to share his. Few people knew of his final illness and his removal from his Island to Montreal. To most of us the news of his death came, sudden and unbelievable, for the moment holding even sorrow numb. Even now it is hard to think that he is gone. As I write this page I recall how gen-erous was his praise of things I wrote, how quick he was to send his scribbled lines of congratulation over this or that, and how much I valued them. And now this, these sentences of appreciation and affection that I would wish him most to see — this he cannot read.

There is a well-worn rubric of the church that runs, "while we have time …" Andrew's death makes me think of it — the pity that we cannot, while we have time, value one another better. We do not see till it is too late. The light has gone.

8

HOW MUCH DOES LANGUAGE CHANGE?

About forty years ago — one of England's ripest scholars — you know what that means; they get so ripe they fall off like pumpkins — said that as far as grammar and structure went, the English language was "probably a finished process." He admitted that new words might come and old words might go, but as for language-making, in the structural sense, it is all over. "The grammar will remain for centuries what it is now." Odd, isn't it, the way old men have of thinking that things have reached the full stop of betterment in their own time! John Stuart Mill thought that political economy was as fixed as Euclid; and now, political economy is a wreck and Euclid is called Einstein.

How does it stand with this idea of an unchanging language? In the forty years since the ripe scholar ripened, has grammar "stayed put," as he expected, or has it moved on?

Of course in one sense there is an aspect of language that can't change. It has a vertebrate anatomy that is, and always has been, the same. The distinction of "parts of speech" rests on fundamental modes of thought, not on shifts of language. A noun will still be a noun in heaven; and a verb is a verb, even in Japanese: put the two together and, even in Japanese, you get what can be charitably called a sentence.

The general notions implied in "parts of speech," and "parsing," and "analysis" are of a fundamental and unchanging character. But "changes of grammar" mean new modes of structure inside this frame. To give an example, the Latin language, the kind we learnt or nearly learnt at school, was succeeded by what was called "low Latin," which we understood was beneath the notice of decent people. The kind of change involved was precisely a change in grammar. Thus in the classical days at Rome, somebody — I forget who — said of his own achievements, *monumentum exegi aere perennius*, i.e., "I have erected a monument more lasting than bronze." But a "low Latin" got down low enough to say *habeo monumentum erectum*, "I have a monument erected" — and the thing proved such a hit that a flood of auxiliary verbs was let loose on Latin and broke it up as rain breaks ice.

In the same way in English "I speak" widened into "I do speak" and "I am speaking," and, quite in our own day, "I am praised" could be expanded into "I am being praised," and we can even say, without taking a fit, "I will be being praised" — a usage which would have made Addison or Gibbon feel faint.

The point then is, are there any more such changes to come? We leave out of count the mere changes of words and phrases that make vocabulary. These of course in their own place are of extraordinary interest and often of marvellous curiosity, at times contain within themselves a whole irony of history. It is strange to think that a word that once meant "to go on a sacred pilgrimage to the Holyland" (*Sainte Terre*) now means "to loaf" (*saunter*); or that the "hocus pocus" of a modern conjurer is the *hoc est corpus* of a medieval bishop.

Yet these developments of language are aside from the present discussion, and indeed, in many cases, are but shifting metaphors that come and go, lose their initial force and pass out or sink into a commonplace. The eighteenth century called a bad young man a "rake" or a "blood"; we call him a "lounge lizard" or a "lobster." But it's all the same thing; he's no worse or better. The Stuart generation called a young woman a "jade," or a "wench." Nowadays we — or, at least, people younger than myself — call her a "skirt," or a "doll," or a "flapper."

Indeed the power of making new words has been accelerated by the continuous need for them. Who ever dreamed, a generation ago, of the "social hostess of a passenger plane"? What landscape painter ever thought of a life insurance "prospect" (meaning a human being). I defy the Duke of Wellington to guess what a "gas mask" is or a "dugout," and Lord Nelson wouldn't know what a "depth bomb" was till you dropped one on him.

These new words are a fascinating study. They seem to indicate a vitality in our spoken language never equalled before. They not only embody a wealth of metaphors but they seem at times to dive down into the fundamental under-tones that preceded definite language, and bring up treasures as from an ancient cave. Consider such words as "stooge" and "boob" applied to a "dumb" young man, or words such as "zoom" to indicate descent through the air accompanied by noise. It is a pity that most of our discussion of such new forms has not reached beyond the stage of making a catalogue, without further interpretation. Such a catalogue is just on the surface as botany was when still confined to the classification of flowers by a ladies' school.

But what about changes in grammar itself? Was the ripe scholar correct about them? I am willing to suggest for the consideration of other scholars — and the school returns of the United States show a total of two million coloured scholars alone — that the ripe English authority was all wrong: he was, to use a new term for it, "all wet."

Proof can only be by examples. Let me proceed to gather and present a few. I will begin with a very simple one, that of beginning a sentence with a verb first and its subject after it without using an introductory word such as *"there,"* or *"now."* For example, instead of saying, "There followed a moment of intense anxiety," ever so many writers of today put, "Followed a moment of intense anxiety." Compare: "Came October" . . . "Broke disaster" . . . "Ensued a pause." They do this not once in a while but they do it all the time, they do it on purpose, for effect, with the idea that it is stronger than what we used to write. Personally, I hate this innovation, with all the unreasoning conservatism of old age. I quite admit — to halt an idiotic objection at its first step — that of course fifty years ago, when I was young, and even the ripe scholar not too old, many writers used such a form sometimes, and it was frequently used in poetry by what was called "poetic license," an indulgence as wide as a "liquor license" in Chicago. But it was no part of regular writing. It is now rapidly becoming so and is helping to add in the new casting of sentences from the continuous flow that was the ideal of Cicero or Milton to the step-by-step prose of today. Thus one of the old-fashioned three-decker love stories which flourished three generations ago, would contain a sentence:

The sudden entry of Elizabeth afforded to John an opportunity for a bold invitation that was no sooner extended than embraced. . . .

The author's ghost might read it now, or soon, in such a rewritten form as this:

Came in John. Appeared Elizabeth. Spoke John, "What about it, Lizzie?" Pondered not Elizabeth. "I'm on," she said.

Call it grammar, or call it what you like, the change in speech is here about as complete as the difference between the famous Strasbourg Oaths of early French (A.D. 842) and an election speech of Mr. Daladier, in 1938.*

That, then, is that, a phrase in itself suggestive of a new era. I pass to another case of usage, very wide and working great change in our colloquial speech. If I wanted to indicate it in a pedantic way so as to give it all the peculiar force of obscurity, I should say that we are reintroducing forms similar to the old Greek reduplicated aorist — a vanishing form belonging in the dawn of written speech whose original force had apparently disappeared. I should then apologize for the lack of Greek type in this article and slip out of proof like Houdini out of handcuffs. But let me say it instead in simple, vulgar language. We have got into the way, colloquially, of putting in front of our verbs such peculiar modifications as "sort of" (pronounced "sorta") and "kind of" (pronounced "kinda"). Such usages as "I sort-of-thought he would come." "I kind-of-suspected he was here," are ghastly as logic, impossible to parse — in fact, utterly unfit for use in the House of Lords. On the other hand they are replete with meaning and they fulfil the entrance test needed for admission into language that they express something that needs expressing and that nothing else will express so well. It is clear to anyone of unclouded vision that we are to have a new kind of mood, made after the fashion of the Greek "reduplicated aorist"

---

*Prime Minister of France from 1938 to the fall of France in 1940. —ED tense — a noble ancestor that will make it respectable. The grammar out of which the Chinese conquerors of Europe will learn their old twentieth century English, will have a section to read:

> Any verb may be removed from the indicative to the dubitative mood by the addition of the prefix "sorta" (derived according to Dr. Woo Hoo from "soror" a sister, but perhaps an abbreviation of "so-it-ought-'er"). Thus the verb "to think" has as its dubitative past:

> I sortathought
> You sortathought
> He sortathought, etc., etc.

> The negative form, which is difficult for foreigners and should be avoided except by writers of special taste and purity, runs:

> I sortadidn'tthink
> You sortadidn'tthink, etc., etc.

Only people who know nothing of language, its origin and its vagaries will find anything odd in this. Let me refer the doubting reader to any grammar of the Zulu language: he will there find verbs with an interpolated middle part of much this sort. But if he has no Zulu grammar, and won't go to Zululand, let me refer him to the more accessible example of Japanese language. He will find there that the Japanese verbs have a great variety of these internal modifications. Thus the Japanese for "put" (OKU) has a tense called (for short) the Indefinite Probable Past, which means "I think-I-very-likely-put," "you think-you-very-likely-put," etc., etc. But in Japanese it has to undergo a second cross variation to distinguish whether I am talking about myself or about you. If I talk of myself it must be indicated in Japanese by some form of change or particle to mean "humble worm," "low form of existence." But if I talk of you it must imply "august-presence-gentleman-Mr.," or have the initial GO in front of it which implies "Just listen to this." So that the tense of which I speak, conjugated out for actual use, would run — as far as it is possible to say it:

First person: Humble worm thinks humble worm likely put.

Second person: Listen to this! August Gentleman Mister thinks High Presence likely put. Etc., etc.

Can you wonder that the Japanese verbal form grows long! I have in front of me a Japanese text book (Chamberlain: page 150) in which the author indignantly complains that foreigners mistake for verbal roots forms which are nothing but the "indefinite potential of the causative conjugation." Simple, isn't it, once you're on to it? And all this out of Chamberlain's Colloquial Japanese — before you get to the real language.*

Let it be observed that the colloquial introduction, and future literary adoption of such a form as "I sort-of-thought" is entirely different from such a form as "I rather thought." The latter is grammatical as it stands with the adverb *rather* to modify the verb thought. But "I sort-of-thought" breaks the mould. It is grammar in the making.

Nor can we smugly brush aside these changes by dismissing them as "colloquial." All language was so, originally. And even now only a small part of our language comes in by the front door of literary creation — such as *cinematograph* and *automobile*. Even these get beaten out by "movie" and "car." In fact there is no front door. Open it as you will it keeps banging to, and cutting off the half of a word as it comes in — leaving us "phone" and "bike," and such. Meantime the crowd of new words, the real ones, squeeze in as best they can at the back door and brush up into respectability.

Verbal changes are being greatly helped by that insidious thing called the "split infinitive"; "insidious" because it has a way of enlarging its consequences like a split in a hemlock log. Personally, I am all for it. I would as soon split an infinitive as split an egg. But grammarians used to shudder — shuddering is their business — at such forms as "to

---

*Japanese verb forms have been simplified since this essay was written. —ED

fully understand," "to entirely agree," and to collapse at such extensions as "to more than half believe." But the split infinitive has made its way into our language by sheer merit. It can say what nothing else can. Even so distinguished a grammarian as Otto Jespersen of Copenhagen, who knows more of our language than a Dane has any business to (see his *Essentials of English Grammar*), is willing to give it his parting blessing in his "Final Remarks on Infinitives." But all grammarians warn us to be careful with split infinitives, as with gasoline or live electric wires. The unthinking public — it is its business to un-think — never heeds the warning and into the gap of the split infinitive pour a host of new verbal forms, like soldiers into a breach. Hamlet could have solved his maddening doubts whether "to be or not to be" if he had made up his mind "to more or less be."

Dr. Hubert Jagger in his *Modern English* cites the case of the Staffordshire County Council being brought up all standing (1924) by a split infinitive that held up the question of slaughtering cattle. They seem to have been perplexed as whether to "ask the ministry seriously to consider it" or "to ask the ministry to seriously consider it," or "to seriously ask the ministry to consider it." Evidently the thing needed was a higher sense of fun in England.

Another wedge is being driven deep and always deeper into the grammatical structure of the English language by its prepositions. All foreigners realize that our prepositions are our chiefest glory. They can only admire without understanding them — like George III with the British Constitution. For example: *to break out, to break up, to break off, to break in!* Thus if a riot *breaks out* in a meeting, the speaker *breaks off*, the police *break in* and — what does the meeting do? It *breaks up*. After which there are arrests and the prosecution *breaks down*. And just as the foreigner thinks he understands it, he finds Tennyson writing, *Break, break, break*, without telling him whether it was up or down, or down and out.

The prepositions once started loose on their evil course, instead of being tightly imprisoned as in Latin, have permeated into our verbal forms like a chemical solution.

What say the waves? is Latin. *What are the wild waves saying?* is Victorian English. But *What are the wild waves being said to?* is something else. Or consider this: *The patient was brought to, but did not know what he was brought to for nor what he was brought to by.* The Japanese for this (much superior) is *Honourable-Sick-Man-Mister, as-for, much-better, cause-non-existent.* Dr. Jagger quotes a still better example in the form, *Whatever did you choose that book to be read out of to for?* He says it is comic; I think so, too.

In other words, stated simply and softly, our prepositional compounds have broken out of any grammatical frame that existed when grammar "became fixed." True, their vagaries had begun, but they hadn't ended, and we don't know yet what they will "pass on over into." As yet no one has fitted a logical grammar around them.

The revolt of the prepositions has been accompanied by an insurrection among the pronouns. It is not yet fully recognized by the grammarians, but has at least acquired belligerent rights. Who is there who still says "It is I"? Or who would be shamed of saying "It is me"? Consider such dialogue as this: "I think you said you lost your gloves. Are these they?" "Oh, thanks awfully, that's them." One would almost prefer the Japanese form: "August-mister-gloves as-for, humble-worm-offer-from-below."

In short, the time has come to bring all these revolted pronouns back under the aegis of grammar by giving them a name, as the French do, and calling them disjunctive forms and forgiving them. The French have used them for so long that in French the other forms, the ones we try to use, sound silly. Compare in the well-known play *Ici On Parle Français* the immortal dialogue, *"Qui est la personne ici qui parle français?"* — *"Je."*

Oddly enough, some few grammatical changes are reversions to old, old types, so old as to be long forgotten and hence not conscious reconstructions. Thus, professors (who know everything) know that "if" meant "give." "If he comes here," was equal to saying, "Give this (let it be granted), he comes here." Compare "Gin a body meet a body comin' through the rye" — where "gin" means "given" and "rye" means only what it says.

Now our language, our colloquial language, in its effort to shake loose from the shackles of long sentences and subordinate clauses, can reach back to the dim ages and revive the remote form. In the most colloquial of English — the English that is almost back-alley and gangsters' English — instead of saying, "If you stay here, the police will get you," the thought is expressed, "Look — you stay here, the cops get you — see?"

The underlying reason is, of course, the impulse we have today, to break up speech so as to make it intelligible step by step as it goes along. This is intensified by the fact that our language is more than ever under the stress of the demand for brevity. We live in an era of traffic signs, street directions, police radio calls, telegram letters and air mail. We have no time even for the old-fashioned politeness that would say, "Gentlemen are requested not to sit down on the wet paint." We just put a sign "paint," and they can sit on it if they like. This pressure extends from the language of written signs to the language of written literature. Our writers begin to find that they need little but a noun and a verb. In fact even the verb can be dropped. Thus Longfellow wrote, "The shades of night were falling fast." A free verse poet of today would just say "Night."

And in the same poem where Longfellow writes, "'Oh, stay!' the maiden said, 'and rest,'" the same idea can be admirably expressed now with the sign "Tourists," or "Fresh eggs." Incidentally, Longfellow's young man in the poem was away ahead of his time, for instead of saying, "I'm so sorry but I really must be moving on," he says "Excelsior." This was bad Latin, as it ought to be neuter, but was wonderful condensation. This single-word brevity, or rather our consciousness of it can easily be reduced to parody, as in the familiar verse:

> A little Boy
> A pair of Skates,
> A hole in the Ice
>   The Golden Gate.

Nor is it only in this way that the isolated use of nouns, substituting images for abstractions, grows upon our language. Two nouns in juxtaposition can, by acting as adjective and noun, replace two nouns connected with verbs and prepositions. A "steamboat" means a "boat moved by steam." A "steamboat company" means a "company operating boats moved by steam." This mode is as old as Anglo-

Saxon, but has grown now to dimensions unrecognizable fifty years ago. We can say, and we do say, "Steamboat Company Dock Agents' Life Insurance Department," and so on, endlessly. If we ran out of new ideas to tack on to the end, we could begin again at the beginning and say, "Lake Shore Steamship Company" — and so on. No Anglo-Saxon could have said that; he couldn't *hold* it; a Roman would have taken a page to say it, and a Greek would be talking yet. Our minds have been trained to a new habit of suspended animation, so to speak, waiting for the end before we make an image. We do with these compounds what the Romans used to do, when they read a long sentence of Cicero's intricate prose. They waited till they got it all. We find Cicero hard to follow because we have long since broken up our prose to make it intelligible as it goes along. The Romans would find our "Steamboat Agency Head Office" stuff quite impossible.

But then what's left of our ripe scholar? Nothing. What with new model verbs and pronouns, split infinitives, interpolated prepositions, traffic sign nouns and buried verbs, our grammar seems to have about as much stability about it as a French franc, or a Japanese treaty or an over-the-counter share in a gold mine, or any other up-to-date phenomenon. No, our ripe scholar has fallen off his stem.

9

FROM THE RIDICULOUS TO THE SUBLIME

[…] [H]umour, in its highest form, no longer excites our laughter, no longer appeals to our comic sense, no longer depends upon the aid of wit.

We have recalled the picture of little Huckleberry Finn floating down the Mississippi on his raft or discussing with his Nigger Jim the mysteries of the Universe. We have seen the poor debtors of Dickens's debtors' prison, with their broken lives, their pots of porter, their tawdry merriment, their pitiable dignity and their unutterable despair. Such pictures as these call forth a saddened smile of compassion for our human lot; it all seems so long past, so far in retrospect, that the pain is gone.

Such is the highest humour. It represents an outlook upon life, a retrospect as it were, in which the fever and fret of our earthly lot is contrasted with its shortcomings, its lost illusions and its inevitable end. The fiercest anger cools; the bitterest of hate sleeps in the churchyard; and over it all there spread Time's ivy and Time's roses, preserving nothing but what is fair to look upon.

Hence comes into being the peculiar legend of the "good old times of the past." Each age sees the ones that preceded it through a mellow haze of retrospect; each looks back to the good old days of our forefathers. In England, people turn back affectionately, and always have, to the days when "England was England"; they can still hear the sound of the village church bells across four centuries of distance. They talk of "Merrie England," and of the Roast Beef of Old England, forgetting that England is older now.

Seen through this refracting prism of past distance all the harsh out-lines are blurred and softened, the colours mingle to a mellow richness. Beside it, all the people and things about us at the moment seem crude and hard. The dead are better companions than the living.

Each of us in life is a prisoner. The past offers us, as it were, a door of escape. We are set and bound in our confined lot. Outside, somewhere, is eternity; outside, somewhere, is infinity. We seek to reach into it and the pictured past seems to afford to us an outlet of escape. When we read of the past, all the pain is out of it; so may we sit buried in some old book of battles long ago, of kings who rose and fell, of multitudes that died of plagues and were swept away in floods. How quaint and sweet sounds now the Plague of London! What terror then; what rumbling of the carts of death passing in the night! But now, what a charm to read of it in the enchanted pages of an Evelyn or a Pepys.

Such too is that escape by the inner absorption of the mind in something utterly unconnected with the pains, the pleasures, the profit and the work of life. Here, for those who can enter it, is the door of the higher mathematics — the conic sections of the Greeks, purposeless and without bearing for them on any art or occupation, but of what infinity of interest. I have often thought that for those absorbed in recondite studies, life must be peaceful indeed. But it is not so. The rapture of isolation is only caught and lost. I used to think, for example, that there must be a wondrous stillness and serenity in the life of a comparative philologist; I thought so till I knew one — a bygone colleague. I realized, as I got to know him that for him life was all storm and stress — the Annual Philological Congress to attend, each one seeming to crowd on the heels of the last; the preparation of "papers," as terrific to him as the manufacture of nitroglycerin. He witnessed and fought all through the great revolution against the Anglo-Saxonization of English spelling, helped to drive out the legend of an Aryan prototype of Sanskrit, and, as his biggest achievement, lived to put the pluperfect subjunctive practically where it is now.

Through all this life and storm he came and went about the college abstracted, muttering, practically unknown; yet to himself a storm centre of seething action.

I saw his queer little funeral — the littlest I ever saw — go past the college gates in a snowstorm. A medical student on the steps lit his pipe and asked, "What the Hell's that?" and when they told him — "I never heard of him," he said. Yet the man had been with us thirty years.

Escape is barred. And yet we look around forward and backward to find it; nor anywhere more eagerly than backward, to those wistful and haunting recollections of our childhood, that search for a vanishing identity connecting us with eternity but lost in the mist of the infinite. How much of our poetry carries the illumination of that retrospect toward childhood, coloured once with the hues of the morning and now changing to those of the fall of night.

I remember, I remember, the house where I was born!

Why should that haunt us? We ought to think, "Certainly I do; it was No.7 John St." So shall we sing:

When you and I were young, Maggie,
And all the world was green
And every lad a King, Maggie,
And every lass a queen! ...

What a preposterous statement, if we take it on its face; only the Royal Family of Roumania living in the green mountains could live up to it.

All through such recollections, all through such sentiments, runs the strain of the highest humour, like gold in the bed of a stream. Here belong our recollections of our school days, never recalled without a pleasant smile for even the worst of our sufferings, a laugh for our simplest adventures.

The other day upon the street I stopped a distinguished friend of mine, a dignified colonel, well up in the sixties, and I said: "Reg, I must tell you. A week or so ago, in Pittsburgh I ran across Eph Lyon."

"Eph Lyon!" he said, brought up all standing with the sudden interest of it! If I had said, "The other day I saw the King of Siam," my old schoolmate would have merely said, "Did you?" but here he stood in the snowflakes, repeating, "Eph Lyon! Eph Lyon! Why, let me see, I haven't seen Eph Lyon for — what! — fifty years."

"Fifty," I said. "That's right, you and I and Eph were all at the school together fifty years ago."

"Eph," said the colonel, standing fixed in his tracks with the snow falling round him — if he had any business he'd quite forgotten it — "Eph was the best half back on the football team."

"Quarter back," I said.

"Half," he protested.

"No," I said, "Gib Gordon was half."

"Why, of course," he admitted. "Gib Gordon! certainly Gib Gordon! Do you remember the day when Beer Ryckert tried to smash his face in?"

And we both laughed, thinking of that angry quarrel in the football field of fifty years ago — all past and vanished but the "humour" of it.

Hear how people talk who have known one another as children and who come together again in later life, and laugh over the angers and quarrels of their childhood.

> "Do you remember that day when I took away your doll and you cried so?"
>
> "Yes, and do you remember I simply got furious and scratched you across the face?"
>
> They both laugh at the recollection.
>
> "Yes, and then your Aunt Mary came in and sent you home and put me in the cupboard."
>
> "Shall I ever forget my rage in that awful dark cupboard?"

So it would seem to me if departed spirits later on would talk and hold converse about their previous lives — far behind them — they would talk as we talk of childhood happenings. The angers, the misfortunes, even the crimes would have faded into happy recollection, into divine retrospect, into "humour."

"Do you remember," thus speaks one of the dead, "the night you broke into my house and my brother and I heard you in the cellar and came down with a gun?" "Do I remember?" laughs the other. "Say, was I scared? I sat there in the coal fumbling with my darned old automatic and then just by luck I got a fair crack at your brother — and just then in hopped the police, you remember?"

They both laughed at the thought of it. "And the trial, do you remember the trial, wasn't it simply killing?" More laughter. "Yes, and the day you were hanged, eh? Say, I'll never forget it. Well, they were great old days!"

If, as the poet Rostand saw it, the armies of the dead still ride and flaunt over the night sky above the battle fields of Europe, there will be no sternness in their faces, no martial anger left.

They would be like the cherished picture of the Duke of Wellington and Marshal Soult riding in London in a carriage together in the eighteen forties, or like the aged men from the North and the South who in 1913 walked over again the ground of Pickett's Charge of fifty years before at Gettysburg, laughing and mumbling of the fierce fight at the Stone Wall. Thus may the dead be standing, side by side, about their cenotaphs of today, talking together, nation with nation, ally with enemy, in a language which the living have not yet learned to use.

Thus does life, if we look at it from sufficient distance, dissolve itself into "humour." Seen through an indefinite vista it ends in a smile. In this, if what the scientists tell us is true, it only offers a parallel to what must ultimately happen to the physical universe in which it exists. Matter, we are told, is not matter in the real or solid sense. It is only a manifestation of force or energy, seeking to come to rest. An atom is not an atom in the sense of being a particle or thing. It is just an area inside whose vast empty dimensions unmatched forces, stresses and strains are trying to come together and neutralize one another. When they do this — at some inconceivable distance of time — then the universe ends, finishes; there is nothing left of it but nothingness.

With it goes out in extinction all that was thought of as matter, and with that all the framework of time and space that held it, and the conscious life that matched it. All ends with a cancellation of forces and comes to nothing; and our universe ends thus with one vast, silent, unappreciated joke.

10

What Is Left of Adam Smith?

ADAM SMITH, *Inquiry into the Nature and Causes of
the Wealth of Nations*, 1776.
IMMANUEL KANT, *Critique of Pure Reason*, 1781.

Here are two sciences — Philosophy and Political Economy — both
bankrupt. The one went through the courts at least a hundred years ago
and is now a cheery old bankrupt, bright and garrulous in old age. It
talks most interestingly about its case, citing a long list of opinions and
judgments that go back to the Greeks. The other bankrupt has just
been thrown into the receiver's hands, still protesting angrily, still
claiming that it has wonderful assets, that everything will be all right.
It cites a wilderness, not of opinion, but of statistics and facts, all apparently bearing on nothing, gets confused, breaks down and cries — a
very picture of senile collapse.

There are those who dislike metaphor; let us say the same thing
in a plain way. Philosophy means the attempt to discover the ultimate nature of existence, of consciousness, of time and space. Has it
found it? No. It is going to? Not a chance of it. Where is it?
Nowhere. Some people do not understand this. They read of the
work of the Mayos and the Carrels and the Rutherfords* and think

---

*Presumably the Mayo family, the most famous group of physicians in the
United States, who established the Mayo Clinic; Alexis Carrel (1873–1944),
Nobel Prize (1912), surgeon who the laid groundwork for further studies of
transplantation of blood vessels and organs; Ernest Rutherford (1871–1937),
Nobel Prize (1908), whose pioneering work in developing the nuclear theory
of atomic structure revolutionized physics. —ED

that they are getting somewhere. In the philosophical sense it is not so. No ultimate dissection of the human body will ever find the human soul. The substitution of Rutherford's atom for Huxley's — replacing a solid particle infinitely small by a huge cavern empty except for centres of force — does not carry us one inch further in our quest of the final relations of mind and matter. Our greatest medical men know no more of the ultimate nature of consciousness than did a horse doctor in Asia Minor B.C. 500. Einstein, as far as the ultimate truth of space, time, and number goes, is no further on than Rodin's "Penseur" — his statue of the primitive man, buried in stubborn thought and trying, let us say, to think out whether two and two is four, or is five.

But let it be noted that the total failure of Philosophy to find its goal is of no consequence. Suppose it did find out what time is or what "being" means. It wouldn't affect anybody or anything. It would be of no practical consequence. Meantime the elusive search is as fascinating as ever: futile but fascinating. "*Cogito ergo sum*", says Descartes; he might as well have said "*Sum ergo cogito*". It's just as good.

Moreover, Philosophy is now able to carry with it a huge catalogue of the opinions of the past, and of the opinions held about other opinions: this gives us Aristotle's opinion of Plato, Bacon's opinion of Aristotle, Locke's opinion of Bacon, Hegel's opinion of Locke, and Professor C. W. Hendel's opinion of Hegel. In the fullness of time someone will have an opinion of C. W. Hendel.*

Thus Philosophy has become a grand college subject, an eager pursuit for the mind, and in old age a delightful *reductio ad absurdum*.

But Political Economy is different. It has *got* to answer. The call made to it is an S.O.S.

Political Economy has been defined to be the science of the production, distribution, and exchange of wealth; or, to make it less material, the study of mankind in pursuit of wealth. At its own face value it has tried to be a "philosophy"; an inquiry as to what *is*, rather than a "precept", a direction as to what to do. It has nothing to do

---

*Charles W. Hendel, professor of philosophy who in the 1930s was well known for commentaries on Rousseau and Hume. —ED

with making an individual rich — a fact on which many students in selecting college courses are gravely in error. That subject belongs under the theological department.

But it is mere affectation to deny that the essential pre-occupation of Political Economy is not a philosophical analysis for its own sake, but an attempt to lay down precepts for the ordinance of society. In other words, it is — as its name meant in Greek and meant to Adam Smith in the only passage where he uses it — "public policy". It is this aspect of it which has assumed extreme importance, an emergency importance in our collapsed and dislocated industrial world. And it is exactly in this aspect that it has gone bankrupt. Unlike Philosophy, its bankruptcy *matters*. Unlike the case of Philosophy, where no answer to its question is ever possible, there *must* be an answer to the great question of Political Economy. How — so it first asked — does mankind produce enough goods for the wants of mankind? That has been answered long ago. How can mankind adjust its production so as not to oversatisfy some, undersatisfy others, and break down in the process? That has *not* been answered. And for that, Adam Smith is mute, Malthus mistaken, and John Stuart Mill only a well-meaning lover of mankind. Yet answer to the problem must be found. Otherwise Political Economy could sit down beside Philosophy mumbling together in toothless old age, as two old chums in the inglenook of the inn of learning. But it cannot be. The inn is on fire.

What I propose to claim, as this essay proceeds, is that the classical Political Economy, whatever it had to offer to the world of a century ago, has nothing for us now, except only two things. First, it probably can still serve as the best college introduction to the study of Economics. What other approach *will* serve? Descriptive Economics only tells, as far as generality goes, what we know already.

You and I may not know how a printing machine works in detail; but we know what a machine is: we may not know the technique of pay-rolls and piece-work and what a time clock is; but we know what work for wages means. Technical detailed studies belong later, for technical uses. They are not the beginning. Neither is history. History cannot prophesy. Nor is the "case system" — the study of actual acquaintance with actual buying and selling — anything but a silly pretence of analogy with engineering science. We all did our "case work" at ten years old when we were first allowed to spend our pennies.

Still worse is the mode of approach which would turn Economics into a technical subject, remove it from the public altogether, camouflage its simplest ideas in make-believe algebraical formulas; overwhelm it, in other words, with all the difficulty and the aridity of a physical science with nothing of its glorious culmination. This form of presentation is a part of that cult of dullness which invades more and more the scholarship of America. The professors kill the flowers and wonder that the root dies with them.

On the whole, then, the formal study of the classical Economics, or of some windy derivative of it, is about the best college approach. Incidentally the subject, at any rate as it is, is of little value to under-graduates. Latin verse would be better. It seems to me that we are see-ing already the difference between the training of the mind given by the old obligatory, disciplinary, studies, and the results effected by the new optional wish-wash which seems to fit students chiefly for endless committees, conferences, and "activities" in premature imitation of the business world.

In one other point, as I shall claim, the classical economists were correct, namely, as to the principle of human selfishness. As they saw it, the world can only run on the principle of every man for himself, the self-interest of the individual. In other words, they assumed the "economic man" — oddly enough the one part of their doctrines which their friends have most eagerly tried to explain away. But they were quite right. Without this principle, namely, that (speaking by and large) we only work for ourselves and because we have to, then socialism goes without saying. Let us start it tomorrow.

But the economists were all wrong in thinking that the pursuit of the individual's own interest made for the welfare of mankind — Adam Smith's "invisible hand". It does not. The welfare of mankind has got to be achieved against it and in spite of it. But it is an equal error to base public policy on a system which does not acknowledge and allow for this individual selfishness. In short, the classical economists said that the only rule of the game needed was to let things alone: we find now we need a whole new set of rules. It isn't a game. It's a handicap.

There was no organized body of Economic Science in the ancient and medieval world. The reason was that relations of man to man were overwhelmingly non-economic, belonged on another plane. They were relations of force, of religion, of custom, or of isolation. Economic Science (discussion of the material relation of the individual to society) only came as the individual got shaken out of his frame, in short became an individual. Labour broke its mould in the fourteenth century, trade in the fifteenth, money and prices in the sixteenth. Each change meant talk. The talk gathered into a body and systematized itself. Adam Smith, with the thoroughness of a Scottish stone-mason, set in the keystone of the rising arch. His successors helped to buttress it on the sides, and erect superstructures on it. The arch is still standing, but you can't walk across the top.

Here is the familiar outline of what Adam Smith wrote — more than familiar to those able, and not afraid, to read this new magazine. He proposed to study the production of national wealth. He was especially pre-occupied, like his generation and the two that succeeded it, with the new and wonderful possibilities of machine production. He opens with an ecstasy on the division of labour and the making of pins. All the classical economists shared this same view of machinery and mankind. Mill, indeed, was presently to doubt whether all the labour-saving machinery invented had ever shortened an hour of human toil. But, for the most part, machine production was the very heart of the system. Of *over*-production the economists hardly thought. Sismondi, it is true, in his *Nouveaux Principes* of 1819, shows another point of view and warns against over-production (glutting of markets) as a sign of the divergence of individual gain and social welfare. But the moving current closed over him. Mill, while admitting the temporary over-crowding of a single market, dismissed with convincing logic all question of a "general glut". His idea was that a "general glut" would right itself. This is no doubt correct, if we admit that the "righting" may take half a generation, may throw fifty million people out of work, and bring disorder, revolution, and bloodshed widespread over the world. On those terms anything "rights itself". The Black Death righted labour; the Reign of Terror righted aristocracy; and the Great War righted nationality. It's a great world if you let it alone. In other words, all that Smith, Ricardo, and Mill ever wrote about production and over-production gives about as much light to us, here and now, as a fire-fly in a tin can.

> Economists themselves [so wrote Charles Gide] have never shared this apprehension [of a general glut]. To them the danger of general over-production seems entirely imaginary and absurd. They do not deny, to be sure, that in certain branches of industry, or even in many of them, production may chance to exceed demand owing to miscalculation. But they deny altogether that *general* over-production can really exist, and they attribute the fear of it to a mere optical delusion.

Yet consider these facts as cited in a recent number (1934) of the magazine *Prosperity:* In the year 1934 Holland, to prevent the consequences of over-production, burned 15,000,000 flower bulbs and destroyed 100,000 pigs; the United States destroyed 2,000,000 sows and 4,000,000 little pigs. Denmark incinerated 25,000 cattle. In New Zealand 5,000 lambs were driven into the sea. In the United States every third row of cotton was "ploughed in". Brazil destroyed 26,000,000 bags of coffee.... and so on through the record, read who will. Whether or not the individual cases are correct, all the world knows that the general picture is true.

Imagine, then, anyone looking for light on the question of over-production of to-day from the pages of the classical economists. They said it cured itself. It does. So does life.

But this question of over-production, destined later to give the *coup de grace* to the system, still appeared of relative unimportance as compared with the general increase of natural wealth obviously and constantly proceeding. The crises and collapses of the epoch had nothing of the disastrous proportions they were later to assume. They seemed attributable, or were attributed, to adventitious causes, not to the system itself. And in any case the impoverishment they caused was largely confined to the lower classes. Society remained unshaken at the top. Countesses distributed soup in soup kitchens, but never needed any themselves. People in those days easily tolerated other people's poverty. At any rate, the "system" seemed unshaken, a success in its main outlines, and supposedly based on a mechanism which operated of itself.

This mechanism was found in the interpretation of the working of demand and supply, market and natural price, given by the economists. It was all so simple that it could be written out, as Mr. Balfour once told the House of Commons, on half a sheet of note-paper. Even he explained it in an hour or so.

The key to the mystery was found in free competition and individual gain. Each man sold his labour for the best he could get. The employer made with it the articles he could make most profit on. The man who made them at the cheapest cost got the sale. The price of goods in any market at any moment was a mere function of demand and supply. But the force of competition, by shortening or increasing supply, tended to keep price at practically the cost of production. This was the law of natural price. Under this law too great a supply automatically stopped production till the glut was carried off like water in the lee scuppers of a flooded deck. This theory of automatic production at the natural cost to the natural extent of the needs of society was extended, outside the home country, to be the theory of free trade. It was, as such, a mere annexed proposition, like the deductions in Euclid, accounted for before it began.

Now this whole theory of cost gives about as much help in estimating the cost of a single manufactured article of to-day as could be found in the Chinese encyclopaedia of the Emperor Ming. But before discussing the total inadequacy of the classical doctrine of costs to explain the industry of to-day, it is necessary to look at the other forces which began, even early in the nineteenth century, to undermine the supremacy of the system. In the first place, its practical success was only partial. It made wealth, but it did not remove poverty. All the world knows the story of the English factories, the "cry of the children", the horrors of the city slum, and the "song of the shirt". This led to the humanitarian protests of Dickens, of Kingsley, of Carlyle, knowing nothing of Economics as a science and caring less. In these men in the light of the hideous revelations of the Factories

Commission of 1833, the idea that the economist N. W. Senior could oppose factory legislation, that Herbert Spencer could demand absolute *freedom* for the employer even in matters of sanitation and disease, that John Bright should sulkily claim the right to "do as he liked with his own" — the thing they called Political Economy created a kind of frenzy. "Of all narrow, conceited, hypocritical, and anarchic and atheistic schemes of the universe," wrote Charles Kingsley, "the Manchester one is exactly the worst."

To this protest in the name of humanity was presently added the indifference and then the hostility of labour, now gradually organizing. The science which taught that strikes could not raise wages, that wage laws could not operate, that there was no hope for the poor except harder work, less children, and escape by emigration from their native land, seemed to the enlightened labourer as contemptible — as it was.

Added to this again was the academic attack of the "historical" school claiming that economic phenomena vary from age to age, from environment to environment; that there are no universal laws, and nothing but a continuous "evolution". This new word was already transforming thought, in part enlightening it, in part putting it to sleep.

Then came the attack from within, Jevons, Menger, and such, the "Austrian" theory of value as the spearhead of the onslaught. This, in a word, undertook to overset the comfortable theory that cost governed value by turning it upside down. Value governed cost. Turning it upside down spilled out of it all its content of social justice.

The nineteenth century closed with painstaking attempts to prop up the falling structure and plaster its outside with reams upon reams of paper. Compromise was the word of the hour; to compromise the historical and the Ricardian school; to compromise the Austrian and classical theories by the comfortable theory that both are true — on the principle of prize-day in a Sunday school. In reality, to compromise the Austrian and the classical theories of value is like trying to compromise God and the Devil.

But the world moved too fast for the compromise and for the system. Organized labour defied it and proved it wrong. Social instinct defied its canon that each man gets, under free competition, what he is worth and is worth what he gets. Legislation took no further account of its so-called principles. Mr. Gladstone himself in the matter of the Irish Land Legislation, had declared it "relegated to Saturn", meaning in American "sent to hell".

With the twentieth century, the current of economic and political development rushed towards the maelstrom of the Great War, carried it on, in defiance of all the conclusions of all the economists, for four years, and ten years later, collapsed and fell into ruin in the slump of 1929 — the like of which never was seen before. Buried under the wreckage is the system of Adam Smith — his production, his machinery, his natural price and natural wage, his social justice arising out of identity of individual and social interest, his "invisible hand" now more invisible than ever. Of it all there only survives the principle that each man must work for himself, under proper rules of the game. I lay continual and repeated stress on this; without this qualification the wreck of Adam Smith means the triumph of socialism — a system even more impracticable than free competition.

I turn to see to what extent, if any, Smith's ideas and precepts apply to the world of to-day (1929–35). Obviously, his ideas on production and how to stimulate it have little bearing to-day. Mr. Stuart Chase* pre-eminently, and others in their degree, have shown that we have exchanged Smith's economics of scarcity for a new "economics of abundance". The mushroom school of the "technocrats" of 1932 at least did one good service to the world before it withered on its stem.** It "sold the idea" of our super-power of production. It made it clear that our future problem is not the control of nature but the control of man. It showed us the machine as a sort of Frankenstein, enslaving

---

*Chase (1888–1985) was a prolific journalist, influenced by Veblen but eclectic, whose book A New Deal (1932) proposed planned production, with minimum wages and maximum hours, planned inflation, and an integration of supply and demand to end competition. —ED

**Technocracy was a movement led by an eccentric engineer, Howard Scott. Also influenced by Veblen and by some of the monetary theories that underlay Social Credit, he argued that all problems of production and distribution could be solved by scientific planning and organization rather than the price system. Technocracy leaped from obscurity into sudden prominence in 1932 and faded just as rapidly. —ED

its creator. When the technocrats undertook to solve the problem by replacing valuation in money and price by computation in "ergs" of the energy put forth in making things, their "system" drifted into imbecility. What is an "erg"? How do you pay a man in "ergs"? How many "ergs" of physical energy is a bank manager "erging" per day? The new "erg", in any shape in which we can think of it, would be just the old dollar "writ large".

The technocrat did more than this. He helped to lay the Malthusian ghost that had whined behind the industrial scene for 137 years. The *Essay on Population* of 1798 was no part of Adam Smith's scheme, except by implication. But his successors built it into their structure as a further locking of the arch. To John Stuart Mill, deeply as he disliked it, it formed along with "diminishing returns", the principal truth of Political Economy. Writing as late as 1883 General Francis Walker could still regard it as impregnable, as open to attack only from the "headless shafts of beginners". But where is it now? As an explanation of how poverty *might* happen — by sheer crowding of numbers against natural resources — it is quite correct. As an explanation of how poverty *does* happen, it is nowhere. Since 1929 countries with a crowded population (England, Belgium) have been overwhelmed in collapse. Countries with a moderate population and heaps of empty resources (the United States) have been equally in collapse. Countries with hardly any population (Canada, Australia), in comparison with their latent resources, have shared the same fate. There have been hard times in Java with over a thousand people to the square mile and bitter times in Pitcairn Island and a slump in Greenland. Where in all this is Malthus, and Mill's restriction of numbers, and population crowding on subsistence, and all the rest of the classic scheme? Nowhere. What has happened is industrial dislocation of which the classicists took no serious account; they never dreamed how much it meant, they never understood that "war" could bring good times because it *integrates* industry, sets everybody working. In war time a quarter of the people, let us say, make and explode gunpowder and keep the rest busily providing for all; economically this is better than peace time with a quarter of the people doing nothing. War means death. War can't last. War speeds up till it breaks. But there is more in the economics of war — while it lasts, integrating all work — than the classicists ever dreamed.

But turn to the central gears of the classical mechanism — the theory that cost of production governs natural value. But what is "cost"? Smith and Ricardo and Mill thought of it as something as simple and uniform as a length of tape. You could cut off an inch, or a yard, or a mile. If one spoon costs a shilling, then two spoons cost two shillings, and a million spoons cost a million shillings. That's as far as the classicists ever got. They lived mostly before the railway taught economics in the form of railway rates, and single individual costs vanished in a midst of totals and overheads and fixed costs and, in the days of Mr. Stuart Chase, the costs of selling. Marshall, it is true, tried to build this new idea of costs into the old structure; but it was like plugging it up with gunpowder. It has blown the building apart. Except in semi-primitive industry, there are no such costs as those of Ricardo and Mill.

More than that. Fitting into this same equation of costs as prices, and of wages as a cost, was the formula of social justice by which the classical economy justified the existence of a *laissez-faire* society. Each man got what he was worth, and was worth what he got. It was a comfortable doctrine for the rich and the capable and the successful. Deplorable though it was that a labourer of 1850 only got three shillings a day, it was based, said the economists, on the sad fact that that was all he produced! Little gleams of light — twilight — reached Adam Smith on this point. "Wages", he said, "are the result of a dispute." If he had followed the thought further it would have taken him a long way. All the factors in economic production would be seen to be in "dispute", and the resulting distribution to reflect its outcome.

The economists should have seen that their equation — value equals cost — was only an equation. They used each side to justify the other. Sweat-shops' wages of shirt-makers are a shilling a day because the shirts they make are only worth a shilling. The shirts they make sell for a shilling because the wages paid in making them are a shilling. What does this tell us of social justice? Nothing. Of why the wages are low, nothing. If I pay a man $2.00 a day to cut hay, I can explain the price of hay per ton in terms of his wages; or I can explain the rate of his wages in terms of the price of hay per ton. But I can't make *both explanations together*.

Hence the classical theory has a circle in the reasoning. It all collapses together. *Magna lapsit ruina*. It is not true that a man is *worth* what he gets and gets what he's *worth*. The truth is that social rewards (wages and salaries and profits) are grossly and cruelly out of harmony with social merit and social production. One doesn't need to be a socialist to admit this. Economists have pursued in vain their ferreting hunt for the *"productive contribution"* of the worker. There is no physical way to measure production contribution, the moment brains as well as hands come in. If an engineer directs a gang of men in building a wooden bridge over a stream, what is his "contribution" and what is theirs? To measure it by his salary and their wages begs the whole question.

The economics of Adam Smith, therefore, if we attempt to apply it to the world of to-day fails utterly as an explanation of production, value, price, population, social justice, riches, and poverty. Is anything left of it? At least, can we try to say, it represents an industrial system that works — works badly no doubt, at times very badly, but still works: under it the world goes on. But *can* we say that? Till 1929 we could, but now — no! The terrible thing is that many of us feel that if, and when, we pass the present catastrophe and depression, a lapse of time under the same system unrevised and uncorrected would bring in another crisis, still more terrible — bringing with it most likely revolution and social destruction. This means that we live conscious of an imminent and terrible danger. We are on the deck of a ship driving towards the breakers that mean death. Up with the helm while there is still the time to change the course!

Nor can the classical system act as a guide towards the legislation that can save us. Adam Smith must turn in his grave at the economic legislation of to-day — violating every canon and principle of what he taught — legislation intensely national, curtailing production, restricting trade, giving bounties to farmers based on the hogs they don't sell and the acres they don't plant. Turn in his grave! He must spin in it.

Few of us can doubt that the trade and tariff nationalism of to-day is utterly overdone; that our present preference of bad money over good is imbecile in the long run; that competitive depreciation of currency is like playing with fire; that to regard a nation as "stealing an unfair advantage" by further depreciation is just crazy. Few of us can doubt that much of the intrusive legislation of to-day, much of Mr. Roosevelt's N.R.A.,* will miss its mark and prove mistaken.

But who could dare to suggest that we could find our salvation in the legislative *laissez-faire* of Adam Smith and his school; that we could dare leave to entire "liberty" and free competition the wages of the workers, the conditions of employment, the lot of the children, the profits of monopoly, the gain of combinations? To turn our industrial world loose and empty to the unrestrained forces of "liberty" and "free competition" would be like turning out people into the fierce blizzard that sweeps our winter landscape as I write these lines.

Rightly or wrongly we must look for salvation in the other direction. Not *laissez-faire* but, if one may twist the French language up by the roots, *"faire-faire"*; not let things happen but "make things happen". And this legislation does not and cannot mean socialism. Straight across that path, like a traffic sign, stands the warning figure of the economic man — sole survivor of the wreck of Adam Smith. This economic man, disclaimed and repudiated by his own creators, is none the less a fact. By this is meant that men can work, in the long run, and as a system, only for themselves. "Every man", wrote N. W. Senior in 1836, in laying down the first of the four principles of Political Economy, "desires to obtain additional wealth with as little sacrifice as possible." "Is it not a patent fact", wrote J. N. Keynes in his *Scope and Method of Political Economy* in 1891, "that in buying and selling, in agreeing to pay or to accept a certain rate of wages, in letting and hiring, in lending and borrowing, the average man aims at making as good a bargain for himself as he can?"

These truths would seem axiomatic. Yet because it seems to give a low view of human nature (a view thoroughly endorsed by John Stuart Mill), kind-hearted people have tried to deny it, and one-eyed people have tried to look the other way. See, for example, Mr. Paul Douglas's discussion in the *Trend of Economics* (a symposium of 1924). "Scientists", he says, "have other motives; so have captains of industry like Mr. Ford." This is cheering but wide of the mark. One might add

---

*National Recovery Administration, one of the first New Deal agencies. —ED

that men work for their wives and children, that Scotsmen read the Bible, and that a chess-club has an *esprit de corps* of its own.

The great fact of individual self-interest remains — not, as Adam Smith thought, as the saving principle of society, but as the sole and only permanent motive force of human work. But for that the solution of the social problem is simplicity itself — work all carried on in common under boards of directors assigning the task, guiding production, helping the weak, and encouraging the faint-hearted — peace and plenty for all the community, and a very philadelphia. But this socialism, this communism, would only work in Heaven where they don't need it, or in Hell where they have it already.

11

THROUGH A GLASS DARKLY

It is to be feared that many readers […] will pass this article by — the modest as too learned, the learned as too ignorant; the light as too heavy, and the heavy as too light. All will be mistaken. What is here said is very real truth — even if softened now and again with an attempt to alleviate it by what is very real fun — and represents a very real and important issue.

The clergy, in their similar despairing call for attention at the opening of a sermon, take a text. Let me, therefore, as the prelude to this essay, take mine from the pages of one of the most eminent and conspicuous works in economics that have appeared in the past few years. The writer of it is the holder of one of the most respected chairs in England, in a university of which I dare not breathe the name. If I did, I should be crushed flat at once under the dead weight of prestige and authority. In any case it would seem invidious and personal to say that in my opinion the particular book of a particular author is tommyrot, when what I really mean is that a hundred recent books by a hundred recent authors are tommyrot.

The author in the case before us is undertaking a discussion of what he calls the "size of real incomes." That is about as near to a plain intelligible phrase as a trained economist can get. An ordinary person would prefer to say "what people get for their money," but that would be just a little too easy to understand. The writer goes on to say that if, conceivably, all people used and consumed one and the same thing, and only one, then we could compare what each got with what every other got by the mere quantity or number. But in reality people consume all kinds of different things with all kinds of preferences.

So far the sky is clear. There has been no warning of mathematics. The readers are as unsuspecting as the crowd in the Paris streets before Napoleon Bonaparte turned on the grape-shots of Vendémiaire.

Now comes the volley: —

It may perhaps be thought that the difficulty can be overcome by comparing real incomes, not in themselves, but in respect of their values. It is, of course, always possible, with a pricing system, to value each of two real incomes in terms of any commodity that we choose, and to set the values so reached over against one another. This is frequently done in terms of money. Unfortunately, however, the two valuations will, in general, be related to one another in different ways according to what commodity is taken as the measure of value. Thus, suppose that we have two incomes each comprising items of three sorts — A, B, C; that in the first income the quantities of these items are a, b, c, with money prices p_a, p_b, p_c and in the second α, β, γ, with money prices π_α, π_β, π_γ. The money value of this first income divided by that of the second is then

$$\frac{a p_a + b p_b + c p_c}{\alpha \pi_\alpha + \beta \pi_\beta + \gamma \pi_\gamma} \ .$$

Call this m. The value of the first income divided by

that of the second in terms of commodity A is $\dfrac{\pi_\alpha}{p_a}$ m;

in terms of commodity B, $\dfrac{\pi_\beta}{p_b}$ m; in terms of

commodity C, $\dfrac{\pi_\gamma}{p_c}$ m. These quantities are obviously,

in general, different. There is nothing to prevent one of them being greater, while another is less, than unity. Thus the result of comparisons depends on the choice we make or the commodity in terms of which valuations are to be made; and this is purely arbitrary. Nothing useful, therefore, can be accomplished on this plan.

As the last echo of the paragraph dies away, the readers are seen to lie as thickly mown down as the casualties of Vendémiaire. The volley has done its work. There will be no further resistance to the argument on the part of the general public. Theirs not to reason why, theirs but to do and die. They will learn to surrender their economic thought to the dictation of the élite. They are not to question where they do not understand.

The last sentence of the paragraph, the final shot, is not without humour. "Nothing useful," it says, "can be accomplished on this plan." No, indeed, nothing much, except getting rid of the readers. For the whole of the "plan" and its pretentious mathematics, when interpreted into plain talk, amounts to something so insignificant and so self-evident that it is within reach of the simplest peasant who ever lived in Boeotia, or failed at Cambridge. It only means that different people with the same money would buy different things; one might buy roses, one cigars, and another concert tickets; and you couldn't very well compare them because the weight wouldn't mean anything, and the colour wouldn't, nor the number. As to what you pay for them in *money* and why you paid — well, that is the very thing we want to find out.

Or shall I state the same thing like this: "It is hard to compare Janie's doll with Johnny's dog." Or let us put it into rural Yorkshire: "There's a mowt of folks i' counthry; happen one loike this aw t'other chap that; dang me if I know 'oo gets best on it." Or in Cree Indian (Fort Chipewyan, H. B. Post, Athabaska Lake): "Hole-in-the-Sky take four guns, two blanket; squaw take one looking glass, one hymnbook."

What the problem means is that he can't really compare what Hole-in-the-Sky got and what the squaw got. That's all.

II

What has been just said is not meant as fun: it is meant in earnest. If the mathematical statement helped the thought — either in presentation or in power of deduction — it would be worth while. But it doesn't. It impedes it. It merely helps to turn economics into an esoteric science, known only to the few. The mathematician is beckoning economics toward the seclusion of the dusty chamber of death, in the pyramid of scholasticism. He stands at the door that he has opened, his keys in his hand. It is dark within and silent. In the darkness lie the mummified bodies of the learnings that were, that perished one by one in the dead mephitic air of scholasticism; of learning that had turned to formalism and lost its meaning, to body and lost its soul, to formula and lost its living force. Here lie, centuries old, the Scholarship of China, the Learning of Heliopolis, the Medicine that the Middle Ages killed, and the Reason that fell asleep as Formal Logic.

All are wrapped in a sanctity that still imposes. They sleep in all the symbols of honour, with a whisper of legend still about them. But the work they would not do, the task they could not fulfill, is left to the fresh bright ignorance of an inquiring world.

Put without prolixity: Any well-established dignified branch of knowledge, finding its problems still unsolved, turns to formalism, authority, symbolism, the inner system of a set of devotees, excluding the world; philosophy becomes scholasticism, science turns to thaumaturgy, religion to dogma, language to rhetoric, and art to symbolism.

Modern economics and philosophy and psychology have so far utterly failed to solve their main problems. So they are beginning to "dig in" as scholasticism. For economics, mathematical symbolism is the means adopted.

III

So few people are accustomed to use mathematical symbols that it is hard to discuss them in an essay of this sort without incurring the very danger here denounced and "sidetracking" the reader. But something of their nature everybody knows. Very often a mathematical symbol or expression does convey an idea very quickly and clearly. Thus the simple and self-evident little charts and graphs used in newspapers to show the rise and fall of production and trade, the elementary index numbers used to show the movement of prices — these things are immensely useful. But they are only a method of presentation of what is known, not a method of finding out what is not known.

Very often we use simple mathematical expressions as a vehicle of common language, as when we say "fifty-fifty," or "a hundred per cent American," or "half-soused," or "three-quarters silly." We could go further if we liked, and instead of saying "more and more" we could say A+n+n.... We could express a lot of our ordinary dialogue in mathematical form. Thus: —

"How is your grandmother's health?"
"Oh, it depends a good deal on the weather and her digestion, but I am afraid she always fusses about herself: to-day she's about fifty-fifty."

Mathematically this is a function of two variables and a constant, and reads:—

$$f(\text{W.D.}+\text{fuss}) = \frac{1}{2}$$

The result is, in all seriousness, just as illuminating and just as valuable as the mathematics quoted above.

We could even go further and express a lot of our best poetry in mathematical form:—

TENNYSON'S "LIGHT BRIGADE"
Half a league, half a league,
   Half a league onward ...
Then they rode back, but not,
   Not the six hundred.

The mathematician would prefer:—

$$\frac{\frac{1}{2} + \frac{1}{2} + \frac{1}{2}}{600} = 600 - N$$

Or, try this as an improvement on Byron:—

CHILDE HAROLD'S PILGRIMAGE
Did ye not hear it! — No; 'twas but the wind,
Or the car rattling o'er the stony street;
On with the dance!

$$d+d+d+d \ldots d(n)$$

Let joy be unconfined;

$$j+j+j+ \ldots \text{infinity}$$

No sleep till morn, when Youth and Pleasure meet.

$$M\text{-}S=Y+P$$

Or, to quote a verse of "Lord Ullin's Daughter" (done as mathematics), in which I once depicted the desperate efforts of the highland boatman:—

The angry water gains apace
Both of his sides and half his base,
Till he sits as he seems to lose
The square of his hypotenuse.

Or, to go a little deeper, by venturing into Descartes's brilliant method of indicating space and motion by means of two or more co-ordinates as a frame of reference, we can make the opening of Gray's "Elegy" a little more exact.

The lowing herd winds slowly o'er the lea.

We can indicate the exact path by a series of points at successive moments of time $(p—p_1—p_2—p_3 \ldots p_n)$, and by dropping perpendiculars from each of these to the co-ordinates we can indicate the area swept by the lowing herd, or rather the area which it ought to sweep but doesn't.

IV

Let me explain here that in this essay I do not wish in any way to deny the marvellous effectiveness of mathematical symbols in their proper field. I have for mathematics that lowly respect and that infinite admiration felt by those of us who never could get beyond such trifles as plane trigonometry and logarithms, and were stopped by a *nolle prosequi* from the penetration of its higher mysteries. Mathematical symbols permit of calculation otherwise beyond our powers and of quantitative expression that otherwise would require an infinity of time. It is no exaggeration to say that mathematical symbols are second only to the alphabet as an instrument of human progress. Think what is entailed by the lack of them. Imagine a Roman trying to multiply LXXVI by CLX. The Roman, indeed, could make use of an abacus — the beads on wires of the Chinese, the familiar nursery toy — but multiplication with beads only, and without written symbols on a decimal or ascending place-plan, is a poor and limited matter. See who will in this connection the medieval work called *Accomptyng by Counters* — A.D. 1510.

Contrast with these feeble expedients the power of expression and computation that symbols give us! The Hebrew psalmist used to ask with awe who could number the sands of the sea! Well, I can! Put them, let us say, at $(100)^{100}$ and we've only used six figures and two crooked lines! And if that is not enough use three more figures:—

$$100^{100^{100}}$$

Where are the sands of the sea now? Gone to mud! Light moves fast and space is large, but symbols can shoot past them at a walk. Take the symbol for a "light-year" and cube it! You can see it all there in half a dozen strokes, and its meaning is as exact as the change out of a dollar.

Consider this. There is a famous old Persian story, known to every-body, of the grateful king who asked the physician who had saved his life to name his own reward. The physician merely asked that a penny — or an obol or something — be placed on the first square of a chessboard, two on the next, and then four, and so on, till all the sixty-four spaces were filled! The shah protested at the man's modesty and said he must at least take a horse as well. Then they counted the money, and presumably the shah fell back dead! The mathematical formula that killed him was the series (1+2+4 ... N), where N=64: the sum of a geometrical progression — and, at that, the simplest and slowest one known to whole numbers.

As a matter of fact, if the king and the physician had started counting out the pennies at the rate of five thousand an hour and had kept it up for a seven-hour day, with Sundays off, it would have taken them a month to count a million. At the end of a year they'd be only on square No. 20 out of the sixty-four; granting that the king and the physician were each sixty-two years old (they'd have to be that to have got so far in politics), their expectation of life would be fifteen years, and they'd both be dead before they got to the thirtieth square; and the last square alone would call for 10,000,000,000,000,000,000 pennies. In other words, they are both alive now and counting![*]

V

But all of this wonder and power and mystery is of no aid in calculating the incalculable. You cannot express the warmth of emotions in calories, the pressure on the market in horsepower, and the buoyancy of credit in specific gravity! Yet this is exactly what the pseudo-mathematicians try to do when they invade the social sciences. The conceptions dealt with in politics and economics and psychology — the ideas of valuation, preference, willingness and unwillingness, antipathy, desire, and so forth — cannot be put into quantitative terms.

---

[*][In original.] If any reader doubts these calculations I refer him to my colleague, Professor Charles Sullivan of McGill University, and if he doubts Professor Sullivan I refer him so far that he will never get back.

It would not so much matter if this vast and ill-placed mess of mathematical symbolism could be set aside and left to itself while the real work of economics went on. Thus, for example, is left aside by the real modern physicists, such as Rutherford and Soddy,[*] the whole mass of the Einstein geometry — which from their point of view is neither here nor there. (Many people don't know that.) But in the case of economic theory these practitioners undertake to draw deductions; to dive into a cloud of mathematics and come out again holding a theory, a precept, an *order*, as it were, in regard to the why of the depression, or a remedy for unemployment, or an explanation of the nature of saving and investment. They are like — or want to be like — a physician prescribing a dose for the docile and confiding patient. He writes on a piece of paper, "$\alpha\Delta\rho\%$" and says, "Take that." Thus one of the latest and otherwise most deservedly famous of the mathematical economists advises us in a new book, heralded as the book of the year, that our salvation lies in the proper adjustment of investment and demand. Once get this right and all the rest is easy. As a first aid the great economist undertakes to explain the relation of investment and demand in a preliminary, simple fashion as follows:—

More generally the proportionate change in total demand to the proportionate change in investment equals

$$\frac{\Delta Y}{Y} \Big/ \frac{\Delta.I}{I} = \frac{\Delta Y}{Y} \cdot \frac{Y - C}{\Delta Y - \Delta C} = \frac{1 - c/y}{1 - dc/dy}$$

To 99.9 per cent of the world's readers this spells good-bye. If economics can only be made intelligible in that form, then it moves into the class of atomic physics. The great mass of us are outside of it. We can judge it only by its accomplishments; and, as economics so far has accomplished nothing, the outlook is dark.

Now I do not know what all that Delta and Y stuff just quoted means, but I am certain that if I did I could write it out just as plainly

---

[*]Frederick Soddy (1877–1956), Nobel Prize (1921), formulated the concept of isotopes; was a demonstrator at McGill 1900–1902; later wrote books on monetary theory that influenced technocracy and Social Credit. —ED

and simply as the wonderful theorem up above about different people spending their money on different things. In other words, mathematical economics is what is called in criminal circles "a racket."

12

So This Is Winnipeg

The visitor to the West — the kind of visitor who writes up his visit — is supposed, on his first morning in Winnipeg, to throw wide open his window and say, "So this is Winnipeg"! I didn't. It was too cold. And there was no one to hear me except the waiter with the tea, and he knew that it was Winnipeg.

But I kept thinking it just the same. For Winnipeg in a sense means more to me, or at least goes back further in my recollections than it does even to most of the people who live in it. It carries me back to the days of the first Manitoba "boom", and the recollections have with them all the colour and wonder of the first recollections of childhood.

"Winnipeg, the capital of Manitoba and chief city of Western Canada, situated at the junction of the Assiniboine and Red Rivers, 60 miles N. of the United States and 45 m. S. of Lake Winnipeg" — so runs its eulogy in the most truthful of the encyclopaedias. The Canadian census of 1931 adds, "pop., 218,000".

Winnipeg is one of the world's cities. Everybody everywhere who has heard of anywhere has heard of it. This is not because of its size. Cities of 218,000 are so common in the world that many of them have never even heard of one another. Winnipeg is a good deal smaller than Stoke, or Dayton, or Stuttgart or Akron: Chin Kiang is twice the size of it, and Bradford and Memphis and Dallas and Mannheim all beat it easily. In the outside world, if it is not wicked to say so, Winnipeg is far better known than Toronto. Indeed I have always found that the only thing in regard to Toronto which far-away people know for certain is that McGill University is in it. Now the betting would be that practically everybody in Bradford and Dallas knows where Winnipeg is, but hardly anybody in Bradford knows where Dallas is, and in that they've nothing on the people in Dallas.

Why then is Winnipeg a world-city, a city known to all the world?

At first sight it seems a little hard to see why. Its name only means "dirty water". Its two rivers lost all economic meaning years ago. They are only useful now to build bridges across. As to being 60 miles north of the United States, you would say the same of Bowmanville, Ontario, and who cares about that?

Worse than that. Winnipeg is cold. It is all right to say that the place has a cosmopolitan atmosphere — I admit that it has — but even a cosmopolitan atmosphere needs a little steam heat. Winnipeg has "six month's winter". So at least its warm admirer Vilhjalmur Stefansson admits in his defence of its climate. The average temperature in January is — I forget what — damn cold, anyway. Even admitting that on bright winter days the thermometer often rises to zero, the place is cold.

Those who love Winnipeg — and they all do — explain that though it is cold it is "dry", and that being dry, you don't feel the cold. People always defend their home town in this way: London explains away its fog, Pittsburgh its smoke and Aberdeen its rain. It appears that the fog is not fog at all but *mist*, that the smoke is only *carbon*, and that the rain isn't really wet. So with that plea that Winnipeg is "dry". It may be, I saw no sign of it while I was there — it seemed, indoors anyway, wetter than Aberdeen.

More than that — the place is not only cold, it's drafty. It has the two widest streets of any capital city in the world, Main Street and Portage Avenue, but even they can't hold all the wind. With the thermometer at 30 below zero, and the wind behind him, a man walking on Main Street, Winnipeg, knows which side of him is which.

No; the only way to defend the climate of Winnipeg is to go the whole way with Vilhjalmur Stefansson[*] and accept the doctrine the

---

[*]Stefansson (1879–1962) was a controversial arctic explorer and anthropologist, best known for *My Life with the Eskimo* (1913) and *The Friendly Arctic* (1915). —ED

"colder the better". In that priceless book of his called *The Northward Course of Empire* he explains that mankind needs the cold, needs the stimulus of it and the energy that's in it. The languor of the tropics kills, the rigour of the north inspires and elevates. The progress of mankind is made by the cold, fights northward into the cold, using each new art of life and artifice of science to live further and further north.

It's a grand theory. Think of it next time you walk on Main or Portage with the January wind astern. Leave the tropics for the bums, the loafers and the poets — let them have "a book of verses under a bough, a cup of wine and thou, singing beside them in the wilderness." But give me a tenderloin steak in a grill room on Main Street with a full-sized woman raised in the cattle country.

No, Winnipeg is an all the world city, because its rise was part of the history of the world, because its creation was one of the romances of the development of North America, and because its fate — its "booms" and collapses, ardent hopes and bitter disillusionments — lie as it were close to the central mysteries of our economic life.

Winnipeg is a world city because the circumstances of its birth drew to it the eyes of all the world. It was like the sudden rise of San Francisco on the shores of the "Southern Sea" or of Johannesburg on the unknown veldt of South Africa. It marked the invasion of mankind into a new and unoccupied territory. Till then "Rupertsland" was one vast unknown emptiness. The stars circled in the Arctic sky over the snow that crackled at 40 below zero. And then, in no time as it were, all was changed, and the Winnipeg that replaced Fort Garry was as widely and as suddenly known to all the world as the Johannesburg of ten years later.

This is why to many people who, like myself, had never seen it, Winnipeg has been a city of far-away memories, that carries in its name all the vividness, the poignancy and the meaning that goes with the memory of childhood.

I remember how the place was born, and those about me, the grown-up people of my family, had a part in its rising fortunes.

The "boom" was of the years '80 and '81, and '82, but the great change began ten years before that with the taking over of the North West Territory as part of the Dominion of Canada, and the setting up of a little corner of it as a province. Till then Fort Garry was a fortified trading post of the Hudson's Bay Company at the junction of the Assiniboine and the Red Rivers. "Winnipeg" was just a name locally given to a group of houses and trading stores scattered along the wagon-road beside the river where it met the portage track that led across the neck of land to the Assiniboine. Here lived the "free-traders", men not connected with the company but trading and dealing on their own.

The creation of Manitoba made a shift in the whole scene, like the "transformation scenes" of the theatre, so wonderful half a century ago. The whole place, Fort Garry and all, went right-about-face, and looked south. Till then, access had been from the north by the one ship a year that the Company sent through the Hudson's Straits: by this way came Lord Selkirk's colonists of 1811: by this way came, in 1842 to the service of the company, R. M. Ballantyne, the story writer whose books for a generation of English children were the only twilight that lit up the northern snow.

The route was over the ocean and through the straits and across the bay to Fort Churchill, up the river to Lake Winnipeg, then 45 miles up the Red River to Fort Garry. Ballantyne took from the middle of May till the end of September to make the journey from Gravesend to Fort Garry.

Quicker access than that was needed now. Lord Wolseley's Expedition had helped to develop the route by Fort William and the Lake of the Woods. The rapid settlement of Minnesota offered a still easier approach. The railways had reached St. Paul in the middle '60s. From there stage coaches ran, even in the '60s, three hundred miles across the Minnesota prairie to Georgetown, Minnesota, on the Red River. They made the trip in five days — fast going! From there, as the crow flies, it was 250 miles to Fort Garry: but the little Red River steamer, "The Pioneer", was no crow: it followed the river and made it 500 miles and took 8 days to it. From railhead to Fort Garry was a fortnight's trip, but you had to wait for the steamer, from one day to three weeks according to circumstances.

As soon as the province was established, everything moved with a rush. There was created a sort of economic vacuum and the air, an inblowing of men and goods, came rushing in. To begin with, settlement was pouring into the Minnesota district. It was beginning to be known in the outside world that the alluvial soil of the Red River district was even richer than Minnesota. Lord Wolseley's expedition had left behind it a regiment of British soldiers and after that had gone, there remained an "Ontario Battalion" for which supplies must be brought in. There was the government to be housed, buildings to be made, and new settlers to be provided for.

So here was Winnipeg, a little place of 250 people in 1870, with its hands full and its beds overfull and its saloons more than overfull — hammering away night and day to make houses, and clamouring for lumber and transport — and traders and adventurers and behind them, slowly gathering to a head, the rising wave of real settlers. ... The economic vacuum kept the little place at high pressure. Lumber that was worth seven dollars a thousand feet in Ontario sold for seventy dollars, coal oil, worth fifty cents a gallon "back east", sold for five dollars "out west". No wonder the freighters could charge four dollars a hundred pounds for the Red River trip alone. It was, in the "economic" sense, "worth" it.

That meant, if you analyse it out economically, that there was lots of money in Winnipeg to buy things and few things to buy; that there was the "money" sent for the soldiers and the money for the government and the private money of the new traders and store-builders and merchants; and this means, after complete analysis of what we call "money" and "credit" that there were a lot of people in Winnipeg who had a "claim" on the goods and services of the East and could say "send me this and send me that": and the only trouble was to find the transport, the way to get it there.

Then came the intensification of economic activity called a "boom". And the whole thing was sound, absolutely. No wind, no bubble about it; just solid economic fact, that can be repeated over and over again — on the Peace River, in British Columbia, on Vancouver Island, in Northern Ontario, more or less all over Canada, wherever undeveloped resources, labour, capital and directing brains all come together. We have never understood the nature of a "boom". We look at it as a sort of economic fever. Not at all; a "boom" is a burst of economic health.

No wonder things move fast in such a world — where everything was young, everything to be done, and where everybody could make money out of everybody else — nothing needed but transport, more transport, and more goods. These were the days when the railroad came into its own, when people laughed and shouted and danced at the sight of the first train and loaded it with flowers, with the bell ringing and with merry girls riding on the cow-catcher! Alas, how different to the grim iron octopus of today, the huge debt-carrier, the farmers' imagined enemy! Something must be wrong somewhere.

Things moved! Especially all sorts of "first things". The "first" parliament met (1871) in "Mr. A. G. Bannatyne's house", in the sitting room — three entire rooms being assigned to its use, one upstairs and two down. The "first oysters" came to Winnipeg in February 1871. In the same month came the "first barber": but his business, I am sure, was trimming beards, not removing them: Winnipeg knew no such effeminacy as a clean shave till many years later. With the barber appeared shortly a "first baker" and a "first harness maker". It was like the days of Pharaoh. Dr. C. J. Bird in the summer of 1871 set up the "first soda water fountain": they had a whisky fountain already. More ominous still is the chronicled record that on December 14, 1870, Mr. Stewart Mulvey gave the "first public lecture" in Winnipeg. He chose as his topic, "True Greatness", and we are told that he was listened to "with great pleasure". It's a cruel phrase to use of any lecturer. Laughter, if you like, derision, anger, excitement — but not "great pleasure".

Music also sprang to life and woke to harmony. We read in the charming volume on *Winnipeg's Early Days*, written by my old friend, Mr. W. J. Healy, the Provincial Librarian, that "the first hand organ was played in Winnipeg in 1876". Mr. Healy adds that it was the only one, then or since, but does not say where the man was buried.

But the main thing in the morning of the life of Winnipeg was the initiation of public enterprises — especially with a charter (from Mr.

Bannatyne's sitting room) or, simpler still, application for a charter. Each new idea was taken up with a hurrah! and if no money came in, they dropped as easily and no one cared. There was a "Bank of Rupertsland" — hurrah! — and then another, the Bank of Manitoba! Neither of them happened. There was an application for a joint stock company for the construction of a railway "passing through the town of Winnipeg to connect with the nearest of the Minnesota railways"; a "Bridge company" that never built bridges; a "General Manufacturing and Investment Co." that never went further; and a "Manitoba Brewing Company" whose future was fully realized.

All this in the early days before the real "boom" began. Measured statistically progress was slow. There were 250 people in Winnipeg in 1870, and 817 in St. Boniface and only 1,565 pure white people in all Manitoba. By 1872 the town still had only reached 1,467, but even in 1882, when all the world had heard of it, the population of Winnipeg was still only 7,900 and that of all Manitoba only a little over 60,000.

But the ground swell that indicated the tidal wave that was to come, appeared years before the boom in the high, the staggering prices paid for real estate while the place was still little more than a hamlet. In 1872 the Hudson's Bay Company, so Grant tells us, sold as building lots thirteen of their five hundred acres about Fort Garry and received $7,000 an acre for them.

The real boom could not come in these early years. The setting was not ready: but the course of the next ten years prepared it. The "railway" reached Winnipeg, by way of St. Paul and Minnesota in 1878. The Homestead Act of 1875 and the surveys that followed it opened up the Northwest for all the world. And the great depression of the '70s that lay with increasing dead weight on Europe, and impoverished the farmers of Ontario, set loose the great migration to the land of hope.

It is here that my own personal recollections, as a boy of eleven years connect with the period. I give them, not for any personal value, but as reflecting the men and things of the "boom" period, the circumstances that occasioned the migration from older Canada to Manitoba, the ardent hopes that went with it and the bitter disillusionment in which it ended. To my mind the tragedy of the "boom" is that it never should have collapsed. Good old Colonel George Ham called it in his memoirs a "fool's paradise". If so it was a paradise lost. We must regain it.

We lived, and had lived, for five years before the Manitoba migration, on a Canadian farm, four miles back from Lake Simcoe, in an isolation not known today, even in the Arctic. The nearest village was four miles away, through great cedar swamps and over narrow roads, a horse and buggy or a sleigh the only means of communication. There was no railway. Newspapers we never saw. No one came and went. There was nowhere to come and go. And the stillness of the winter nights was as silent as eternity.

Then came all about us the hard times brought about by the fall of all farm prices. Mortgages fell like great snowflakes on the farms. People were "turned out" and "sold up" and moved away or "went to the States", or simpler still, died. And then all of the people began talking of the place we then called Manitobah — and they used to ask "Does your father think of going tò Manitobah?" They didn't know that the word meant "God's country", but it sounded like that to them.

Just at that time there came to us from England my uncle, my father's youngest brother, E. P. Leacock, still dimly remembered in Winnipeg as an outstanding "character" of the boom. He was an adventurous spirit, full of brains, and attraction, as visionary as Tartarin, as loud as Falstaff, bearded and jovial as a Plantagenet. Nothing would do him but my father must go with him to Manitoba. The "Star of Empire" he told us children, "glitters in the West". So it was to, for a little while.

So we had a "sale" at our farm, as countless other Ontario people did. The whisky for the sale cost more than the thin animals and broken imple- ments brought in. But that didn't matter. The star was glittering. My uncle wiped out all disappointment with a laugh and off they went. We children stayed behind to follow later: though as a family we never followed. But my father and uncle "hit" Winnipeg just as the boom rose to its height and my uncle, at least, rode on the very crest of it, triumphant.

I have always felt that there must be something exhilarating, stimulating, superhuman in the rushing, upward life of a boom town — a San Francisco of the '50s, a Carson city of the '60s, a Winnipeg of the '80s. The life of the individual fits into the surroundings as into a glove — the "world" no longer means something far away, something in the papers — it is right there. In the life of the great cities of today the individual is crushed, lost, is nothing. In the boom town his life is life itself. There everybody is somebody. "Character" springs like a plant and individuality blooms like a rose: and forthwith there are gay people, brave people, and queer people — room for everybody to be something; not the crushed dead-level uniformity of the metropolis. Everybody becomes, as in Charles Dickens's America, "a remarkable man": indeed we all are, in reality, if looked into deeply enough.

In such a setting politics swell into grandeur: social life becomes a whirl — life itself a day-to-day adventure, and the future an infinite vista. So was it with Winnipeg of the boom, as beside which the New York and London of today are dull and commonplace.

My father and my uncle arrived in Winnipeg just as the boom was rising to its height. George Ham has described for us the frantic activity of speculation which went with, indeed sprang from, the economic basis of the opening-up of a new country —

"Auction sales", he writes, "were held daily and nightly. Property changed hands quickly at greatly enhanced values. The craze spread to the rural districts. Surveyors and map artists worked overtime to fill orders. If ever there was a fool's paradise, it sure was located in Winnipeg. Men made fortunes — mostly on paper — and life was one continuous joy-ride."

But I am convinced that Colonel Ham, like so many others, has mistaken the mere surface for the foundation, the foam for the water. If there is room for 300,000 people in Winnipeg now, so there was then — for a prairie population of nearly three million now, so there was then. No part of the world is full till mankind exploits and uses its uttermost resources. Leaving out of count the places — London, Belgium and such — where people live not on resources under their feet, but on resources carried in and out, the filling up of the world has happened so far in only a few crowded areas of India, China, Java and the like. Most of it is still relatively empty — our country and Australia almost completely so. Our only trouble is that we don't know how to begin.

But the outward and visible sign of the real meaning of the boom in Winnipeg in 1881 was that there was "bread and work for all"; jobs for everybody, plain or skilled it didn't matter. Everybody was counted a skilled labourer till he blew himself up or broke his leg and proved that he wasn't. I recall that a young man who went out with my father and uncle, straight off an Ontario farm, got a job the first day running the engine in a steam laundry. He didn't know how to run it but that didn't matter. No one else did. He blew himself up the same day. That didn't matter either. I doubt if they even went to look for him.

My father opened a "real-estate office" with a sign in blue and gold thirty feet long. He had with him an English partner, a Captain Desborough — the type of those drawn from the old country by the magnet of Manitoba. The captain had been a "public school" boy, still knew the first line of the first book of Virgil and commanded great respect with it in the saloons on Main Street. He and my father lasted nearly a year before they blew up.

My uncle had a larger career — went up like a rocket; was in everything — railway companies, land companies, and in the parliament of Manitoba. I remember how a group of them came down to Toronto a little later (when I was a schoolboy there) along with John Norquay, the famous prime minister. I remember what huge men they seemed, all bearded like Assyrians and wearing the buffalo coats of the period! There are no such men now. That barber who first insinuated himself into Main Street, has got in his work.

So the boom broke: and after its collapse arose a foolish theory as if the mere buying and selling had anything to do with what happened. Buying and selling back and forward is as empty economically as a poker game. Collectively no one is richer or poorer. It was not because the buying and selling stopped that the boom broke, but because the hammerers stopped clattering on Main Street, our navvies stopped digging on the prairies. We "called it a day" too soon.

This problem when the new boom begins we shall have to face again. The essential point for its solution will be to keep the economic, physical life of development of resources by work and capital running well ahead of its mere reflection in pecuniary values. There must be the substance or the shadow vanishes.

One last feature remains to record and to commend in the Winnipeg of the bye-gone days — a feature that left upon it a mark that it still wears. This is the cosmopolitan, world-wide outlook of Winnipeg, that shows itself in the city press, in the public organisations and in the university and learned societies. The city runs true to its first form. It was from its birth a cosmopolitan place, a meeting place of people from all over the world. It was born, so to speak, into the sunlight of the larger world, and had nothing of the long slow twilight of the growth of other cities. George Grant, the later principal of Queen's, noticed this when he visited the place for the second time, in 1881. "Winnipeg", he said, "is London or New York on a small scale. You meet people from all over the world." A result of this was the appearance in the little town of almost every known form of institution and patriotic society, a historical club, a St. Andrew's society, with another society for St. George and one for St. Patrick. The whole social life was buttressed, perhaps stimulated, with a supply of saloons that attracted the notice of every visitor.

Winnipeg, like the rest of us, was born in mingled sin and righteousness. Purged now of its sin, it keeps the virtue of its cosmopolitan outlook. Buried in the heart of a continent, it still looks over the rim of it in all directions.

13

THE LAND OF DREAMS

Nearly half of Canada lies outside of the provinces and to the north of them — a land area of 1,500,000 square miles out of 3,500,000. This is made up of the Yukon, between the Rockies and Alberta; the Mackenzie District between Alberta-Saskatchewan and the Polar Sea; Keewatin, chiefly the "barren lands" between Manitoba, the Hudson Bay and the Polar Sea; and Franklin, the vast territory of broken islands reaching to an apex at the pole. It is, in point of human life, an empty country — in all 14,000 people on an extent of land equal to that in which 300,000,000 souls live, or try to, in British India: emptier still as far as white people go, there being 2,500 in the Yukon and about a thousand in the Territories.

But it is far from empty in its resources, its future, and in its inspiration. The great forests of Canada reach away beyond the sixtieth parallel: they carry a frontier line that lies in a north-west slant from Fort Churchill to Great Bear Lake. In the Mackenzie basin there are still plenty of big spruce trees of 100 feet height and of a diameter up to eighteen inches. A last skirmish line of stunted spruce and scrub willow reaches to the Arctic Sea itself, at the mouths of the Mackenzie Delta. In the Mackenzie District local lumber suffices for all needs of building. The mineral wealth of the Yukon, in this new age of metals, may at any time restore the lost glory of Dawson City and its fellow camps. The reindeer just introduced into the Arctic grazing lands, may soon rival the herd of 700,000 now feeding in Alaska, where none existed a generation ago. Our far North has pasture, so says the Porsild report of 1928, for at least three quarters of a million animals.* The furs

---

*Alf Erling Porsild (1901–1977) was a Danish biologist hired in 1926 by the Department of the Interior to investigate the feasibility of reindeer grazing in arctic Canada. —ED

from the Territories, chiefly from Mackenzie, number about 250,000 skins a year with muskrat as the chief item, and about 7,000 beaver and 11,000 white fox, a total value running from a million to a million and a half dollars.

The Mackenzie District, if not a land flowing with milk and honey, at least flows with petroleum and natural gas. The secret store of radium in the rocks of the Great Bear Lake may make Croesus of Lydia look poverty-stricken. The district has already a steam boat commerce that covers 1,300 miles of navigation. The aeroplane is as familiar a sight to the native Indian as a bus to a Cockney. Even the "barren lands" carpeted with flowers blush with red copper.

But to me this far away north suggests not modern commerce, but a land of dreams, of infinite horizons, of blue, blue sky and of bright sunshine on the snow, more invigorating than warmth itself. Such dreams carry back to the far away days when first the ships of the Hudson's Bay Company sailed into the waters of the mid-night sun.

Some years ago I was engaged in Montreal in what is called "historical research", a thing done by professors in the heart of the summer in the depth of a library where there is no one to check up their time. Often it takes years and years to write a chapter.

But the point is that I wanted to make a reference to the foundation of the Hudson's Bay Company over two and a half centuries ago, and I wanted to be certain of their official name. The companies of those days had queer names, all alike and yet all different — "gentlemen" of this and "adventurers" of that, or "merchants" of the other. I couldn't remember whether the Hudson's Bay Company were called gentlemen, or adventurers, or business men, or captains of industry, or crooks. I looked into a lot of old volumes and got no wiser. Then a sudden idea came to me: "I'll telephone them!" It had occurred to my mind that the Hudson's Bay Company of Charles the Second were still right there down town in Montreal and doing business. So I called the number and asked, "Would you mind telling me the full official name of your company?" "Certainly.

We're often asked for it. We're the Governor and Company of Adventurers of England trading into Hudson's Bay."

It seems wonderful, doesn't it? I almost imagined myself going a little further and saying, "Hullo, Prince Rupert, can I speak with your cousin Mr. Charles the Second?" "Hold the line a minute and I'll see. I'm sorry, our Mr. Charles is in conference with our Miss Nell Gwynne, and we don't like to disturb him."

The thoughts aroused by such an incident characterize the size and majesty of the Great North; the fascinating sweep of time and space that its name involves; the North, where man scribbles in vain a little history and Nature buries it in a blizzard of snow.

The North is the only place where Nature still can claim to rule, the only place as yet but little vexed by man. All over the globe there spreads his noisy failures; the North alone is silent and in peace. Give man time and he will spoil that too; but the time has not, thank Heaven, as yet arrived. The fascists, we read, are mowing down the reds, or the yellows, or whatever they are, in Barcelona with machine guns. But the Eskimos of Ungava are not troubling the Algonquins. Someone is dropping bombs all round Gibraltar, but none fall on the delta of the Mackenzie. The organization of the air defence of London hums as loud as the mosquitoes of the Great Slave Lake, but all is quiet on the Coppermine. The Poles are so worked up about their corridor to the sea that there may be a first class war about it; but the Indians are using the same old portage route from the Moose to the Albany, and going right across the railway track, and no one worries about it.

Compared with the rest of a troubled world, the North seems a vast realm of peace.

No great war, no war on a real scale, ever devastated the great north-west. But listen to this forgotten — or rather unknown — episode of history. That arch-disturber of mankind, Napoleon Bonaparte, once tried to make such a war, once planned to strike at England by means of a great sweep to be made from the snow-covered plains and mountains of the West. This was to take the Canadas and the settlements of the seaboard from the rear. Students of military science like myself (I like it best when it's about a hundred and fifty years old) do not need to be told that a crack in the rear is about the most deadly thing that one general can administer to the other. That is why a great commander like Marlborough or Napoleon was always careful to have his rear resting on something reliable — like a marsh, or broken rock or a field of cactus. And that was why a great mind like that of Napoleon would turn to grandiose schemes of hitting, not merely another general in the rear, but a whole nation. Napoleon went to Egypt, not to kill the Egyptians — that was just done on the side — but with a view to getting at the rear of Turkey, and he planned the still vaster enterprise of throwing India on the rear of Europe. But for the defeat of Tippoo Sahib at Seringapatam this might have been done. Readers who don't know about this "rear" business often wonder how people like Tippoo Sahib and Zenghis Khan get into our history. That's it — by the rear entrance.

Well, at any rate Napoleon's plan was to organize the vast tribes of the Northwest — presumably the Crees and the Doukhobors and the Albertans — to overwhelm Ottawa and Montreal. His idea was correct in a way and came true later on, but it was premature. It was characteristic of Napoleon's profound ignorance of America, to imagine the Northwest filled with likely looking Indians who could be recruited into Kellerman's dragoons and Milhaud's cuirassiers and descend (in four or five days) from the Rocky Mountains on Montreal with cries of "Vive l'Empéreur!"

So Napoleon set out to get information. All that could be found out in Paris (the year was about 1805) was that a man called Mackenzie had been right across the continent to the Pacific Ocean and had written a book about it, published in 1801 under the title "Voyages on the River St. Lawrence and Through the Continent of America to the Frozen and Pacific Oceans" — which, for a Scotchman, was short and snappy. Napoleon ordered the book translated in French and printed. Only two or three copies were made, beautifully bound and embellished. There is no trace of any of them left except of the copy given to General Bernadotte, afterwards, by Napoleon's influence, made Crown Prince of Sweden, and great-grandfather to the present King. Napoleon wrote to

Bernadotte about the scheme, and hence our knowledge of it. The information gathered showed its emptiness — at the time — but later on the notion of a descent from Alberta to take Ottawa in the rear has been worked out with success.

When I write about the North I speak with a certain authority. For I know the North, as few people know it. In the corporeal, bodily sense, I have never been there. But in my arm chair, in front of the fire in my house on Côte des Neiges Road in Montreal, I have traversed it all, from the portages back of Lake Superior to where the Mackenzie delta washes into the tidal seas. I have been with Franklin on the Coppermine and Coronation Gulf, with Hudson till I lost him owing to his own folly, with Mackenzie over the divide, in Red River ox-carts with Butler, and in the foothills with Milton and Cheadle. In the snow-storms and Arctic blizzards I feel perfectly at home; if it gets really bad I just lie down in the snow, along with Stefansson, and let it bury me completely and lie there for a day or two and read a book till it moderates. But I must say I don't think I ever felt such intense cold as on crossing the Coppermine running hard with ice through barren treeless country of slate and stone. Imagine trusting oneself on a river like that on a sort of raft or boat made of willow sticks, wet to the skin, in piercing cold. I had to get up and mix a hot whisky and stir the fire and leave Franklin and Richardson to freeze awhile till I rejoined them. A fine story that, "The Journey to the Polar Sea," by John Franklin: not the narrative of his immortal adventure and heroic death, but the earlier journey down the Mackenzie and along the polar shores with Richardson and young Back. There is a very human little incident in the tale of how Lieutenant Back, youthful and ardent, nearly got left out of the expedition — stayed behind to go to a dance. They sailed without him and he caught them at the Orkneys or somewhere. Back later became a knight and an admiral, returned to the North, again as an explorer, and discovered the Back river, not the one at Montreal but the one that commemorates his name.

Let no one think, from what was said above, of the silence and peace of the North that I am trying to depict it as a vast frozen emptiness. Far be it from me to fall into that worn-out fallacy of the lifelessness of the North. If I ever shared it, I was cured of it long ago by an angry letter I once received from Vilhjalmar Stefansson, an angry letter that proved the beginning of a personal friendship of over twenty years. I had written a little book called "The Adventurers of the Far North," and had spoken in it of the North as if "Here in this vast territory civilization has no part and life no place. Life struggles northward only to die out in the Arctic cold."[85]

Stefansson, who takes a personal pride in the North and regards Baffin Bay as a superior social centre to Naragansett Beach, felt affronted and wrote, in substance: "You may be a hell of a humorist, but what you don't know about the North would fill a book. Don't you understand that the North is full of flowers and butterflies and life everywhere?" I answered back mildly: "I meant further north still. The thing must stop somewhere." But I learned the lesson, and I know now that it is just a poet's fancy to speak of the Great North as "silent and untenanted." I am well aware, without being told again by Tyrrel or Stefansson, or anyone touchy about it, that the north "teems every-where with animal and plant life." I read the other day a rather spiteful account, by an English settler, of the mosquitoes on the shores of the Great Slave Lake that made me quite envious. I happen to be the president of the Anti-Mosquito Society of East Simcoe, one of the few active offices that I still retain in retirement. What with coal oil and such things, we have killed off so many mosquitoes that we are beginning to run out of them and may have to send for more. It is good to know that if a real shortage comes the Great Slave lake district can supply an adequate "carryover".

But if the North, even at its emptiest, still waves with Arctic flowers and hums with a mist of insects, there is a sense in it which contrasts with all other parts of the globe. The role of man and nature, as seen elsewhere, are reversed. The elemental forces still rule; and over it falls, inevitable and eternal, the winter night.

Vilhjalmar Stefansson is not the only one of the great explorers of our time whom I have been privileged to know. I recall a wonderful evening in my home at Montreal, listening to Raoul Amundsen, just back from his discovery of the South Pole. The eminence of that exploit makes it part of the history of the world, and makes people lose from sight Amundsen's earlier achievement: his accomplishment, in the little *Gjoa*, of the north-west passage, which gives him a place in the heroic annals of Canada. Amundsen,[*] when I met him, was lecturing — a job which he hated as much as all good lecturers do — in order to get enough money to make another polar voyage, anywhere so long as it was polar. I was to be chairman of his meeting, and so I called upon him after breakfast with a list of social invitations — things he abominated. I said, "Captain Amundsen, the Ladies' Morning Musical would like to invite you as their guest this morning." "Thank you," he said, "but I would rather not." I went on to the next item. "Sir William Peterson would like to know if you would care to come up at ten o'clock and see McGill University?" "Thank you; I would rather not see it." "The Women's Canadian Club are holding a lunch and would like you to come as a guest of honour." "That is very kind, but I would rather not." "The Ski Club want to give a tea." "No, thank you." "The Norski, Danski, and Svenski Associations would like to escort you with torches from the hotel to the hall." "It is very kind, but no, I would rather take a cab."

"Now," I said, "we come to the last item. After your lecture is over, will you come up to my house and have some Scotch whisky?" "Yes, very gladly, indeed; that is most kind." And at my house that night Amundsen talked till the small hours of his South Pole experience, talking chiefly with Jack McCrae of Flanders Fields, who was also a polar explorer of sorts, having just made a trip through the Hudson Straits.

I also knew Captain Bernier,[**] our own Canadian explorer, who saw more of our arctic seas than any other living man. I met him at a big dinner in New York, where he was the chief guest. He had some moving pictures — very new and very imperfect things then — of polar scenes. Bernier apologized for them. "I 'ave to hapologize," he said, "for the pictures. We didn't know ver' well how to take them. This one is call' 'Heskimo Loading Coal'!"

------

[*]Amundsen (1872–1928) was the first to travel the Northwest Passage in 1903–06. In 1911 he reached the South Pole, a month before Robert Scott, whose famous expedition perished in the attempt. —ED

[**]Joseph-Elzéar Bernier (1852–1934) led government expeditions into the Arctic between 1904 and 1911, certifying Canada's claim to the archipelago. —ED

Load it they certainly did! The picture had been taken with a wrong timing; the Eskimos dashed in one hop a hundred yards from the ship to a great cliff of coal; their picks moved so fast you could not see the points; they filled bags of coal in four seconds; and were back on the ship in one hop. Next to me at the banquet sat an American coal man. "Gee," he said, "I wish I had those fellers at thirty cents an hour!"

Ernest Shackleton I knew also, and well. It is not generally known, for it has never been made history, that after the war Shackleton planned a Canadian polar expedition to explore the Beaufort Sea. He had wanted to go south again, but the British admiralty were very half-hearted about giving him support. So he turned to Canada, and came to Montreal to raise money. I was one of those who tried to help in this, and, with the government's and private generosity, we soon had plenty of money in sight for the expedition. Exploration is as cheap as human life itself. I arranged on behalf of Shackleton for the services of a corps of young McGill scientists. Then he asked me if I would like to go as historiographer, and I said yes. I knew McGill would spare me. Any college would send its staff to the Beaufort Sea any time. I said I needed no pay, and so for twenty-four hours I was historiographer of the Beaufort Sea Canadian Expedition.

But it came to a sudden end. I said to Shackleton that I would supply all my own Scotch whisky for the year's trip, as I didn't want to be a charge on the ship. And he said they didn't take whisky on polar expeditions and, outside of the medicine chest, didn't allow it. Another illusion of the North shattered! I always thought that explorers, the ship once well set in the ice and buried in snow, went down below with a pack of cards and a keg of whisky. But it seems not. They take observations. I resigned, and a little later news came that the admiralty had gone right about face and Shackleton was given a ship, and he went south and never came back.* But all of this that I have said of the North is supposed to move gropingly towards a general idea, to throw a dim light upon a general conclusion. Here

---

*This occurred in 1922. Shackleton died at age 48, just as the expedition was getting underway, worn out, it is said, as much by the exertions of fundraising as of the expedition. —ED

is this vast, beautiful space — the last part of human heritage to be reached and explored by man. Not much longer can it remain in isolation. Its infinite distance is gone. It thrills with the waves and currents of talking voices: over it hovers the searching aeroplane. Mankind has taken the empty savannahs of the West and is moving on the North. Human life and human livelihood have learned easily to adapt themselves where once was hyperborean darkness.

We, speaking collectively for all mankind, have for the present at least made a mess of the rest of the world. Our contriving wits and calculating selfishness had somehow cheated us of what seemed our inheritance. Man struggles in the grasp of his own machinery.

For the North let us make it different. If the vast lands that edge the polar seas — Scandinavia, Russia, Canada — are to be filled with electric light that dims the aurora, with power that defies the cold, and resources that supply the world, let us see to it that in the new trust of the future of the North we make fewer errors than in the old.

14

I'll Stay in Canada

You were kind enough to suggest that I might, being now free from work, come home to England. But no, no, don't tempt me. It wouldn't work. I know it wouldn't. It sounds fine. But there are all kinds of difficulties, things you wouldn't think of at first — questions of language and manners; a lot of them. Honestly, I don't think I'd better try it.

You see, it's been sixty years, this early spring, since I came out from England as a little boy of six, so wise that I knew all about the Trojan War and which Gods fought for which side, and so ignorant that I had never seen a bark canoe or a bob-sleigh and didn't know what a woodchuck was. We crossed the Atlantic, which I recall as continuous ice; were in river steamers for four days; then in a train with a queer little engine that threw hemlock sparks all over the bush; and then thirty miles in a lumber wagon — and we were *there*.

After that my brothers and I never saw a railway train again for three years, till someone built a railway to Lake Simcoe and the "cars" came. There followed another three years, and then we went away to school and to the world. But the "stamp" I carry is that of the farm in Georgina Township and my predilection is for the soil and the Canadian bush. Forever, I like the sunrise.

I worked at teaching. I taught for three months, in training, eighteen years old, at the old Strathroy High School with General Sir Arthur Currie, our greatest Canadian, as my pupil.

Then I taught for a year at Uxbridge High School. Then I taught ten years at Upper Canada College. Then I got quite a good job at McGill University and held it for thirty-five years. My life has been as simple as one of Xenophon's Marches. But at least my jobs grew longer. The next, I think, will be what you'd call permanent.

But now, as you say, I am free to do as I please; and, if I like, after sixty years I could come "home." Certainly it sounds tempting. Yet, as I say, there are difficulties. The first is the question of language. When I left Hampshire I spoke English. But I've lost it, and it might be too late to pick it up again. You see, we speak differently here. I don't mean uneducated people, I mean educated men, like my friends at my club (The University Club, Montreal — you can't miss it; it's just opposite McGill University).

We used to be ashamed of our Canadian language, before the war, and try to correct it and take on English phrases and say, "What a ripping day," instead of "What a peach of a morning," and "Ah you thah?" instead of "Hullo Central," and "Oh, rather!" instead of "O-Hell-yes." But now, since the Great War put Canada right on a level with the Portuguese and the Siamese and those fellows who came from — ah! one forgets the names, but it doesn't matter — I mean, made Canada a real nation — we just accept our own language and are not ashamed of it. We say "yep!" when we mean "yep!" and don't try to make out it's "yes," which is a word we don't use; and if we mean "four" we say so and don't call it "faw."

So you see, there's the question of language. Then there's the difference of education. I don't mean that we are not educated — us fellers in the University Club — because we are: only in a different way. At first sight you English people would not think we *were* educated because we learned different things. Any member of the club knows what a kilowatt is, and you don't; but on the other hand, our members would think that a "perfect aorist" is either a vacuum cleaner or an Italian trombone player.

It is just that difference. I remember a few years ago a distinguished English bishop, speaking at our club, said that he felt that Greek had practically made him what he was; we felt exactly the same about him and thought it very manly and British of him to admit it straight out.

Then, there's the question of manners. There it would be pretty hard for me or for any of my friends here to "get by." You see, we are not just quite what you call gentlemen. Not quite. In the dark and if we don't talk, you could hardly tell us. But when we begin to feel easy and at home the thing comes out. I don't just know what it consists of: I think we are a little too unrestrained and we have a way of referring to money, a thing of which you never definitely speak in England.

I remember, in making conversation with that bishop, I asked him if his salary went right on while he was out here, and when he said, "I beg your pardon," all I could say was, "Forget it." Of course, the bishop didn't know that in Canada we never feel at ease with a man till we know what his salary is, and which of the gold mines he bought shares in last.

All this means we lack "class." There isn't a sufficient distinction between us and those lower down in money. Personally I can go bass fishing with a taxi driver and a Toronto surgeon and an American tourist and the "feller that rents the boat" and can't see any difference. Neither can they. There isn't any.

That brings me to the Americans! There's another reason for not wanting to leave Canada for England. I'd hate to be so far away from the United States. You see, with us it's second nature, part of our lives, to be near them. Every Sunday morning we read the New York funny papers, and all week we read about politics in Alabama and Louisiana, and whether they caught the bandits that stole the vault of the national bank, and — well, you know American news — there's no other like it. And the Americans come-and-go up here, and we go-and-come down there, and they're educated just as we are and know all about kilowatts but quit Latin at the fourth declension.

Their colleges are like ours and their clubs are like ours and their hotels are like ours and Rotaries and Lions and Kiwanis like ours. Honestly, you can't tell where you are unless you happen to get into a British Empire Society; and anyway, they have those in Boston and in Providence, and the Daughters of the American Revolution is practically a British organization — so all that is fifty-fifty.

Our students go and play hockey with their stoodents and our tourists going out meet their towrists coming in. The Americans come up here and admire us for the way we hang criminals. They sit in our club and say, "You certainly do hang them, don't you!" My! they'd like to hang a few! The day may be coming when they will. Meantime, we like to hang people to make the Americans sit up.

And in the same way we admire the Americans for the way they shovel up mountains and shift river-courses and throw the map all round the place. We sit in the club, fascinated, and listen to an American saying, "The proposal is to dam up the Arkansas River and make it run backward over the Rockies." That's the stuff! That's conversation.

There you are again — conversation. It would be hard for me or any Canadian to learn to "converse" in England. You see, English conversation turns upon foreign politics and international affairs. It runs to such things as — "But don't you think that the Singapore Base would have been better if it had been at Rangoon or at least on the Irrawaddy?" "Ah, but would that really control Hoopow, or, for that matter, Chefoo?"

Now, we don't talk about that. Listen to us in my club and you hear, "He told me that in Central Patricia they were down to the second level and that there was enough stuff *right in sight* to make it a cinch. I bought 100 at 2.30 and yesterday it had got to three dollars...."

That's real talk. And that's our country, anyway — our unfailing interest, for all of us, in its vast development, its huge physical future. In this last sixty years — since I've known it — we have filled it in and filled it in like a huge picture lying in a frame from the frozen seas to the American line, from Nova Scotia to the Pacific. What the English feel about the Armada and the Scottish about Bannockburn, the Canadian, consciously or not, feels about the vast geography of Canada.

There is something inspiring in this building of a new country in which even the least of us has had some part. I can remember how my father went — from our Lake Simcoe farm — to the first Manitoba boom of over fifty years ago — before the railway. He had an idea that what the West needed was British energy and pluck. He came back broke in six months. Then Uncle Edward went; he had a gifted mind and used to quote to us that "the Star of the Empire glitters in the West." He did better. He came back broke only after four years.

Then my brothers Dick and Jim went. Dick was in the Mounted Police and then worked in a saloon and came home broke. Jim got on fine but he played poker too well and had to leave terribly fast. Charlie and George and Teddy went — they all went but me. I was never free to go till now, but I may start at any time. Going West, to a Canadian, is like going after the Holy Grail to a knight of King Arthur. All Canadian families have had, like mine, their Western Odyssey.

It's the great spaces that appeal. To all of us here, the vast unknown country of the North, reaching away to the polar seas, supplies a peculiar mental background. I like to think that in a few short hours in a train or car I can be in the primeval wilderness of the North; that if I like, from my summer home, an hour or two of flight will take me over the divide and down to the mournful shores of the James Bay, untenanted till yesterday, now haunted with its flock of airplanes hunting gold in the wilderness. I never have gone to the James Bay; I never go to it; I never shall. But somehow I'd feel lonely without it.

No, I don't think I can leave this country. There is something in its distances and its isolation and its climate that appeal forever. Outside my window as I write in the dark of early morning — for I rise like a farm hand — the rotary snow ploughs on the Côte des Neiges Road are whirling in the air the great blanket of snow that buried Montreal last night. To the north, behind the mountain, the Northern Lights blink on a thousand miles of snow-covered forest and frozen rivers.

We are "sitting pretty" here in Canada. East and west are the two oceans far away; we are backed up against the ice cap of the pole; our feet rest on the fender of the American border, warm with a hundred years of friendship. The noise and tumult of Europe we scarcely hear — not for us the angers of the Balkans, the weeping of Vienna and the tumults of Berlin. Our lot lies elsewhere — shovelling up mountains, floating in the sky to look for gold, and finding still the Star of Empire in the West.

Thank you, Mother England, I don't think I'll "come home." I'm "home" now. Fetch me my carpet slippers from the farm. I'll rock it out to sleep right here.

15

THIS INTERNATIONAL STUFF
For Men Like Myself

Today, out in my garden picking peas, I found myself thinking about the ominous situation in Europe and everywhere, and the fact that at any time noisy cities and quiet countrysides may be devastated by war. I use the tall kind of peas that grow from five to six feet high; it takes the birds longer to get them; often you have some left.

But they grow so high that you sit in the shade of them. And when they are staked up they look something like the long rows of vines along the valleys of the Rhine and the Danube and the Yangtze Kiang and in all the soft sunny corners of the earth where people are soon going to kill one another, if one believes the headlines. So I thought of all the people everywhere tending the vines, and planting the red brown fields, all warm with sun and nature's happiness, but in a short time to be turned loose — no one knows why — to kill one another. They don't want to — any more than I do.

I'd kill a crow — any gardener would — but I wouldn't kill an Australian or a Hungarian. I'd rather have the Hungarian make *goulash*; in fact I think without exaggeration, rather than kill him, I'd eat it. And yet, perhaps this summer, regiments of furious cavalry will be shouting *Goulash! Goulash!* as they charge on the enemy; and the enemy will answer defiantly with the yell *Chile con Carne!* or *Chianti!* or *Vive le Fromage de Brie!* Then the crazy pretense that nations hate one another will be turned by bloodshed into unbelievable reality.

The truth is that the world has long since outgrown nationalism, and yet we don't seem to realize it. National isolation, national war, national exclusiveness, are in reality things of the past. Every art and mechanism of our economic life, our manufacture, our transport, our flights in the clouds, our voices in the ether of space, all proclaim the unity of the globe. Everything has been unified — except man himself.

What the world needs now is internationally minded men — I'll put it very simply — men like myself. You ask, where on earth can you get them? I admit it's hard.

In my own case, I really feel that I am an internationally minded man. I have no prejudices. As a Canadian, I am willing to admit, if you like, that perhaps the Canadians are just a little bit bigger and brainier than any other people. But then the Americans to the south of us are a mighty fine people, and even over in Europe and Asia and Africa there are a lot of fine people, too.

I met a little feller from Europe the other day — a Croat, or a Chick, or a Slick, or something. Where was it he said he came from? Toschen or Poschen — anyway, somewhere. And he seemed all right, a nice little feller. So they all do.

How often do you hear people say, "I met a German and he seemed all right," "I met a New Zealander and he seemed fine," "I met a Norwegian and I couldn't see anything wrong with him." Of course not. There's nothing wrong with any of them.

All the people of the world, taken by and large, are mighty fine people, with energy and kindness and love, valuing just the same things that we do, with the same care for their children and their friends, and their home town. All these things we value, they value.

The international man (my kind, the kind we need more of) is able to enter into the patriotism and pride of the history of other peoples, to admire and value what they have done in the past, to look with veneration at the tattered flags that recall their battles, and to thrill at the music of their national airs.

A year or so ago I was at a great gathering of one of the big service clubs of the world. And as a part of the pageant of the occasion, they had a march of delegates from different states and nations, with their flags and music.

I watched a detachment from New England marching by to the sound of *When Johnny Comes Marching Home Again, Hurrah! Hurrah!* and I thought to myself, "That's the stuff! The real old Massachusetts spirit, you can't beat that," and I felt that the one place nearest my heart (being international) was old New England.

But the next minute another crowd burst into sight, with a band playing, *Way Dawn South in Dixie,* and with Texas Rangers in sombrero hats and Louisiana Tigers all ready for a spring. Then I could feel my heart move south of Mason and Dixon's line, and throb at the glory of the Lost Cause.

I could even feel a southern accent rising on my tongue — till just at that moment I heard the *skirl* of the bagpipes — you can't even pronounce *skirl* unless you live north of the Clyde — and the music, or rather the sound of *The Campbells are coming, er-er, er-er!!* and I saw the kilts and bonnets of bonny Scotland — the grrreatest country in the world! I thought to myself, where can you get another country to compare with Scotland?

But the question answered itself a minute later as the next detachment passed in a torrent of tossing emerald green and a band that loudly called with drum and fife to ask, *Oh! Denis Dear, and Did You Hear the News That's Going Round?*

But if you think the Scotch or the Irish an inspiring sight, wait till you see what a detachment of French, the most martial nation in the world, can look like, all tanned and brown with the Algerian sun, all dingy red and dusty blue with a march step that has in it the precision of centuries, the prestige of the great wars, rising and falling in tune to the music of *Madelon! Madelon! Madelon!* ... Even the English walking as if at a funeral to the music of *Nearer My God to Thee,* and the Canadians never quite keeping step and trying to sing the words of *Oh! Canada* — which they never quite remember — are impressive and inspiring by their very lack and scorn of sentiment.

Anyone looking at such a pageant as this — duplicated every day, for those who can see it, in the life and art of our time — ought to feel the wish to be an international man, to take his part in welding the world together so that no discord can break it asunder.

How do we do it? Well, I can tell at least a good way not to do it, and that is the method that the world has been following, the method of compacts and covenants and scraps of paper and naval agreements — otherwise disagreements. These things only accentuate national differences, only emphasize national inequalities, and instigate national wars.

"Rules of war" is a contradiction in terms. The only proper rule of war is to say that we pledge ourselves never to use any kind of weapon or any kind of attack which we don't think is the kind of weapon or the kind of attack we care to use. That hits the point to a nicety.

There was, long ago, a dear old melodrama of New England life in which an angry old-fashioned farmer, protesting at his daughter's getting "new-fangled" ideas, exclaimed, "I don't want my daughter to read no books that I don't want her to read." The speech always got a laugh. But in reality the man said just what he meant, and the diplomats would do well to follow his precept. A naval agreement should read, "We aren't going to build any ships bigger than what we feel we want to build, and we won't build any greater number than the number that we're going to build."

With a distinct understanding like that, the world could stop being preoccupied and obsessed with facts and treaties and the peace and war question, and could just go on living.

What is needed is for people to know one another, to cultivate every relationship that runs crosswise of international lines, to read one another's books, to admire one another's art, to taste one another's foods. Bring me *Caviar* and I'll eat it; fetch me *Ravioli* and I'll get it down, yes, even that South American stuff, what is it, *Chile con Carne* — I forget — anyway, I'll consume it. I'll eat *Wiener Schnitzel* with the Germans, and *Tripe à la Mode de Caen* with the French, *Yum Cha* with the Chinese, *Sukiyaki* with the Japanese, yes, and even *Haggis à la McGinnis* with the Scots. I'll smoke South African tobacco, and if there's any worse I'll try to smoke that. I'll play checkers with the Czechs, polo with the Poles, and basketball with the Basques.

At any rate, I mean that is the *attitude*. This world can never be made right by force, never by fear, never by power. In the long run nothing conquers but ideas, nothing governs but the spirit. Those of us who think that way — the international boys like myself — have got to do each our simple best in that direction. At any rate, that's how it looks to me.

16

CANADA AND THE MONARCHY

If you were to ask any Canadian, "Do you people *have* to go to war if England does?" he'd answer at once, "Oh, no." If you then said, "*Would* you go to war if England did?" he'd answer, "Oh, yes." And if you asked, "Why?" he would say, reflectively, "Well, you see, we'd *have* to."

And with that you would receive a first introduction into the peculiar political mystery that one may call the paradox of the British Empire. We in Canada never saw it better illustrated than in the emergency of the Czechoslovakian crisis. All men of sound nationality and allegiance old enough to remember the suffering and sacrifice of the Great War, and above all those who had served in it, seemed to be of one mind. They heartily damned the Sudeten Germans and the Czechs with them; they even damned all Europe and denied all connection with the place; but they took no interest in mere legalistic discussions as to whether Canada was *bound* — legally, if such a silly word can be used — to go to war.

As they themselves said, that was not the point; nobody was talking of that. The point was that they couldn't see any way out of a war if England was in it: to be a *neutral* country, with bombs dropping on England, the British people fighting for life, enemy ships in and out of our ports, recruiting forbidden, aid prohibited — why, the thing just seemed damned silly; did and still does. It is fit only for futile discussions by the people called "pink" professors for whom academic abstractions take the place of reality.

Yet, on the other hand, here we are, Canadians living in Canada — what real interest have we in the people on the Elbe and the Danube? What do we really know about whether the Czechs lorded it over the Sudetens or the Sudetens undermined it under the Czechs?

Or, for the matter of that, what does India matter to us? We have nothing to do with it economically, spiritually, or in any other way, and we don't want its people over here. Or Japan — or no, wait a minute — that's different. As you go round the world you reach us again on our Pacific side: Japan is of vital interest to us, and of course to deal with the Japanese we must have England behind us. But if England safeguards us from Japan, then we can't keep out of Europe, can we? So there you are, round the full circuit of the centrifugal and centripetal forces of the British Empire — and even at that we have left out the whole problem of Africa.

One asks, then, what really is the British Empire, and in what direction are these internal and external forces moving it? If we look for a constitutional definition of what the British Empire is, the only approach to it is found in the resolution of the Imperial Conference of 1926 on which was based the Statute of Westminster of 1931. The resolution declared that the United Kingdom and the Dominions are "autonomous communities within the British Empire, in no way subordinate to one another in any aspect of their domestic or external affairs though united by a common allegiance to the Crown and freely associated as members of the British Commonwealth of Nations."

This pronouncement is as much a riddle of the Sphinx as was the United States Constitution in regard to state sovereignty in the ante-bellum period. "Freely associated" can mean anything or nothing. Indeed, it is felt that the constitution of the Empire is so nebulous that it can't be solidified. It is like the Polynesian gods surrounded by a taboo which forbids even naming them. They have to be just called "Oom," which isn't really their name. "Nothing would be gained," so resolved the same Conference, "by attempting to lay down a constitution." So the ensuing Statute of Westminster became the "Oom" of the British Empire.

Even the indicated existing bonds that hold the "free association" look fragile when you examine them. There is a common allegiance to the Crown; but as a matter of fact George VI began reigning in South Africa one day before he reigned in England, and did not begin reigning in Ireland till one day after that. "Legalistically" speaking, there were two Kings at once. More than that, the reign of the King in Ireland, now properly called Eire, is only a sort of twilight. By the Constitution (Amendment No. 27) Act of December 1936, also a product of the abdication, the King is King of Ireland *outside* of it but not *in* it. The bond of union formerly represented by a common court of first appeal (the Judicial Committee of the Privy Council) shakes loose at a trick like a conjuror's knot. It is only there unless the Dominions refuse it. Ireland has done so.

The Dominions are members of the League of Nations, and three of them hold mandates under it; academically it is held that that makes them "sovereign states" as far as international law is concerned — in other words, what one might call sovereign states in the Pickwickian sense, international law being now an abstraction. In the British Empire there is no common citizenship, no common taxation, no common army or navy, no common currency or legal tender, no common foreign policy. Are not, then, the parts of the Empire sovereign states? Not at all — they are just "freely associated." It sounds about as logical as Amos 'n' Andy or Huckleberry Finn.

And yet, the great majority of those who have occasion to think most about it will, I am certain, agree with me in saying that the British Empire was never as closely bound together as now, never as far from any thought of dissolution or secession, and is moving, in its own peculiar path, into closer, more organic union. The legal aspect of its structure — or rather the lack of legal aspect — merely reflects the fact that the days of legalistic structure, compacts, and scraps of paper are passing away. They are ropes of sand, holding nothing that will not join — at best a bandage round a healing limb, worthless without nature.

II

To read the present right we must look back to the past. The starting point for the constitutional study of imperial relations must be found in the monarchy of the eighteenth century, when the "Glorious Revolution" of 1688 and the Act of Settlement that followed it in 1701 had established in Great Britain the "supremacy of parliament" as the basis of law and government. Parliament here meant "King,

Lords and Commons," and an "Act of Parliament" enjoyed a plenary sovereignty with no (legal) limitation of prerogative, custom, or moral right. Incidentally, this made the jurisdiction over the American colonies a misfit in common sense and led to disunion. But no English lawyers questioned the pure law of the matter as to sovereignty. Indeed, the Declaratory Act of 1766 said that it was so.

This theory of parliamentary supremacy lasted from 1766 till 1926. Formulated by Bentham and Austin, rehearsed by a hundred law schools, it took its place, for British lawyers, alongside of Newtonian gravitation and the axioms of Euclid. But its inherent insufficiency was there all the time: the "Lords and Commons," who with the King made up the "Supreme Parliament," were Lords and Commons of Great Britain and Ireland. Settlers in outlandish parts had no share and no say in it. This did not matter much when the settlers were still few and the parts truly outlandish. Nor did it matter at all with populations not settlers, but natives, living on their own ground. "King, Lords and Commons" was good enough for them. And the white settlers at first found dependence natural and necessary. The 40,000 Loyalists (1783–1790) who came into what is now Canada owed everything to the fostering care of the mother country — transport, food, land. Infant colonies, of course, clung to the leading strings of their mother's apron.

But as settlement grew and colonies changed to communities, the misfit that had led to the separation of the American Colonies was felt again. It is true that a measure of self-government existed from the start. Elected assemblies had been given to the two Canadas in 1791. Nova Scotia was allowed an Assembly as far back as 1759, by a sort of prescriptive British right, based on those of the other American plantations. The refugee-loyalist Colony of New Brunswick (1784) had an Assembly from the beginning. The Australian settlers received one each in due course, as did the Cape and Natal. But these popular assemblies conferred the name of freedom without the fact. The royal governor still controlled the executive and the purse.

To this sentimental grievance, the inferiority complex, of the colonies were added various practical injustices — about the public lands, the status of the churches, and so forth — things impossible to understand or to regulate from England. When Governor Simcoe told his log-house parliament at Newark (Niagara) in 1792 that they enjoyed an "image and transcript of the British Constitution," the image was distorted by the alien mirror and the transcript by the alien hand. By the time the two Canadas had half a million people, English and French, this misfit of government had become intolerable to free people — meaning people allowed to grumble. The result was the sudden rebellion of 1837. The British Government suppressed it, hanged all the leaders within reach, and sent out Lord Durham to ask what had happened.

Durham, a British Liberal, wrote a famous report which said that what these people needed was British Liberalism prescribed in those days by the Cobdenite School for peoples of all races, colours, and environments, like a salve for rheumatism sold from a street wagon. Its special application took the form of "responsible government," meaning an executive cabinet responsible to the elected house. This was duly installed in Canada in 1842,* and became, in the following twenty years, the standard system of the British (white) colonies. The Duke of Wellington, still alive and living on the memory of Waterloo, was declared "thunderstruck" when he heard of it. He considered it "fatal to our connection with the colonies." But that to the Liberals was the chief merit of it. The example of the United States was interpreted as "manifest destiny." The future of all colonies was independence — a painless dissolution of the Empire in which the colonies were to float away on a sea of the milk of human kindness. Even the Tories wanted to be rid of them. "These wretched colonies," said Disraeli, "will all be independent some day, and meantime are like millstones round our neck." The Manchester School revelled in "little Englandism" and the dream of a "right, tight little island."

So the next thirty years after the Duke had been thunderstruck in 1842 witnessed a progressive loosening of the bonds of empire. After 1846 the colonies began making their own tariffs. Canada and Victoria

*In 1842 the governor of Canada appointed for the first time a prime minister whose party commanded a majority in the Assembly but did not undertake to accept all their recommendations. Responsible government, in this fullest sense, was only achieved in 1848.—ED

(Australia) plunged for "protection." British ministers explained this to British manufacturers as a temporary aberration of ignorance. British garrisons were removed from colonial towns; the last garrison of Montreal went away to music in 1870. There was relief when they went. Their uniforms had turned the girls' heads: a farmer is a shabby lover beside a hussar, and a merchant smells of coffee rather than of gunpowder. The men of the colonies decided to defend themselves — and there wasn't any war anyway.

A severe jolt to complacency came with the American Civil War. The crisis over the Trent Affair (1861), and the new outlook it gave, helped to make possible the British North America Act of 1867, creating the Dominion of Canada. But the Act altered nothing as to the ultimate constitution of the Empire. Parliament was still supreme — indeed its supremacy was used (1871, 1884, and so forth) as a mechanism, as the *only* mechanism, for amending the government of Canada. Amendment was made only when asked for by both the Canadian Houses, but that was usage, not law. There was no other way — nor is there even to-day. Oddly enough, there is no power findable in the present Dominion which could, let us say, abolish the Canadian Senate, or alter the jurisdiction of the federal government. The voters can't, parliament can't, a convention can't — so, unless the British Parliament can, nobody can.*

Freedom under responsible government kept on "broadening down" as Tennyson had said it would. The Governor-General lost, bit by bit, his remaining independent powers. He stopped using his power of disallowance, and it died. After 1878 the Dominion hanged its own criminals, the Minister of Justice becoming the fountain of mercy and the Governor-General merely signing on the (fatal) dotted line. Goldwin Smith, in 1891, called him a rubber stamp. By the turn of the century, or just a little after, Canada was entirely separate from the British Army; the Navy had gone from Halifax and Esquimalt, and the Governor-General presided not over councils but over drawing-rooms.

---

*This situation ended with the Constitution Act 1982. —ED

III

But in another aspect the situation had entirely changed. "Little England" hadn't come off. In place of it was "big Germany." The milk of human kindness was too thin to float colonies. Free trade was bankrupt, and universal peace replaced after1854 by wars that never stopped. The constituents of the Empire found themselves in a new world — a world grabbing for territory, dividing up Africa, reconquering Asia, searching the earth for rubber, oil, metals, markets, resources.

Hence the new movement for imperial unity — the mixed creed of imperialism, partly good and partly bad — inspired by grandeur and by courage, by meanness and by fear, but above all guided, as the event has shown, by instinct.

The movement aimed first at formal Federation (the Imperial Federation League of 1884). The colonies were all found singing "God Save the Queen" at hundreds of meetings, in colonial towns, in the bush, and on the prairie. The song stopped as soon as it turned out that there would be a "collection" after the meeting — that is, that imperial federation meant imperial taxes. The league divided, dissolved, vanished.

In place of taxes to unite the Empire, the next expedient was imperial pageantry, the Colonial Conferences or the Golden Jubilee of 1887 and the Diamond Jubilee of 1897. Assembled London marvelled to see colonial prime ministers actually wearing silk hats and riding in open barouches with maharajahs from Hyderabad and native chiefs from the Cannibal Isles. Rudyard Kipling's "Recessional" anthem marked the high tide of imperial sentiment: the only trouble was to find a mould to pour it into and let it solidify. The Conferences — from 1897 till the war — proved a vain hope. All attempts at closer union split on the rocks of taxation and representation. "If you want our aid, call us to your councils," said the grandiloquent premier of Canada, Sir Wilfrid Laurier. "If at any time you are prepared to share the burden of Empire," answered the equally eloquent Joseph Chamberlain, "we are prepared to give you a proportionate share in the councils of the Empire." The two phrases matched and met. England didn't want advice, but money; the colonies had advice to give, but not money. And the advice, anyway, was merely to let them alone. The situation reached an impasse. A blunt Prime Minister, Mr. Asquith, said (1911): "Our responsibility cannot be shared."

Equally unattainable was any form of commercial union. The colonies — called Dominions after 1907 — had protective tariffs and proposed to keep them. They gave "preferences" to England, but adjusted them with great nicety not to prefer. The foreigner had to jump a high wall and John Bull only a low wall; but he couldn't jump it anyway. Later on, much later, a still blunter British Minister, Mr. Jim Thomas (1930), called preference "humbug." Blunt people say things which polite people have known and not said for years. This separation, in point of fact — of government, of defence, of tariffs — presently got itself a theory and called itself Colonial Nationalism. Political theory always means wisdom after the fact, a post-mortem, not a prophecy. "Nationalism" meant being let alone and letting freedom broaden down some more. "We are happy as we are," said a distinguished French Canadian.

Thus there were two schools — those for closer formal union and those too happy to want it. The Unionists being a band of crusaders, Mr. Lionel Curtis's* organization, "The Round Table," went round the Empire like the Old Federation League. I myself, the writer of this article, shared in these mistaken activities, lectured round the Empire under the auspices of the Rhodes Trust, and was one of those to expound the case of security by formal Imperial Union. Our chief argument was that, in case of war, united action was impossible without imperial unity. Speaking broadly, New Zealand was all for formal union. Itself a reproduction — in climate, resources, and nationality — of the British Isles upside down in the Pacific, New Zealand is the most "loyal" (a Victorian word) of the Dominions, still calling England "home" and

---

*Curtis (1872–1955), a British advocate of imperial federation, organized The Round Table, a network of influential intellectuals in Britain and the colonies dedicated to uniting the empire; coined the term "Commonwealth of Nations" in 1916, helped found Royal Institute of International Affairs; later a world federationist. —ED

without major ambitions. All for union also was Natal — hemmed in by the Dutch — till the Union of 1909 amalgamated it with South Africa. Dead against unity, and bitterly against it, were all the Dutch — many, perhaps most of them, dreaming still at that date of independence, and the rest, under Botha and Smuts, held only as honest men keeping their compact of Vereenging (1902) Dead against unity, with the deadness of inertia, was Canada. Australia, federated in 1901 into a Commonwealth, faced both ways, wanting lots of British ships and British money but not British interference. Under these forces the Empire drifted like the star drift of the great constellations across the sky, slow, majestic, in part retrograde, and moving nowhere.

Then came the war. It turned out that the Imperial Unionists were quite wrong. The Empire fought better in sections. Local patriotism draws best. The war sealed the fate of the Federal Empire and at last fashioned its mould — a "Commonwealth of Nations." After the war the Commonwealth ran as true to form as had the Dominions and the colonies. It kept on disintegrating. Canada, Australia, New Zealand, and South Africa became signatories of the Treaty of Versailles and members of the League of Nations. South Africa took over "German Southwest" and "German East" (Tanganyika)[*] as "mandates." The Union govern- ment expressly declared that it would never give mandates back; it refused to make returns to the League as to how the mandates were getting on. That kind of thing doesn't do for white people isolated among myriads of blacks. Australia took over Kaiser-Wilhemsland and called it Papua, to take the German taste out if it. New Zealand got a piece of Samoa, for the sake of prestige and class — and felt as proud as a poor white with a slave.

The drift continued unabated. When Mr. Lloyd George suggested that the colonies might join in the Turkish War of 1921 (which didn't happen) the answer from Canada was that Parliament would look into it.[**] Southern Ireland — admitted as a Dominion, the Irish Free State

---

[*]Actually, Tanganyika was a British mandate. —ED

[**]The British called for assistance when the Turks under Kemal Ataturk repudiated the Treaty of Sèvres in 1922 (not 1921) and pinned down British occupation troops at Chanak. The crisis abated and a new peace treaty was signed with Turkey. —ED

of 1921, in preference to having a permanent civil war — became the Peck's Bad Boy of the Commonwealth, tore up the account books of the land debts, cancelled all appeals from the courts, pretended it could talk Gaelic (its sole official language: English is only by necessity and courtesy), called itself Eire, appointed its own Governor-General, and finally made a new constitution in 1937, in force after 1938, which cuts out the Crown altogether except for relations abroad and sets up a President with a cabinet of ministers and a citizenship all its own as far as it can make it. The Irish since then are thinking what to want next. The weak spot of their position is that at the abdication of December 1936 they had independence lying at their feet and wouldn't pick it up.

The other Dominions shared the drift without the animus. Newfoundland, like a retrograde star, drifted the other way: crippled in resources, half-frozen, half-starving, it called on the mother country to take it back, and in 1933 became again a colony with the supremacy of parliament warm around it like a winter blanket, and a sustaining diet of British loans to revive its industry. Not too much is said about this by any of us — it looks somehow like freedom broadening backwards.

But the other Dominions steadily and without animus have slackened each remaining formal bond. They make their own treaties; since 1929, no British Minister is needed even for the signature — the Dominions can write their own names. They have now, as far as they wish to, their own diplomatic staff. Canada has ministers at Washington, Paris, Tokyo — we prefer not to have one among the Nazis. We remember too well the missionaries among the Iroquois. So in such cases the obliging United Kingdom — the phrase now replaces "mother country" — acts for us without charge.

IV

As far as the situation has a constitutional basis, it rests on the (Imperial) Statute of Westminster of 1931. This was intended, not as introducing anything new or abolishing anything old, but merely as a recognition of existing fact. Nearly all British constitutional statutes, from the Magna Carta downwards, prefer to do this and nothing more, as notably the Magna Carta itself, the Petition of Right of 1628, the Bill of Rights of 1689. This is what is called the British genius for government: the British can tell themselves anything and believe it. The Statute of Westminster had its genesis thus — the war conferences, viewing the actual innovations of the war organizations, recommended reconsideration of imperial relations after the war. The Imperial Conference of 1926 drafted resolutions. These carried of course, "no legal sanction." The Dominions, on the report of the Conference, expressed a general approval of embodying the resolutions in an imperial statute. As drawn, it contained the definition of the status of the Empire already quoted — "autonomous communities, and so forth." It enacted that henceforth no imperial legislation could override dominion legislation: both are without limit, territorially or extraterritorially. The obvious possibility of conflict is left to look after itself. The Statute declared itself inoperative in regard to Australia and New Zealand till expressly ratified by their parliaments, this being in accordance with their declared views. Ratification was not completed in fact till 1938. But the Statute was accepted as applying to the other Dominions on the strength of their antecedent approval.

In strict law the Statute is as full of holes as a sieve. On the face of it, it leaves the Dominion of Canada bound hand and foot beyond constitutional amendment with a chain and padlock of which it has thrown away the key. Anomalies like this don't matter a particle in British government. We've lived on them since Edward the Confessor. But, as far as it has a general apparent meaning, the Statute dissolves the Empire into seven (now six) separate sovereign parts, free to secede and indissolubly bound together. It thus proudly takes its place on the shelf with Magna Carta and the rest. Americans will recall their "Confederation of 1777" and understand the idea exactly. They also share in the genius of government.

An observer who had eyes but no mind, looking at this, would tell us that the British Empire was visibly drifting apart — indeed, that it had already drifted apart. But an observer who could interpret what his eyes saw would form a judgement exactly the other way. The British Empire, disunited in legalistic form, represents at the present time a closer union than ever before in its history, with every evidence, as far as observation can penetrate, of a permanent unity, one that will not be lost except by submergence in a wider union.

Consider this. What parts or sections of the Empire at present want independence? Absolutely none. Contrast with this the situation of the opening century. After the bitter end of the inglorious Boer War in the forced compact of Vereeniging, forced by sheer weight of numbers, destruction of homes, and death of women and children in concentration camps, nearly all the South African Dutch still dreamt of independence. It was for independence that old De Wet and his associates rebelled in 1914. Ultimate independence, peacefully obtained, was the inspiring thought of Heb Volt and Judge Hertzog (formerly) and of the Dutch Nationalist parties. Those of longer vision, Botha and Smuts, would have none of it; against it stood not only their given word but their vision of the long future. And now the long future has come, and with it the idea of independence in South Africa has floated away like mist over the mountains in the new winds of world danger.

The South African elections of 1938 showed an overwhelming majority for Hertzog's United National South African Party. Their opponents on the right were the "Ultra-British" group, on the left the "Ultra-Dutch" of Dr. Malan. But even for these last the demand for "independence" as an actuality has faded away. It lives on only in symbols and side issues. All Africa bubbled with mimic fury last summer over whether to sing "God Save the King" or "God Save South Africa' — the song is literally "Die Stem von Suid Africa." The government decided to save both: the bands play now either twice or not at all. But this is not independence. It is just what they call in England the old school tie.

Forty years ago South Africa stood by itself, protected by infinite distances, by harbourless coasts, by an impassable hinterland. Organize its port defence and all Europe could not harm it. Dr. Jameson (of the Raid of 1895) used to say — I have heard him say it — that if the Boers had moved faster to the sea in 1899 they would have licked all Britain.

But now — what are a few thousand miles to aerial flight? What coast is closed against bombardment? What better gun platform than an empty hinterland? South Africa can no more stand alone than

Czechoslovakia — and the South Africans know it. Mr. Pirow, the energetic Defence Minister of the Union, stated officially in the parliament a little while ago that South Africa is free to stay out of a British war. Such a statement now is merely a chewing of old straw. Nobody doubts it, and it doesn't matter anyway; it's not what people are free to do, but what they are going to do. In short, the typical attitude among South Africans is that, as long as it is understood that they can leave the Empire overnight, they'll stay in it forever.

The last statement sounds Irish. It *is* Irish: it represents exactly what Ireland did at the time of the abdication. Indeed, the abdication of Edward VIII acted as a peculiar test of the imperial structure — or, if one will, a peculiar revelation in a strong light of its mode of operation. Technically the abdication in England took place as follows. The King wrote a letter in which he said, "I want to abdicate." Of itself that wouldn't effect anything. The King has no power to put himself off the throne. So a bill was presented to Parliament and passed by the Commons and the Lords. Then the King assented to the Act, and the abdication became operative at an exact day and hour indicated in the Act.

But the Union of South Africa refused to see it that way. What to it was the action of Lords and Commons? They don't affect South Africa. For South Africa the abdication took place as soon as its government heard of the King's desire and said yes — which beat the Lords and Commons by a day. Ireland, meaning Eire, did not agree to either idea; it never does. As Eire saw it, the King couldn't abdicate till the parliament of Eire let him out: that took one extra day over England. But the essential point is that both the formerly dissentient Dominions had their free choice of green flags and *vierklur* flags, and of slipping painlessly out of the Empire under a new King or without any — and both commonwealths instinctively drew back as one shuts the door against cold weather.

Ireland is a queer place, a lovable place. It was just like it to stay in the Empire; and, what is more, the two parts of Ireland — Northern Ireland and Eire — will be joined before so very long as a single imperial unit. I know no statement calculated to enrage Irishmen as much as this. Ulstermen shout with indignation at the idea of such a union with republican idolatry; Free State Irishmen scorn to think of any union based on concessions to monarchy. But the shouts sound hollow, the anger overloud — like the voice of age raised in the dispute that the young must settle. People shout most against what they know is coming; and peaceful settlement seems tame after a hundred years of grievance and excitement and fun.

V

Now take Canada. To those of us who live here, separation from the Empire is quite unthinkable — not from the anger of patriotism, but because we can't think it. Union with the United States — we have it now: a peculiar beautiful union of hearts, with old quarrels asleep, and surrounded with the reverence of slumber. Independence? What from? A little group of our French people — a group only in the sense that four-leaf clovers are a group, one here, one there — like to talk of a sort of dream republic called Laurentia.* It is a lovely place: there are no English there, and no capitalists or power companies, and there are no soldiers and armies, and it never goes to fight in Europe; in this dream world the government is all by orators — young orators — and they talk and talk, and write newspapers and pamphlets, and fall asleep and wake up and talk. No one quite knows where this Laurentia is, whether Montreal is in it, whether it has ports and ships that block the outlet of a continent, or whether it is up somewhere in the snow near Peribonka, in the country of Maria Chapdelaine. But what is life without dreams?

Thus does the British Empire, as the clouds grow over Europe, Asia, and Africa, draw close together. The earlier grievances, like the inferiority complex that magnified them, are all forgotten now. Even the most unreflecting realizes how fortunate has been our escape from dissolution, how fortunate has been the evolution of our monarchy, unique in the world's history, reconciling or offering an opportunity to reconcile liberty with sovereignty, democracy with kingship, prestige and pageantry with plain equality.

---

*Followers of Abbé Lionel Groulx. —ED

And in this new process of "getting together," this new phase of history, repudiating all the false starts, the mistaken aspirations of the past, where do we find our new bond of union, our common centre towards which to draw? In the monarchy: that at least remains. The worn-out fetters of authority are broken and thrown away, but the golden links of a voluntary union of hearts hold tighter. That phrase "a union of hearts" is too sentimental for British taste. Put with it, as a Scottish addendum, that it is "highly advantageous": admit, with an Irish grumble, that there's nothing else; add the cheerful Australian expression "good enough" — and you get the idea.

At any rate, the new union is symbolized and embodied in the monarchy alone. Legislative union, economic union, judicial union, military union — all these are gone. But the monarchy, so easily explained away at home as a constitutional nullity by Walter Bagehot and abroad as a rubber stamp by Goldwin Smith — this has become the central fact, the real effective bond of the Empire. What if the band plays "The Stem of South Africa" in Pretoria and "O Canada" in Ottawa? It still plays "God Save the King" in both. What if four-colour flags fly over Johannesburg, and Kangaroos over Canberra, and Maple Leafs over Ottawa? The Union Jack floats beside every one of them.

This new sense of unity under our monarchy has come over us in the Empire like a new wave of consciousness. It palpitates in the common thought of the common people, as at once our destiny and our salvation. They have no time for the professorial argument about neutrality, a monkey on a stick, lifeless: they seize by instinct the larger fact.

This is for us in Canada the real significance of the hoped-for visit of the King and Queen. It is the new inauguration of the British monarchy in the hearts of the people. The past is gone. Its mistakes are forgotten. This is the beginning of the future.

So we want the King and Queen to come, not just the King — King and Queen both, because "King and Queen" spell princesses, and princesses spell the long fairy tale of the future. We want the King and Queen to see what a wonderful place Canada is — full of water power, and quintuplets, and the best wheat they ever tasted.

We are like children with treasures to show. They must see it all — from the apples of the Annapolis Valley to the giant trees of Vancouver — because it's as much theirs as ours.

All this is not because we are "loyal" — that old world went out with Queen Victoria. We just "belong."

17

BONDS OF UNION

Nations cannot be held to one another by written compacts. Malevolence can tear them up and then only force remains. In such one-sided bargains, sin beats righteousness at the start since the one is free to break its word and the other cannot help but keep it. A nation that throws away its arms on the strength of a piece of paper, is lost. The paper is only good if what is written on it is already in the heart.

A spring can rise no higher than its source. Laws and institutions cannot exist till the spirit first comes. They are the expression of it. Laws against theft arise from the fact that the great mass of the people are determined not to steal. The philosopher Kant thought that a social compact of laws could be made even among devils. But he was wrong. Why the devil should a devil keep a compact if he wants to break it? Kant would say that two or more devils could make a devil keep a compact. But so they could without the compact. The word is worthless without the inspiring spirit.

It is this that renders fruitless much of the current discussions of the future federations to be formed, presumably, of present devils; of a new League of Nations, or of a super-state to be made by mixing devils half and half with honest men.

All these things are ropes of sand, nothing — Kant's devils over again. In the world about us we must look around for ties that hold.

If a League of Nations has no armed forces of its own, it cannot of itself use any coercive control. It can only say what it thinks; and any of us can do that. If it has armed forces, but not superior to those of ordinary nations, then it only adds one more to join in a fight; only turns a private fight into a public one. But if the League of Nations is turned into a super-state armed with force over disarmed nations, powerless against it, then this is nothing but committing hari-kari. In the world in which we now know we live, the proposal is so silly as to be beyond discussion. It is silly in the good old English sense, meaning innocent. It belongs among the nebulous illusions of people too kind and too credulous to realize facts or of people cunning enough to think that they can fool others with it.

A League of Nations can do admirable service. It can serve as a voluntary agent for international discussion, for arbitration. It can serve as a world clearing house for statistics and economic research. It can gather information to aid the social progress of the world. But it can never exercise a coercive control. Its weapon is the pen, not the sword. Its member is a professor, not a statesman and still less a soldier.

We must therefore look about to find what real bonds of union there are to connect the Empire with enduring peace. These we find in its association with the United States. The peace of North America has risen on the horizon as a light for all the world. We can read the future by it. We can see from it how nations can remain in peace and harmony with neither force nor compact.

With America, and in a sense with all the world, the Empire is united by the English language, and by the community in literature that it brings. A single world-language is as yet only a world dream. But English is already, or already becoming, the second language of all the world. It is spoken as a mother tongue by 200,000,000 people. Russian, at a glance, seems to approach it with 140,000,000. But Russian is shut into its own area. It is an island. England is an atmosphere. Outside of Russia you cannot buy a cup of tea in Russian. You can feed in English all over the world. Where Russia changes into Mongolia, you can see printed signs for travellers, we are credibly informed, that read "English spoken; American understood." English is the language of the sea. And when the continents and islands of the Empire end, English still washes forward in broken waves of "pidgin English" (business English) of the Orient, of the Beach-la-mar talk of the Pacific Island or the queer jabber in which West Africa trades gin and coconuts. The outside people who have *handled* English — from the Normans on — have knocked out of it all the grammatical nonsense of suffixes and affixes, and fitted it for world consumption. It carries its awful spelling like a ball and chain on its foot, but it marches on. There is no doubt of the power of language to unite, or rather of the power of diverse language, to separate. In the United States, as colonies, the English language got enough rootage to hold its place and spread across the continent. Without that, the world's history would be different. If the German immigrants to the Middle West had made a German speaking bloc, if the Creole French speech had spread to cover a larger Louisiana, with a Spanish area from Texas to California, and if a Scandinavian country had appeared in Minnesota and the Dakotas, it is hard to believe that there could exist the united republic that we see.

Still more intimate is the bond of literature common to us and the Americans from Shakespeare to King James's Bible down to Gray's *Elegy written in a Country Churchyard* — common till then, and since then shared in common. American boys and girls at school charge with Tennyson's *Light Brigade*. English children climb *Excelsior* with Longfellow's mysterious boy, as ignorant of where he is trying to get as American children themselves. Mr. Pickwick and Rip Van Winkle, the Deer Slayer and Gunga Din, the Boy on the Burning Deck and Huck Finn on his Raft, are the common possessions of Britain and America.

But most intimate and powerful of all is that union of intercourse and ideas that is seen as between Canada and the United States. Here Canada acts as a middle term between the Empire and America. It is well to dwell on this for in it we can see the living outline of a world to come — that or chaos.

Turn back the pages of our history to the American Revolution that ended with the surrender of — or not that, it sounds a little painful — let us say, that ended with the Peace of 1783. It turned out and has been turning out more and more as kindlier eyes looked at it, in the colours of the sunset, that it wasn't a revolution at all — just a sort of triumph of British freedom on the soil of America.

The British themselves saw it first. They discovered after the Revolution, as I say, that it was a great triumph for British freedom, and that George Washington was a typical English country gentle-man. In fact, they annexed the whole thing, made it part of British school history, called it "manifest destiny," and recommended it to all other, quieter colonies — just as a mother always likes best the bad boy of the family.

After the Revolution came the "Loyalists" to settle in Upper Canada. But they none the less remained Americans, in their way. They brought with them from New England their Thanksgiving Day turkey, and from New York the "York shilling," that was our count of money till yesterday. From them, too, came the "little red school house" in its "school section" framed on the Massachusetts model; and later the local government and the township that they themselves had brought out of Lincolnshire.

Presently there came the war of 1812. We can't get it quite straight now, what it was all about. It makes fine moving "pictures." But what that war was *for,* we can no more make out now than old Caspar could with his. It was something to do with "pressing" sailors, but it's all gone now — "pressed and cleaned" like the rest of our history, as fragrant as old lavender in a cedar chest. As a matter of fact, as in all our conflicts and quarrels, both kinds of people seem to have been on both sides. Why, in the Upper Canada of that day, of its 80,000 inhabitants only 35,000 represented the Loyalists and their children, and 25,000 were "American" settlers who had come in on their own account, and the rest (20,000) had wandered in from the old country. And, per contra, ever so many Americans thought the declaration of war was a policy of madness and the Governor of Massachusetts issued a proclamation (June 26th, 1812) for a public fast for a wrong committed "against the nation from which we are descended and which for many generations has been the bulwark of the religion we possess."

So that was how our history started and that was the way it kept going on. Quarrels that refused to turn to hate, animosities that broke down into friendship, seeds of dissension sown in a soil that brought them up as flowers. Angers that passed like April showers, or summer thunder, only to clear the air. The underlying reason of all this is the queer intermingling of our history and our population. The loyalists were only just the beginning of it. All through a century and a half our populations have washed back and forward over the line. Why, if at the present moment you count up all the people born in Canada and still alive, fourteen out of every hundred are living in the United States, a total of 1,250,000 in all. And conversely, 350,000 American born peoples are living among us.

All this interchange of population one might think would have to lead to amalgamation, to the "annexation" of Canada by the United States, or of the United States by Canada. "Annexation" indeed used to be the bogey of our Canadian politics, the turnip on a stick with a candle in its mouth, used to frighten the electors. It is a dead topic now.

Annexation made its last appearance in 1911, a period that begins to seem like ancient history now, all peace and sunshine and such a thing as a "World War" just a fanciful dream of the imagination. Elections in days like those had none of the grim reality of life and death struggle in which we live now. They were made up of 50 per cent business and 50 per cent humbug. You had, of course, to start an "issue," and if there was none in sight in a clear sky you had to make one, as an Alberta rain-maker makes rain. So this time the Liberals said to the Conservatives "How about annexation?" — and the Conservatives said, "First rate, which side do you want?" — because both sides had had each. It was like the way in which the "scholars" in the little red school house used to decide on who should have first innings by throwing a baseball bat and matching hands on it. So the Liberals took Annexation and lost out on it.

Looking back on it now after nearly forty years it all seems coloured with the evening light of retrospect. Nor were there any great angers over it at the time. One of the great arguments of the platform was to quote a letter of good Mr. Taft, the President, in which he had spoken of our becoming an "Annex" of the republic. He probably meant it as a compliment, just as one speaks with pride of the expansion of an hotel. But naturally for us "Taft's letter" became the target of heroic denunciation. They used to carry it round, copies of it, to election meetings and have it on the speaker's table, beside the water jug, as Exhibit No. 2 — right after the telegrams from all the distinguished people who would not be at the meeting — a little touch that lends class to a political gathering. It's not who's there, that counts, it's who's not.

Years after they gave a big dinner to Mr. Taft at the University Club in Montreal, when he had long finished being President and was up here as an "arbitrator" to decide whether the Grand Trunk Railway was worth nothing or less than nothing. In introducing Mr. Taft the Chairman read out from bygone newspapers those old denunciations of Mr. Taft and added "Look at him! The man has the face of a Mephistopheles!" And Mr. Taft, smothered with laughter, admitted that he had.

But if anyone wants to understand our relations with one another better than history can tell or statistics teach, let him go and stand anywhere along the Niagara-Buffalo frontier at holiday time — July 4th or July 1st, either one — they're all one to us. Here are the Stars and Stripes and the Union Jacks all mixed up together and the tourists pouring back and forward over the International Bridge; immigration men trying in vain to sort them out: Niagara mingling its American and Canadian waters and its honeymoon couples ... or go to the Detroit-Windsor frontier and move back and forward with the flood of commuters, of Americans sampling ale in Windsor and Canadians sampling lager in Detroit ... or come here to Montreal and meet the Dartmouth boys playing hockey against McGill ... or if that sounds too cold, come to Lake Memphremagog in July and go out bass fishing and hook up the International Boundary itself.

But all of such fraternization is only all the more fraternal because we know that we are satisfied on each side of the line to keep our political systems different. Annexation in the old bygone sense has vanished out of the picture. And in the other sense of a union of friendship that needs neither constitution nor compacts, we have it now and mean to keep it.

It is on this basis that we can build for the peace and safety of the world. There is no question here of a formal federation or a written compact. These things can defeat their own end. They indicate as much what will not be done, as what will. They invite a grudging dispensation of assistance, a measured allotment of goodwill. But goodwill cannot be measured and allotted; and without it a federation is just a chain, weak as its weakest link, and an axis a weather-cock, turning with every wind.

The world needs a standard to which all honest men may rally, a barrier to shelter the weak against iniquity. As the keystones of such an arch, the government of free men that arose in Saxon England, and became in America government by the people and for the people, will have fulfilled its final purpose.

18

PARADISE LOST
Leacock's Retirement Speech

This is my last lecture; I have kept it purposely for you — for you, my old pupils who have had so many from me in the last 35 years that one more cannot hurt you. The harm is already done, and you carry, on all the familiar faces which I see about me, that stamp which is set on all my students — an irremovable look of resigned despair.

The subject of our lecture tonight gentlemen — for I insist on calling you so — is "Paradise Lost" — not Milton's but mine and yours, the "Paradise Lost" of all those whose college days are over. For the college, gently and firmly as life itself, tells us when our time is out. For most of you, just when you were at your happiest, the college made a thin pretense that you knew enough, gave you a degree and told you to go; for others (a few of the brighter faces I see here tonight) the college said you couldn't get a degree in a hundred years and warned you to leave town; and for others of us, your teachers, the time came when the college said it had heard our lectures so often that it would pay us not to give any more.

But for all of us, however removed, the college that we have left sinks back into that soft colouring of retrospect better and kindlier than the garish light of daily life. And I feel that in honouring me tonight with your presence here, your generous gifts and your affectionate attention — it is not merely my own person that you honour, but the memory and the meaning of the college in which I have had the honour to serve and the long years during which I have done so.

I have at least tried to do the best that was in me, and in doing it have enjoyed a freedom of action, a liberty of thought and expression for which our college has ever been distinguished. I admit that my lectures have not always been attended with success. My opening lecture in

January, 1901 on the Monarchy of England, was immediately followed by the news that the good Old Queen was taken ill. She did not survive long enough to hear my lecture on the President of the United States which might have saved her. I admit that my lectures on Colonial Freedom were followed by the Banana Riots in Trinidad; that the introduction of my *Elements of Political Science* into China drove the people into a frenzy of indignation and ended the Manchu Dynasty; and that the attempt of the Abyssinians to read Part III — the part of the book never yet reached by a white student, has proved fatal. Yet on the whole, I look back with pride over what I have done, and when I look at you tonight I feel convinced that no other kind of teaching, no teaching at all, could have made you any different.

I can join with you then in turning this occasion rather to the honour of our Alma Mater than to my own. Very often the evening sun, breaking out below the clouds that have obscured the day, affords the best and widest view across the landscape; so with our retrospect of college. We can see how little matter the small disputes, the petty quarrels of the day or hour, how much the long achievement of a century. The college lasts longer than we do; no single mind, no single life controls it. It represents for each of us, as it were, a part of ourselves, something greater than the worn body and the troubled mind that is our soul's companion of the day.

I am convinced that there is for each of us a sort of super-self that comes out in emergency, in the effort of sacrifice, in the heroism of war, and in the creative ecstasy of the artist. Nor is there any environment that better can develop it than a college; we can see it in the ideal professor — careless and even comic in his dress, gullible to the edge of imbecility, an easy mark for the idler spirits of his class, but carrying somewhere within him, that higher idealism lifted above life, that in the end endears him; and we see it in the graduate looking back upon his alma mater, with a view detached from all the meaner considerations of personal gain, from all the hard necessities of daily life — and seeing in it only the fleeting vision of the ideal, of things as they might be, that stands for us as a consolation for things that are.

May I say in conclusion that I appreciate more than I can tell you your gift of a set of my works to the college library, and of another set to my son. I am told that you were in some doubt whether to let it be Shakespeare's works or my own. You have chosen wisely. I have not only written more than Shakespeare, but what I have written is worth more. Shakespeare's books can be had anywhere at 15 cents each, while mine run from a dollar up.

And with that, gentlemen, I will say — as I have these 35 years, and now, for the last time, "that will be all for today."

19

LOOKING BACK FROM RETIREMENT

I was retired — or rather I was fired on the grounds of senility — last year from the college where I had been a professor for thirty-five years. Before that I had been a schoolmaster for ten years, making in all forty-five years of teaching. On this mere pretext, I was invited to go.

In other words, I am what is called a *professor emeritus* — from the Latin *e*, "out", and *meritus*, "so he ought to be." These old professors go drifting out of the colleges, so many every year, as when the harness is slipped off old horses, and they go wandering down into the pasture. The world is always very kindly about it. When they leave there is always a gentle pretence that now in retirement they will do greater things. "Professor Rameses, we understand, will now at last have time to complete his monumental work on the Assyrian epoch." Oh, no, he won't; not all eternity would be enough for that. But he'll sit there in front of a blotter in his study and his wife will put the ink-pot beside him, and through the open door will come the scent of the laburnum, and the late summer flies will buzz around his head! No, no, he'll never finish. Look, he's asleep already!

Or of another professor, it is said, "We understand that Professor Dream intends, now that he is free, to devote himself to journalism!" Will he? That only means that he'll sit and read the newspaper all morning in a barber shop. But notice that kindly little touch "now that he is free!" The idea is that the old fellow has been held back from all kinds of accomplishment, and, once set him loose, and he's supposed to dash off at a tremendous pace! It reminds me of the old days when we used to hire a horse and buggy at a livery stable, and the livery man would drag the horse out, shouting, "Whoa! Whoa! there!" and stand at his head while we got in, as if it were a close call for life to drive behind that horse. When he let go with the final "Whoa! Back! Get up there!" the old horse hadn't the strength to shake the fly-net. So with the professors. Complete their study of Horace! Bring their work on ichthyology up to date! Don't believe it — autumn flowers and buzz flies for them — "Whoa! Back! Get up!"

I recall long ago the resignation of one of my own old professors, and how we got up a dinner for him. I sat next to him and said, "I suppose now you'll be able to complete your translation of Faust?" and he said, "Eh?" I said, "You'll be able to complete your translation of Faust?" "What?" he shouted. "Faust!" I yelled. "No; thank you," he called back. "I've had plenty." An idea struck me and so I took the dinner card in front of me and wrote "Faust" on it and put it in front of him. "I can't read it," he shouted.

So in my own case I've taken warning. When people say to me, "You'll be able now to finish your book on the *History of Political Theory,*" I answer, "To hell with it."

They're a queer lot, the old professors. I suppose that forty or fifty years in the little empire of the classroom is bound to affect a man's character and make-up. In business there are certain standards, certain normal ways of talking and dressing and acting that all men have to fall into as part of business life. Not so with the professors. Take their dress; they've never thought about it. As young men they had no money to dress, and by the time they had they'd lost any sustained interest in it, and so they buy their things spasmodically as the whim seizes them. I recall, from my days as a Chicago student forty years ago, the case, or rather the appearance, of a very distinguished old professor who came over from England to teach some kind of dead language. It was in the summer quarter. He wore a round straw hat — the kind that kids wear — a black morning coat with tails — that was a little bit of London — a pair of duck pants — that stood for the sea — and a pair of ox-blood tanned boots that were meant to represent the eager life of a newer continent. You see, if you analyse that costume, there is life in every bit of it.... The white pants were for the foam of the sea; he got them, no doubt, the day Sir Thomas Lipton invited him on his yacht. The London morning coat meant Piccadilly and the fashion of England; it was all there. Add to it, as the last touch, a string tie, to recall the

Confederate campaign in Missouri, and there you have the man! I remember that he evidently looked on himself as pretty nattily dressed, quite an up-to-date piece of chocolate. The case is actual; anybody of the Chicago of the late nineties could give you the professor's name — or no, they couldn't; they'd have forgotten it. The flies are buzzing round them too.

In other words, professors, if they go on long enough, turn into "characters."

Much of what has been said about professors is naturally true not only of them but of all old men. More nonsense and guff has been talked about old age than of any time of life. Cicero, when his hair began to fall out, wrote a whole book *On Old Age*. Rabbi Ben Ezra — in Browning, isn't it? — said, "Grow old along with me, the best is yet to be!" and the same note has been struck a thousand times, but will never blend into a chord. Cicero and the rest talk of the "serenity" of old age — in fact, a "serene" old age has been a phrase in all languages! Serene old Men! Have you ever seen one of them in a sudden temper, because he couldn't find his fishing line, or had lost his ever-sharp pencil? Old age is supposed to be quiet, restful, at peace with all the world. Don't believe it! Old men live in a world of horrors. At a sniff, they are sure the kitchen stove has set fire to the house! The world is closing in on them. They feel that they are going to be overwhelmed at any minute by terrible changes — Bolsheviks, labour agitations, Mussolini — anything!

I remember a year or two ago, one such stopped me in the street, an old man, just old enough to be getting a nice shake on him even when he stood upright; in fact he had himself buttoned up pretty high in his collar and neckerchief. "These Bolsheviks!" he said. "These Bolsheviks, they'll overrun the whole world, mark my words; we'll live to see it!" Well, he didn't, anyway; he blew up the next week.

And if it's not public dangers it's private ones — the dangers to themselves and to their poor old body that walks with a shadowed figure beside it. Do you realise, my dear young friends in the early twenties who read these lines, that for old people the world is full of death? Those notices that you hardly look at, those obituaries, of what seem to you old people dropping off — and why shouldn't they? —

that, to them, is their world going out one by one, people waiting to be called across a gangway, so many names called every day. Youth is careless of death. It is the price at which humanity lives. Wordsworth, you remember, said, "A simple child that lightly draws its breath and feels its life in every limb, what can it know of death?"

And Captain Harry Graham, the English humourist of yesterday (a tear to his memory), said it with even greater point in the little verse, "Grandpapa fell down the sewer; that's one grandpapa the fewer!" For people of insight and philosophy, Harry Graham's stanza reaches further than Wordsworth's sentimentality. Wordsworth is putting his own ideas into the child — you recall, no doubt, how the We-are-seven poem runs along in its cheerful discussion in a church yard — "and often after sunset when all is bright and fair, I take my little porringer and eat my supper there!" Nonsense! Wordsworth as an old man might take a little porringer, provided he took it regularly and not too near bedtime, but the child wouldn't.

A little porringer! That strikes again the note of the terrors of old men; they're wearing out, they're running down, and so they get the "death bug" that ticks and ticks beside their consciousness, so that they feel the flight of time as it goes by, carry a scale of hours and days such as younger people can't imagine. It is as if one looks down an avenue, all lined with evergreen trees — a little mist, indeed, at the end, but the end can't be so far away after all.

So the old men are preoccupied. "Have you ever," they whisper, "had any trouble with your esophagus?" The answer to this is "Never!" Don't humour or encourage them. Let them take it on the esophagus! They seem to know of parts of the body younger people have never heard of. "The membranous coating of my diaphragm," bleats the old fellow, "is pretty well worn out. I've had to cut out all proteins altogether."

Cutting them out! They start cutting things out like a captain lightening a ship. "I cut out whisky," says the old fellow, "and I don't feel any the worse for it all." No, certainly not; you couldn't feel worse if you tried. "I've cut tobacco right out." Certainly, you haven't got suction enough left in you to keep a cigar alight. Then they cut out meat, and cut out coffee, and cut out all the things they know of, and then begin to cut out things that are just names. Ask them; just let them start and they'll tell you they cut out all nitrogen and glycerine, and gun-cotton, and tabloids — the things they cut out would supply a Spanish army.

This I suppose is a pessimistic discussion. I can't help it. To my mind, the quotation given above, "that's one grandpapa the fewer," goes to the root of the matter. In fact even this business of looking back on life and writing memoirs should be begun earlier, and by younger people. In fact I am glad to observe that it is. A generation ago people never wrote reminiscences till they could cover a long lapse of time. Reminiscences had some such title as: My Hundred Years in the U. S. Cavalry, or Pink and Punk: My Eighty Years of Fox Hunting. Then, thank goodness, someone began Looking Back From Forty! and then someone else realized that you could turn round quicker than that, and a crop of memoirs began to appear on Looking Back from Thirty; and then Looking Back on College, and Looking Back from High School, and finally Looking Back on Kindergarten, or Where Are Those Girls Now?

Youth will have its way; soon the old men won't even write the old-age stuff.

20

BASS FISHING ON LAKE SIMCOE
WITH JAKE GAUDAUR

Among the pleasant memories of my life is the recollection of my fishing days on Ontario's Lake Simcoe with Jake Gaudaur — little excursions that extended over twenty or twenty-five years. If you don't know the name of Jake Gaudaur it only means that you were born fifty years too late. Half a century ago Jake was for several years the champion oarsman of the world — a title won on the Thames at Henley. In those days, before motor-cars and aeroplanes, rowing was one of the big interests of the nations, and Jake Gaudaur was a hero to millions who had never seen him. The fact that his name was pronounced exactly as Good-Oar helped to keep it easily in mind.

Jake was of mixed French and Indian descent but belonged in the Lake Simcoe country and English had always been his language — the kind we use up there, not the kind that they use at Oxford. I can talk both, but the Lake Simcoe kind is easier and, for fishing, far better. It cuts out social distinction. Jake was a magnificent figure of a man; he stood nicely over six feet in his stocking feet — the only way we ever measure people up there. He was broad in the shoulders, straight as a lath, and till the time when he died, just short of eighty, he could pick up the twenty-pound anchor of his motor boat and throw it round like a tack-hammer. Jake — standing erect in the bow of his motor boat and looking out to the horizon, his eyes shaded with his hand — might have stood for the figure of Oshkosh, war chief of the Wisconsin Indians.

When Jake's championship days were over he came back to Canada and "kept hotel" in Sudbury. That was the thing for champions to do; in the unregenerate days of the old bar, thousands of people spent five cents on a drink just to say they had talked with Jake Gaudaur. I wish that retired professors could open up a bar. It must be a great thing to be an ex-champion, or a quintuplet, and never have to work.

So Jake made his modest pile and then came back to our part of the country, the Lake Simcoe district, and set up at the Narrows, at the top end of the lake, as a professional fisherman, taking out parties on the lake for bass fishing.

Now, who hasn't seen Lake Simcoe has never seen a lake at all. Lake Simcoe on a July morning — the water, ruffled in wavelets of a blue and green and silver, as clear as never was: the sky of the purest blue with great clouds white and woolly floating in it! Just the day for fishing! — every day is, for the enthusiast.

The lake is just right in size to be what a lake ought to be — twenty to thirty miles across in any direction — so that there's always a part of the horizon open where you can't see the land. The shore is all irregular with bays and "points" and islands and shoals, so that any roads there-abouts are away back from the water, and the shore line of trees and sand and stone looks much as Champlain saw it three hundred years ago. Over it in the summer air of July there hovers an atmosphere of unbroken peace. When I think of it I cannot but contrast it with the curse that lies over Europe where mountain lakes are scarped and galleried for guns, and every church steeple on their shores a range and target. I wish I could take Hitler and Mussolini out bass fishing on Lake Simcoe. They'd come back better men — or they'd never come back.

So here we are at ten o'clock in the morning helping Jake load the stuff out of our car into his motor boat! Notice that — ten o'clock. None of that fool stuff about starting off at daylight. You get over that by the time you're forty. The right time to start off bass fishing is when you're good and ready to. And when I say ten o'clock, I really mean about ten-thirty. We just call it ten o'clock and when you look at your watch after you're actually started, it's always ten-thirty, or not much past it. Anyway there's no finer time in the day on the water than ten-thirty — still all the freshness of the morning and all the day in front of you — half way between windy and calm with little ruffled waves in the sunlight, and a cool breeze, partly made by the boat itself.

As for the bass, they bite as well at any one time as at any other. The idea that they bite at daylight and don't bite after lunch is just a myth. They bite when they're ready to; the only reason they don't bite after lunch is that the fishermen are asleep till three.

Jake's boat is no "power" boat, to hit up twenty-five miles an hour. That fool stuff came to our lakes later and is out of keeping with bass fishing. Jake's is a big roomy open boat with a front part for Jake and a big open part at the back where we sit — a broad stern seat with leather cushions and wicker arm-chairs on a linoleum floor. Solid comfort. No rough stuff for us: we're not sailors. And no cover to keep off the sun; who cares a darn about the sun when you're fishing; and nothing to keep off the wind — let it come; and no protection against the rain. It won't rain. Any man who thinks it's going to rain shouldn't go fishing.

"Will it rain, Jake ?"

"I don't think so, Professor; not with that sky."

We've gone through that little opening dialogue, I suppose, a hundred times. That's the beauty of bass fishing: always doing the same things in the same way, with the same old jokes and the same conversation.

"I was thinking we might go out and try the big rock at McCrae's point first, Professor," says Jake.

Seeing that we've never done anything else in twenty years, it seems a likely thing to do.

This gives us two miles to go — down from the Narrows to the open lake and then sideways across to the first point. For me this is always the best part of the day — the cool fresh air, the anticipation better than reality, the settling into our wicker chairs and lighting up our pipes, with the stuff all properly stowed around us, the fishing-gear, the lunch and the box with the soda on ice. Not that we take a drink at this time of the day. Oh, no! We're all agreed that you don't need a drink on a beautiful fine morning at ten-thirty — unless perhaps just as an exception today because it's such a damn fine day that you feel so good you'd like a drink. There are two reasons for taking a drink when you're out bass fishing — one, because you feel so good, and the other — because you don't feel so good. So perhaps this morning, "Eh what?"

"Well, just a starter."

"Jake, can I pass you along a horn ?"

"Thanks, Professor, I don't mind."

There are four of us, mostly, apart from Jake, so it takes most of the time of the run to mix up and serve the drinks. I am thinking here especially of one party, though really it was just like all the others. There was my brother George and George Rapley, the bank manager (a tear to his kind memory), and Charlie Janes, the railroad man of a Lake Simcoe town. George Rapley always came because he could fish, and Charlie Janes because he *couldn't*. You may have noticed that bank managers are always good fishermen; it's something in their profession, I think, a kind of courtesy, that gets the fish. And I am sure that everybody who goes bass fishing will agree that to make the party right you need one fellow who *can't* fish. In fact in any bass fishing party of friends who go out often together, there is always one who is cast for the part of not knowing how to fish. No matter how often he's been out, he's not supposed to know anything about fishing and he good-naturedly accepts the role. If he loses a fish, that's supposed to be because he didn't know how to land it; if *we* lose a fish it's supposed to be because it was *impossible* to land it. It's these little mutual understandings that fit life together.

So almost before the "horn" is finished, here we are bearing down on the big rock off McCrae's point. It's nearly a quarter of a mile from shore and six feet under water, but Jake steers to it like a taxi to a hotel door. The anchor goes down with a splash, our swing on it timed to throw us right over the rock! There it is! See it — big as a wagon! — and in another minute down go the baited lines trailing to go under the edge of the great rock.

This is the great moment of fishing, the first minute with the lines down — tense, exhilarating. It's always the same way — either something big happens, or nothing. Perhaps — bing! the lines are no sooner down than a bass is hooked — by Charlie Janes, of course — just like the luck of the darned fool! And while he's still hauling on it — biff! there's another one — and Jake, it seems, has quietly landed a third one when the other two were plunging round. With which there's such a period of excitement and expectation that it's nearly three quarters of an hour before you realize that those three fish are all there are — or rather *two* fish: George Rapley lost his — too bad! he was playing it so beautifully. Charlie Janes, the darned old fool, flung his over the side of the boat, right slap into the ice-box.

Or else — the other alternative — the lines go down and nothing happens.

In either case we fish on and on under the rock till excitement fades into dullness, and dullness into dead certainty. That's *all*. At last some-one says, "I guess they ain't biting here any more." Notice "*They're not biting*"; we never say, "*they're not here.*" Any man who says, as I have heard some of our odd guests say, "Oh, hell, there are no fish here," is not fit to be brought again. The only theory on which bass fishing can be maintained as a rational pastime is that the bass are *everywhere* — all the time. But they won't bite. The wind may be wrong, or the air just too damp, or too dry, or too much sun, or not enough — it's amazing how little will start a bass not biting. But the cause must always be one that can change in five minutes, or with a move of five yards. These beliefs are to a fisherman what faith is to a Christian.

"We might try out past Strawberry Island," says Jake. This means a change farther out, right out in the open water of the lake with the whole horizon of wind and wave and sun open for twenty miles all around to the south. This is not exactly a shoal. The bottom of the lake drops here from twelve feet to thirty feet of water — like the side of a hill. Jake explains it all fresh every time, and he makes each new spot seem so different and so likely that we go at each with new hope eternal. If we don't get any fish as each half hour stop goes by, Jake tells the story of how he and I fished once and never had a bite till after sundown and then caught thirty-three bass in half an hour off McGinnis's reef. "You mind that evening, Professor?" he says (to "mind" a thing is to remember it). "It was thirty-three, wasn't it?"

"Thirty-four I think, Jake," I answer, and he says, "Well, mebbee it was." We've brought those fish up a little every year.

Or else Jake tells the story of the young girl from Toledo who came up with her father and had never been fishing before and never even in a motor boat, and it was a caution how many she caught. This story, of course, conveys the idea that if inexperienced fishers, like the young lady from Toledo, can catch fish, experienced people like ourselves could hardly expect to.

Then all of a sudden as it always seems, comes the idea of lunch — all of a sudden everybody hungry and ready for it. And does ever food taste better than out in the wind and sun in a motor boat? — salmon sandwiches, cold chicken in a salad, chunks of home-made bread, mustard pickles; all eaten partly off a plate and partly with your fingers and with bottled ale to wash it down.

People who go fishing but are not real fishermen land on shore for lunch, light a fire and, I believe, even cook the fish caught. Some of them go so far as to have a game of poker or, in extreme cases of mental derangement, go for a swim. All of this to a proper fisherman is just deplorable, just lunacy. The true fisherman eats right in the boat with the lines still hanging in the water. There seems to be a sort of truce during lunch time; I never knew a bass to touch a hook till it's over. But lunch on the other hand isn't hurried. It's just eaten in the natural way. You put into your mouth all it will hold; then eat it; then start again. Eating in the open air knows no satiety, no indigestion.

The whole point is that the longest day is all too short for fishing, and no one who really loves bass fishing can bear the thought of knocking off from it even for an hour. As a matter of fact, we *do* take time off but we never admit it. For there also came in our fishing with Jake a drowsy part of the day when we took a sleep. Not that we ever called it that deliberately. The sleep was just a sort of accident. A little while after we'd eaten all the lunch we could hold Jake would say: "I thought we might go and try for a spell down round the corner of that shoal — just off that way apiece. You mind we was there before?"

"Yes, sure, I remember it, Jake."

The place is a sort of convenient little nook among the shoals — nothing showing on top of the water. We always reckoned as if the bottom were in sight. It had the advantage that the waves couldn't reach it, because of the shallows, and it was always quiet, and no fish ever came there. Jake could anchor the boat where there were just enough waves to rock the boat gently and just enough light breeze to murmur a lullaby — and with the two-o'clock sun to make you pull your straw panama away over your eyes, a man seated like that in a wicker chair, with two pounds of sandwiches and six ounces of whisky in him, is as drowsy as a flower nodding on its stem, and asleep in five minutes. The lines dangle in the water; there is no conversation, no sound but the breeze and the lapping of the little waves. Up in front we could see only Jake's broad back, but there was slumber in every line of it.

It didn't matter who woke first. After about an hour anybody could straighten up and say: "By Jove, I believe I was almost asleep. Were you?" And the others would answer, "Darn near!" And then Jake would say, as if he'd never stopped talking, "I was thinking we might go out and try the dry shoal."

This rouses us to a new search for bass, hither and thither half a mile, a mile, at a time. Even then we are only covering one corner of Lake Simcoe. The lake is just big enough to seem illimitable.

Bass fishing on Lake Simcoe is not like the bass fishing you can get a hundred miles north of it, on the rivers in the bush, out of easy reach. Up there it's no come-and-go business in a day; you must stay at least two nights. You catch one hundred bass in the first day and the next day you don't even keep them; you throw them back. The third day you hate the stinking things; a bass two days dead, with its skin discoloured, would sicken even a cannibal.

Not so Lake Simcoe. There are just not enough bass, just never too many — some dead, dull days without any — they're there, but they won't bite. But even on the deadest, dullest day, always the hope of a strike.

You might wonder, if you don't know the life, why the afternoon never gets dreary, what there can be to talk about — especially among men often and always out together on the same ground. That's just ignorance. In bass fishing there are vast unsettled problems, to be discussed forever. For example, do you need to "play" a bass, or is that just a piece of damn nonsense imitated out of salmon fishing? The school to which I belong holds that "playing" a bass is just a way of losing it. What you need is a steel rod with the last section taken out and an "emergency tip" put in — making a short firm rod about six feet long. When the bass nibbles, *wait* — then wait some more — then strike — with such power as to drive the hook right through his head — then shorten the line — not with a reel; that's too slow — haul it in beside the reel with your left hand and hold it firm with your right — shove the rod close to the water, if need be *under* the water — by that means the bass *can't* jump out of the water, there isn't line enough — drag him against his will till someone else holds the net — and in he comes.

Contrast this with the artistic "playing" of fish that *looks* so skilful — paying out line — the fish leaping in the air thirty feet from the boat — and all that show stuff — only good for a picture book!

Now can't you see that the discussion of that point alone can fill an afternoon?

Personally I am always an extremist for a short rod and rapid action — the bass right in the boat in twenty seconds. I think that in his heart Jake Gaudaur agreed with this. It's the way all Indians fish and always have. But Jake's calling demanded compromise. He favoured both sides. Rapley, like all bankers, played a fish as they play a customer with a loan, taking it in gradually.

We always knew that the afternoon was closing to evening when Jake said:

"Suppose we go out and try that big rock inside McGinnis's reef. You mind, Professor? The place where you caught all them bass, that night; thirty-four, wasn't it?"

"Yes, or thirty-five, Jake. I'm not sure. Let's try it."

This sunken rock is the triumph of Jake's navigation of the lake. It's a mile from even the nearest point of land, and sunk six feet down. Beside it the big rock at McCrae's is child's play. That one you can find if you keep on looking for it. This one, never. It's all very well to say that you can do it with "bearings"; any amateur yachtsman that ever wore Panama pants will tell you that. But try it. Try to get bearings that are good at all hours and all lights and shadows on the shores, good in rain and good in mist, and you soon see where you are — or are not.

Jake, erect at the bow as he steers, is as straight as Oshkosh; the boat gathers speed in a curve that picks up one of the bearings and then straight as a pencil line over the water for a mile — then a stop with a reversed engine, without a turn, or the bearings would be lost, and there we are — right over the rock. In a clear light it's as plain as day, but on a dull day you can just make it out, a great rock sunk in a wide basin of water for the bass to get in.

Here we try our final luck. We can't leave. If the bass are there (I mean if they are biting) it's too good to leave. If we don't get a bite, we just *can't* leave.

We haven't realized it, but the afternoon has all gone. The sun is setting behind the hills on the west side of the lake. Just before it goes its beams light up for a moment the windows of unseen farm-houses ten miles the other side of us — and then, before we know it, the sun is gone. But we can't leave. It's still broad daylight yet.

"There's two or three hours good fishing yet, Jake, eh?"

"All of that, Professor."

Somehow it seems as if the day were suddenly all gone. "Have another horn, Jake?" Surely that'll hold the daylight a little, giving Jake a horn. Anyway we can't leave. The light is fading a little. A cold wind begins to move across the lake; the water seems to blacken under its touch as the boat swings to it.

"The wind's kind o' gone round," says Jake. "I thought it would." It's not surprising. The wind has gone round and the air turned chill after sundown every evening of the sixty years I've known Lake Simcoe. But we can't leave. Charlie Janes has had a bite — or says he has. We never take Charlie's word, of course, as really good; he may have caught in a crack of rock. But Rapley thinks he had a nibble. That's better evidence. So we stay on — and on — till the dark has fallen, the shores have all grown dim and then vanished and the north-west wind is beginning to thump the waves on the bow of the anchored boat.

"I guess, gentlemen, it's about time to pull up," says Jake. If we had caught fifteen or twenty bass he'd have said, "Boys, I guess it's about time to quit." But "gentlemen" brings us back to the cold cruel reality.

So the anchor is up and the motor boat at its full power set for home. It's quite rough on the water now; the boat slaps into the waves and sends the spray flying clear astern to where we have our chairs huddled together, back to the wind. It's dark too. You have to use a flash-light to open the soda for the "consolation drinks" that mark the end of the fishing.

"Have a horn, Jake?"

"Thanks, Professor."

Jake, with his oil clothes on, can't leave the wheel now; he sits there all in the spray with one hand for steering and one for the drink.

It's amazing how a lake like Lake Simcoe can change — a few hours ago a halcyon paradise, still and calm — and now with the night and the wind gathering over it —

"Oh, well, Jake knows the way," and anyway it's only three miles till we'll be in shelter of the Narrows! — Whew! that was a corker, that wave! "Here, put these newspapers behind your back, Charlie, they'll keep off the spray."

Just enough of this to give one a slight feeling of night and mimic danger — and then, in no great time, for the distance is short, we round into the shelter of the Narrows with just a mile of water, smoother and smoother, to run.

All different it looks from the morning; what you see now is just lights — a perplexing galaxy of lights, white and green and red here and there on the unseen shore — and great flares of moving white light that must be the motors on the highway.

"What's the red light away up, Jake?"

"That's the one above the railway bridge." We always ask Jake this and when he answers we know we are close in. The water suddenly is quite smooth, a current running with us — the summer cottages and docks come in sight, with "young fellers" and girls in canoes and the sound of a radio somewhere discussing war in Europe.

We're back in the world again, landed at Jake's dock with a little crowd of loafers and boys standing round to see "how many fish Jake got" — not us, *Jake*. We unload the boat and take a look at the string of fish. "Let's see that big one that Rapley caught, eh?" But where is it? Surely it can't be this small dirty-looking flabby thing — I'm afraid it is.

We divide the fish. Jake won't take any. We try to work them off on one another. Fishermen want *fishing*, never fish — and end by slinging them into the car all in one box. "Well, we certainly had a fine day; good night, Jake." And another fishing day has gone — now never to return.

I can only repeat, in tribute to a fine memory, "Good night, Jake."

21

COMMON SENSE AND THE UNIVERSE

Speaking last December at the annual convention of the American Association for the Advancement of Science, and speaking, as it were, in the name of the great 100-inch telescope under his control, Professor Edwin Hubble, of the Mount Wilson Observatory, California, made the glad announcement that the universe is not expanding. This was good news indeed, if not to the general public who had no reason to suspect that it was expanding, at least to those of us who humbly attempt to "follow science." For some twenty-five years past, indeed ever since the promulgation of this terrific idea in a paper published by Professor W. de Sitter in 1917, we had lived as best we could in an expanding universe, one in which everything, at terrific speed, kept getting farther away from everything else. It suggested to us the disappointed lover in the romance who leaped on his horse and rode madly off in all directions. The idea was majestic in its sheer size, but it somehow gave an uncomfortable sensation.

Yet we had to believe it. Thus, for example, we had it on the authority of Dr. Spencer Jones, the British Astronomer Royal, in his new and fascinating book of 1940, *Life on Other Worlds*, that "a distant universe in the constellation of Boötes has been found to be receding with a velocity of 24,300 miles a second. We can infer that this nebula is at a distance of 230,000,000 light-years." I may perhaps remind my fellow followers of science that a light-year means the distance travelled in one year by light, moving at 186,000 miles a second. In other words, this "distant universe" is now 1,049,970,980,000,000,000,000 miles away!

"Some distance!" as Mr. Churchill would say.

But now it appears that that distant universe has *not* been receding at all; in fact, it isn't way out there. Heaven knows where it is. Bring it back. Yet not only did the astronomers assert the expansion, but they proved it from the behaviour of the red band in the spectrum, which blushed a deeper red at the revelation of it, like the conscious water that "saw its God and blushed" at Cana in Galilee long ago. One of the most distinguished and intelligible of our astronomers, Sir Arthur Eddington, had written a book about it, *The Expanding Universe*, to bring it down to our level. Astronomers at large accepted this universal explosion in all directions as calmly as they once accepted the universal fall of gravitation, or the universal death in the cold under Carnot's Second Law of Thermodynamics.

But the relief brought by Professor Hubble is tempered, on reflection, by certain doubts and afterthoughts. It is not that I venture any disbelief or disrespect toward science, for that is as atrocious in our day as disbelief in the Trinity was in the days of Isaac Newton. But we begin to doubt whether science can quite keep on believing in and respecting itself. If we expand today and contract tomorrow; if we undergo all the doubled-up agonies of the curvature of space, only to have the kink called off, as it has been; if we get reconciled to dying a martyr's death at one general, distributed temperature of 459 degrees below zero, the same for all, only to find that the world is perhaps unexpectedly warming up again — then we ask, where are we? To which, of course, Einstein answers, "Nowhere," since there is no place to be. So we must pick up our little book again, follow science, and wait for the next astronomical convention.

Let us take this case of the famous Second Law of Thermodynamics, that inexorable scroll of fate which condemned the universe — or at least all life in it — to die of cold. I look back now with regret to the needless tears I have wasted over that, the generous sympathy for the last little band of survivors, dying at 459 degrees below our zero (-273° centigrade), the absolute zero of cold when the molecules cease to move and heat ends. No stove will light at that, for the wood is as cold as the stove, and the match is as cold as both, and the dead fingers motionless.

I remember meeting this inexorable law for the first time in reading, as a little boy, a piece of "popular science" entitled *Our Great Timepiece Running Down*. It was by Richard Proctor, whose science-bogeys were as terrifying as Mrs. Crow's *Night Thoughts*, only slower in action. The sun, it appeared, was cooling; soon it would be all over. Lord Kelvin presently ratified this. Being Scotch, he didn't mind damnation and he gave the sun and the whole solar system only ninety million years more to live.

This famous law was first clearly enunciated in 1824 by the great French physicist, Nicolas Carnot. It showed that all bodies in the universe kept exchanging their temperature — hot things heated cold, and cold things chilled hot. Thus they pooled their temperature. Like the division of a rich estate among a flock of poor relations, it meant poverty for all. We must all share ultimately the cold of absolute space.

It is true that a gleam of hope came when Ernest Rutherford and others, working on radioactivity, discovered that there might be a contrary process of "stoking up." Atoms exploding into radioactivity would keep the home fires burning in the sun for a long time. This glad news meant that the sun was both much older and much younger than Lord Kelvin had ever thought it was. But even at that it was only a respite. The best they could offer was 1,500,000,000 years. After that we freeze.

And now what do you think! Here comes the new physics of the Quantum Theory and shatters the Second Law of Thermodynamics into gas — a word that is Dutch for chaos. The world may go on forever. All of this because of the final promulgation of the Law of the *Quantum* — or shall we say, the Law of Just So Much — of which we shall presently speak. These physical people do not handle their Latin with the neat touch of those of us who knew our declensions as they know their dimensions. Of course they mean *Tantum* — but let it go at that. *Quantum* is drugstore Latin, *quantum sufficit*. *Tantum* is the real thing — *Virgilium vidi tantum* ("I saw something of Virgil").

At this point I may perhaps pause to explain that the purpose of this article is not to make fun of science, nor to express disbelief in it, but only to suggest its limits. What I want to say is that when the scientist steps out from recording phenomena and offers a general statement of the nature of what is called "reality," the ultimate nature of space, of time, of the beginning of things, of life, of a universe, then he stands exactly where you and I do, and the three of us stand where Plato did — and long before him Rodin's primitive thinker.

Consider this. Professor Hubble, like Joshua, has called upon the universe to be still. All is quiet. The universe rests, motionless, in the night sky. The mad rush is over. Every star in every galaxy, every island universe, is at least right where it is. But the old difficulty remains: Does it go forever, this world in the sky, or does it stop? Such an alternative has posed itself as a problem for every one of us, somewhere about the age of twelve. We cannot imagine that the stars go on forever. It's unthinkable. But we equally cannot imagine that they come to a stop and that beyond them is nothing, and then more nothing. Unending nothing is as incomprehensible as unending something. This alternative I cannot fathom, nor can Professor Hubble, nor can anyone ever hope to.

Let me turn back in order to make my point of view a little clearer. I propose to traverse again the path along which modern science has dragged those who have tried to follow it for about a century past. It was, at first, a path singularly easy to tread, provided that one could throw aside the inherited burden of superstition, false belief, and prejudice. For the direction seemed verified and assured all along by the corroboration of science by actual physical results. Who could doubt electricity after the telegraph? Or doubt the theory of light after photography? Or the theory of electricity after reading under electric light? At every turn, each new advance of science unveiled new power, new mechanism of life — and of death. To "doubt science" was to be like the farmer at the circus who doubted the giraffe. Science, of course, had somehow to tuck into the same bed as Theology, but it was the theologian who protested. Science just said, "Lie over."

Let us follow then this path.

II

When the medieval superstition was replaced by the new learning, mathematics, astronomy, and physics were the first sciences to get organized and definite. By the opening of the nineteenth century they were well set; the solar system was humming away so drowsily that Laplace was able to assure Napoleon that he didn't need God to watch over it. Gravitation worked like clockwork, and clockwork worked like gravitation. Chemistry, which, like electricity, was nothing but a set of experiments in Benjamin Franklin's time, turned into a science after Lavoisier had discovered that fire was not a thing but a process, something happening to things — an idea so far above the common thought that they guillotined him for it in 1794. Dalton followed and showed that all things could be broken up into a set of very, very small atoms, grouped into molecules all acting according to plan. With Faraday and Maxwell, electricity, which turned out to be the same as magnetism, or interchangeable with it, fell into its place in the new order of science.

By about 1880 it seemed as if the world of science was fairly well explained. Metaphysics still talked in its sleep. Theology still preached sermons. It took issue with much of the new science, especially with geology and the new evolutionary science of life that went with the new physical world. But science paid little attention.

For the whole thing was so amazingly simple. There you had your space and time, two things too obvious to explain. Here you had your matter, made up of solid little atoms, infinitely small but really just like birdseed. All this was set going by and with the Law of Gravitation. Once started, the nebulous world condensed into suns, the suns threw off planets, the planets cooled, life resulted and presently became conscious, conscious life got higher up and higher up till you had apes, then Bishop Wilberforce, and then Professor Huxley.

A few little mysteries remained, such as the question of what space and matter and time and life and consciousness really were. But all this was conveniently called by Herbert Spencer the *Unknowable*, and then locked in a cupboard and left there.

Everything was thus reduced to a sort of Dead Certainty. Just one awkward skeleton remained in the cupboard. And that was the peculiar, mysterious aspect of electricity, which was not exactly a thing and yet was more than an idea. There was also, and electricity only helped to make it worse, the old puzzle about "action at a distance." How does gravitation pull all the way from here to the sun? And if there is *nothing* in space, how does light get across from the sun in eight minutes, and even all the way from Sirius in eight years?

Even the invention of "ether" as a sort of universal jelly that could have ripples shaken across it proved a little unconvincing.

Then, just at the turn of the century, the whole structure began to crumble.

The first note of warning that something was going wrong came with the discovery of X-rays. Sir William Crookes, accidentally leaving around tubes of rarified gas, stumbled on "radiant matter," or "matter in the fourth state," as accidentally as Columbus discovered America. The British Government knighted him at once (1897), but it was too late. The thing had started. Then came Guglielmo Marconi with the revelation of more waves, and universal at that. Light, the world had learned to accept, because we can see it, but this was fun in the dark.

There followed the researches of the radioactivity school and, above all, those of Ernest Rutherford which revolutionized the theory of matter. I knew Rutherford well as we were colleagues at McGill for seven years. I am quite sure that he had no original intention of upsetting the foundations of the universe. Yet that is what he did, and he was in due course very properly raised to the peerage for it.

When Rutherford was done with the atom, all the solidity was pretty well knocked out of it.

Till these researches began, people commonly thought of atoms as something like birdseed — little round, solid particles, ever so little, billions to an inch. They were small. But they were there. You could weigh them. You could apply to them all the laws of Isaac Newton about weight and velocity and mass and gravitation — in other words, the whole of first-year physics.

Let us try to show what Rutherford did to the atom. Imagine to yourself an Irishman whirling a shillelagh around his head with the rapidity and dexterity known only in Tipperary or Donegal. If you come anywhere near, you'll get hit with the shillelagh. Now make it go faster; faster still; get it going so fast that you can't tell which is Irishman and which is shillelagh. The whole combination has turned into a green blur. If you shoot a bullet at it, it will probably go through, as there is mostly nothing there. Yet if you go up against it, it won't hit you now, because the shillelagh is going so fast that you will seem to come against a solid surface. Now make the Irishman smaller and the shillelagh longer. In fact, you don't need the Irishman at all; just his force, his Irish determination, so to speak. Just keep that, the *disturbance*. And you don't need the shillelagh either, just the *field of force* that it sweeps. There! Now put in two Irishmen and two shillelaghs and reduce them in the same way to one solid body — at least it seems solid but you can shoot bullets through it anywhere now. What you have now is a hydrogen atom — one proton and one electron flying around as a *disturbance* in space. Put in more Irishmen and more shillelaghs — or, rather, more protons and electrons — and you get other kinds of atoms. Put in a whole lot — eleven protons, eleven electrons; that is a sodium atom. Bunch the atoms together into combinations called molecules, themselves flying round — and there you are! That's solid matter, and nothing in it at all except disturbance. You're standing on it right now: the molecules are beating against your feet. But there is nothing there, and nothing in your feet. This may help you to understand how "waves," ripples of disturbance — for instance, the disturbance you call radio — go right through all matter, indeed right through *you,* as if you weren't there. You see, you aren't.

The peculiar thing about this atomic theory was that whatever the atoms were, birdseed or disturbance, it made no difference in the way they acted. They followed all the laws of mechanics and motion, or they seemed to. There was no need to change any idea of space or time because of them. Matter was their forte, like wax figures with Artemus Ward.

One must not confuse Rutherford's work on atoms with Einstein's theories of space and time. Rutherford worked all his life without reference to Einstein. Even in his later days at the Cavendish Laboratory at Cambridge when he began, ungratefully, to smash up the atom that had made him, he needed nothing from Einstein. I once asked Rutherford — it was at the height of the popular interest in Einstein in 1923 — what he thought of Einstein's relativity. "Oh, that stuff!" he said. "We never bother with that in our work." His admirable biographer, Professor A. S. Eve, tells us that when the German physicist, Wien, told Rutherford that no Anglo-Saxon could understand relativity, Rutherford answered, "No, they have too much sense."

But it was Einstein who made the real trouble. He announced in 1905 that there was no such thing as absolute rest. After that there never was. But it was not till just after the Great War that the reading public caught on to Einstein and that little books on "Relativity" covered the bookstalls.

Einstein knocked out space and time, as Rutherford knocked out matter. The general viewpoint of relativity toward space is very simple. Einstein explains that there is no such place as here. "But," you answer, "I'm here; here is where I am right now." But you're moving, you're spinning around as the earth spins; and you and the earth are both spinning around the sun, and the sun is rushing through space toward a distant galaxy, and the galaxy itself is beating it away at 26,000 miles a second. Now, where is that spot that is here! How did you mark it? You remember the story of the two idiots who were out fishing, and one said, "We should have marked that place where we got all the fish," and the other said, "I did; I marked it on the boat." Well, that's it. That's *here*.

You can see it better still if you imagine the universe swept absolutely empty: nothing in it, not even *you*. Now put a *point* in it, just one point. Where is it? Why, obviously it's nowhere. If you say it's right there, where do you mean by there? In which direction is there? In *that* direction? Oh! Hold on, you're sticking yourself in to make a direction. It's in *no* direction; there aren't any directions. Now put in another point. Which is which? You can't tell. They *both* are. One is on the right, you say, and one on the left. You keep out of that space! There's no right and no left. Join the points with a line. Now you think you've got something, and I admit this is the nearest you have come to it. But is the line long or short? How long is it? Length soon vanishes into a purely relative term. One thing is longer than another: that's all.

There's no harm in all this, so far. To many people it's as obvious as it is harmless. But that's only the beginning. Leave space alone for a moment and take on time and then things begin to thicken. If there is no such place as here, a similar line of thought will show that there's no such time as now — not absolutely now. Empty the universe again as you did before, with not a speck in it, and now ask, What time is it? God bless me, how peculiar! It isn't any time. It can't be; there's nothing to tell the time by. You say you can feel it go; oh, but you're not there. There will be no *time* until you put something into space with dimensions to it — and then there'll be time, but only as connected somehow — no knowing how — with things in space. But just as there is no such thing as absolute top or bottom in space, so there is a similar difficulty as to time backward and time forward.

The relativity theory undertakes to explain both space and time by putting them together, since they are meaningless without one another, into a compound called "space-time continuum." Time thus becomes, they say, the fourth dimension of space. Until just recently it was claimed further that to fit these relationships together, to harmonize space and time, space must have a curve, or curvature. This was put over to the common mind by comparing what happens in space with what happens to a fly walking on a sphere (a globe). The fly walks and walks and never gets to the end. It's curved. The joke is on the fly. So was the joke long ago on the medieval people who thought the world was flat. "What happened to the theory of the earth," writes Eddington, "has happened also to the world of space and time."

The idea was made plainer for us by comparing space-time to an onion skin, or rather to an infinite number of onion skins. If you have enough, you can fill all space. The universe is your onion, as it was Shakespeare's oyster.

The discovery by Einstein of this curvature of space was greeted by the physicists with the burst of applause that greets a winning home run at baseball. That brilliant writer just mentioned, Sir Arthur Eddington, who can handle space and time with the imagery of a poet, and even infiltrate humour into gravitation — as when he says that a man in an elevator falling twenty stories has an ideal opportunity to study gravitation — is loud in his acclaim. Without this curve, it appears, things won't fit into their place. The fly on the globe, as long as he thinks it flat (like Mercator's map), finds things shifted, as by some unaccountable demon, to all sorts of wrong distances. Once he gets the idea of a sphere, everything comes straight. So with our space. The mystery of gravitation puzzles us, except those who have the luck to fall in an elevator, and even for them knowledge comes too late. They weren't falling at all: just curving. "Admit a curvature of the world," wrote Eddington in his Gifford Lectures of 1927, "and the mysterious agency disappears. Einstein has exorcised this demon."

But it appears now, fourteen years later, that Einstein doesn't care if space is curved or not. He can take it either way. A prominent physicist of today, head of the department in one of the greatest universities of the world, wrote me on this point: "Einstein had stronger hopes that a general theory which involved the assumption of a property of space, akin to what is ordinarily called curvature, would be more useful than he now believes to be the case." Plain talk for a professor. Most people just say Einstein has given up curved space. It's as if Sir Isaac Newton years after had said, with a yawn, "Oh, about that apple — perhaps it wasn't falling."

Now with the curve knocked out of it, the space-time continuum, with these so-called four dimensions, becomes really a very simple matter; in fact, only a very pretentious name for a very obvious fact. It just means that information about an occurrence is not complete unless we know both where it happened and when it happened. It is no use telling me that Diogenes is dead if I didn't know that he was alive.

Obviously "time-when" or "place-where" are bound together and coexist with one another. If there were no space — just emptiness — there could be no time. It wouldn't count itself. And if there were no time, there could be no space. Start it and it would flicker out again in no time — like an electric bulb on a wobble-plug. Space-time continuum is just a pretentious name for this consequence of consciousness. We can't get behind it. We begin life with it, as the chicken out of the egg begins with its cell memory. All the mathematics based on "space-time continuum" gets no further, as far as concerns the search for reality. It gets no further than the child's arithmetic book that says, "If John walks two miles every day for ten days," etc., etc. The child hooks space and time with a continuum as easily as the chicken picks up gravel.

III

But, unhappily, we can't get away from the new physics quite as simply as that. Even if we beat them out on space and time, there is far worse to come. That's only the start of it, for now, as the fat boy in *Pickwick* said, "I'm going to make your flesh creep." The next thing to go is cause and effect. You may think that one thing causes another. It appears that it doesn't. And, of course, when cause and effect go, the bottom is out of the universe, since you can't tell, literally can't, what's going to happen next. This is the consequence of the famous Quantum Theory, first hinted at by Professor Max Planck about forty years ago and since then scrambled for by the physicists like dogs after a bone. It changes so fast that when Sir Arthur Eddington gave the Gifford Lectures referred to, he said to his students that it might not be the same when they met next autumn.

But we cannot understand the full impact of the Quantum Theory in shattering the world we lived in, without turning back again to discuss time in a new relation, namely, the forward- and backwardness of it, and to connect it up again with the Second Law of Thermodynamics — the law, it will be recalled, that condemns us to die of cold. Only we will now call it by its true name — which we had avoided before — as the Law of Entropy. All physicists sooner or later say, "Let us call it Entropy," just as a man says when you get to know him, "Call me Charlie."

So we make a new start.

I recall, as some other people still may, a thrilling melodrama called *The Silver King*. In this the hero, who thinks he has committed a murder (of course, he hasn't really), falls on his knees and cries, "Oh, God, turn back the universe and give me yesterday." The supposed reaction of the audience was, "Alas, you *can't* turn back the universe!"

But nowadays it would be very different. At the call, the Spirit of Time would appear — not Father Time, who is all wrong, being made old — but a young, radiant spirit in a silver frock made the same back and front. "Look," says the Spirit, "I'm going to turn back the universe. You see this wheel turning around? Presto! It's going the other way. You see this elastic ball falling to the floor? Presto! It's bouncing back. You see out of the window that star moving west? Presto! It's going east. Hence accordingly," continues the Spirit, now speaking like a professor, so that the Silver King looks up in apprehension, "time, as evidenced by any primary motion, is entirely reversible so that we cannot distinguish between future time and past time: indeed, if they move in a circle both are one."

The Silver King leaps up, shouts, "Innocent! Innocent!" and dashes off, thus anticipating Act V and spoiling the whole play. The musing Spirit, musing of course backwards, says, "Poor fellow, I hadn't the heart to tell him that this only applies to primary motion and not to Entropy. And murder, of course, is a plain case of Entropy."

And now let us try to explain. Entropy means the introduction into things that happen of a random element, as opposed to things that happen and "unhappen," like a turning wheel, good either way, or a ball falling and bouncing as high as it falls, or the earth going around the sun. These primary motions are "reversible." As far as they are concerned, time could just as well go backwards as forward. But now introduce the element of random chance. You remember how Humpty Dumpty fell off the wall? All the king's horses and all the king's men couldn't put Humpty together again. Of course not. It was a straight case of Entropy. But now consider a pack of cards fresh from the maker. Are they all in suits, all in order again? They might so arrange themselves, but they won't. Entropy. Take this case. You show a motion picture of a wheel spinning. You run it backwards; it spins the other way. That's time, the time of primary motion, both ways alike. Now show a motion picture of a waiter with a tray of teacups. He drops them; they roll in a hundred fragments. Now run it backwards; you see all the little fragments leap up in the air, join neatly into cups, and rest on the tray. Don't think that the waiter smiles with relief. He doesn't: He can't smile backwards: He just relaxes from horror to calm.

Here then is Entropy, the smashing down of our world by random forces that don't reverse. The heat and cold of Carnot's Second Law are just one case of it. This is the only way by which we can distinguish which of two events came first. It's our only clue as to which way time is going. If procrastination is the thief of time, Entropy is the detective.

The Quantum Theory begins with the idea that the quantities of disturbance in the atom, of which we spoke, are done up, at least they act that way, in little fixed quantities (each Quantum — no more, no less), as if sugar only existed by the pound. The smallness of the Quantum is beyond comprehension. A Quantum is also peculiar. A Quantum in an atom flies around in an orbit. This orbit may be a smaller ring or a bigger ring. But when the Quantum shifts from orbit to orbit, it does not pass or drift or move *from one to the other.* No, sir. First, it's here and then it's there. Believe it or not, it has just shifted. Its change of place is random, and *not because of anything.* Now the things that we think of as matter and movements and events (things happening) are all based, infinitely far down, on this random dance of Quantums. Hence, since you can't ever tell what a Quantum will do, you can't ever say what will happen next. Cause and effect are all gone.

But as usual in this bright, new world of the new physics, the statement is no sooner made than it is taken back again. There are such a lot of Quantums that we can feel sure that one at least will turn up in the right place — by chance, not by cause.

The only difficulty about the Quantum Theory has been that to make the atomic "orbits" operate properly, and to put the Quantum *into two places at once,* it is necessary to have "more dimensions" in space. If they are not in one, they are in another. You ask next door. What this means I have no idea.

Nor does it tell us any ultimate truth about the real nature of things to keep on making equations about them. Suppose I wish to take a holiday trip and am selecting a place to go. I ask, "How far is it? How long does it take to get there? What does it cost?" These things all come into it. If I like I can call them "dimensions". It does no harm. If I like I can add other dimensions — how hot it is, how much gold it has, and what sort of women. I can say, if I wish, that the women are therefore found out to be the seventh dimension of locality. But I doubt if I can find anything sillier to say than the physicists' talk of ten and twelve dimensions added to space.

Let it be realized, I say, that making equations and functions about a thing does not tell us anything about its real nature. Suppose that I sometimes wonder just what sort of man Chipman, my fellow club member, is. While I am wondering, another fellow member, a mathematician, comes in. "Wondering about Chipman, were you?" he says. "Well, I can tell you all about him as I have computed his dimensions. I have here the statistics of the number of times he comes (t), the number of steps he takes before he sits down (s), his orbit in moving round (o), aberrations as affected by other bodies (ab), velocity (v), specific gravity (sp), and his saturation (S)." He is therefore a function of these things, or shall we say quite simply:

$$F \int \frac{s.v.o.sp.S}{t.ab}$$

Now this would be mathematically useful. With it I can calculate the likelihood of my friend's being at the Club at any particular time, and whether available for billiards. In other words, I've got him in what is called a "frame" in space-time. But just as all this tells me nothing of ultimate reality, neither do the super-dimensions of the new physics.

People who know nothing about the subject, or just less than I do, will tell you that science and philosophy and theology have nowadays all come together. So they have, in a sense. But the statement, like those above, is just a "statistical" one. They have come together as three people may come together in a picture theatre, or three people happen to take apartments in the same building, or, to apply the simile that really fits, as three people come together at a funeral. The funeral is that of Dead Certainty. The interment is over, and the three turn away together.

"Incomprehensible," murmurs Theology reverently.

"What was that word?" asks Science.

"Incomprehensible; I often use it in my litanies."

"Ah, yes," murmurs Science, with almost equal reverence, "incomprehensible!"

"The comprehensibility of comprehension," begins Philosophy, staring straight in front of him.

"Poor fellow," says Theology, "he's wandering again; better lead him home."

"I haven't the least idea where he lives," says Science.

"Just below me," says Theology. "We're both above you."

22

THREE SCORE AND TEN
The Business of Growing Old

Old age is the "Front Line" of life, moving into No Man's Land. No Man's Land is covered with mist. Beyond it is Eternity. As we have moved forward, the tumult that now lies behind us has died down. The sounds grow less and less. It is almost silence. There is an increasing feeling of isolation, of being alone. We seem so far apart. Here and there one falls, silently, and lies a little bundle on the ground that the rolling mist is burying. Can we not keep nearer? It's hard to see one another. Can you hear me? Call to me. I am alone. This must be near the end.

I have been asked how old age feels, how it feels to have passed seventy, and I answer in metaphor, as above, "not so good."

Now let us turn it round and try to laugh it off in prose. It can't be so bad as that, eh, what? Didn't Cicero write a book on old age to make it all right? But you say he was only just past sixty when he wrote it, was he? That's a tough one. Well, what about Rabbi ben Ezra, you remember — "Grow old along with me." Oh, he was eighty-one, eh? No, thanks, I'll stay right here around seventy. He can have all his fun for himself at eighty-one.

I was born in Swanmoor, a suburb of Ryde in the Isle of Wight, on December 30, 1869. That was in Victorian England at its most Victorian, far away now, dated by the French Empire, still glittering, and Mr. Dickens writing his latest book on the edge of the grave while I thought out my first on the edge of my cradle and, in America, dated by people driving golden spikes on Pacific railroads.

It was a vast, illimitable world, far superior to this — whole continents unknown, Africa just an outline, oceans never sailed, ships lost over the horizon — as large and open as life itself.

Put beside such a world this present shrunken earth, its every corner known, its old-time mystery gone with the magic of the sea, to make place for this new demoniac confine, loud with voices out of emptiness and tense with the universal threat of death. This is not mystery but horror. The waves of the magic sea called out in the sunlight: "There must be a God." The demoniac radio answers in the dark: "There can't be." Belief was so easy then; it has grown so hard now; and life, the individual life, that for an awakening child was so boundless, has it drawn into this — this alley-way between tall cypresses that must join somewhere in the mist? But stop, we are getting near No Man's Land again. Turn back.

Moving pictures love to give us nowadays "cavalcades" of events, to mark the flight of time. Each of us carries his own. Mine shows, as its opening, the sea beaches of the Isle of Wight. ... Then turn on Porchester village and its Roman castle.... Queen Victoria going past in a train, in the dark, putting her head out of the window (her eight heads out of eight windows).... Now shift to an Atlantic sailing steamer (type of 1876) with people emigrating to Canada.... Then a Canadian farm in a lost corner of Ontario up near Lake Simcoe for six years.... Put in bears, though there weren't any ... boarding-school, scenes at Upper Canada College — the real old rough stuff ... University, cap and gown days, old style; put a long beard on the president; show fourteen boarding-houses at $4.50 a week.... School teaching — ten years — (run it fast — I want to forget it)....

Then make the film Chicago University with its saloons of forty years ago, a raw place, nowhere to smoke.... And then settle the film down to McGill University, and run it round and round as slowly as you like for thirty-six sessions — college calling in the Autumn, students and co-eds and Rah! Rah! all starting afresh, year after year.... College in the snow, the February classroom; hush! don't wake them, it's a lecture in archaeology.... All of it again and again.... College years, one after the other.... Throw in, as interludes, journeys to England, a lecture trip around the Empire.... Put in Colombo, Ceylon, for atmosphere.... Then more college years....

Then loud music and the Great War with the college campus all at drill, the boys of yesterday turned to men.... Then the war over, lecture trips to the U.S.... Pictures of Iowa State University.... Ladies' Fortnightly Club — about forty of them.... Then back to the McGill campus.... Retirement.... An honorary degree ("this venerable scholar").... And then unexpectedly the war again and the Black Watch back on the McGill campus.

Such is my picture, the cavalcade all the way down from the clouds of the morning to the mists of the evening.

As the cavalcade passes down the years it is odd how gradually and imperceptibly the change of outlook comes, from the eyes of wonder to those of disillusionment — or is it to those of truth? A child's world is full of celebrated people, wonderful people like the giants and magicians of the picture books. Later in life the celebrated people are all gone. There aren't any — or not made of what it once meant.

I recall from over half a century ago a prize-day speaker at Upper Canada College telling us that he saw before him the future statesmen, the poets, the generals and the leaders of the nation. I thought the man a nut to say that. What he saw was just us. Yet he turned out to be correct; only in a sense he wasn't; it was still only us after all. It is the atmosphere of illusion that cannot last.

Yet some people, I know, are luckier in this than I am. They're born in a world of glamour and live in it. For them there are great people everywhere, and the illusion seems to feed itself. One such I recall out of the years, with a capacity for admiration all his own.

"I sat next to Professor Buchan at the dinner last night," he once told me. "He certainly is a great scholar, a marvellous philologian!"

"Is he?" I said.

"Yes," my friend continued. "I asked him if he thought the Indian word *snabe* was the same as the German ward *knabe*."

"And what did he say?"

"He said he didn't know."

And with that my friend sat back in quiet appreciation of such accurate scholarship and of the privilege of being near it. There are many people like that, decent fellows to be with. Their illusions keep their life warm.

But for most of us they fade out, and life itself as we begin to look back on it appears less and less. Has it all faded to this? There comes to me the story of an old Carolina Negro who found himself, after years of expectancy, privileged to cast a vote. After putting the ballot paper in the box he stood, still expectant, waiting for what was to happen, to come next. And then, in disillusionment: "Is that all there is, boss? Is that all there is to it?"

"That's all," said the presiding officer.

So it is with life. The child says "when I am a big boy" — but what is that? The boy says "when I grow up" — and then, grown up, "when I get married." But to be married, once done and over, what is that again? The man says "when I can retire" — and then when retirement comes he looks back over the path traversed, a cold wind sweeps over the fading landscape and he feels somehow that he has missed it all. For the reality of life, we learn too late, is in the living tissue of it from day to day, not in the expectation of better, nor in the fear of worse. Those two things, to be always looking ahead and to worry over things that haven't yet happened and very likely won't happen — those take the very essence out of life.

If one could only live each moment to the full, in a present, intense with its own absorption, even if as transitory and evanescent as Einstein's "here" and "now." It is strange how we cry out in our collective human mind against this restless thinking and clamour for time to stand still — longing for a land where it is always afternoon, or for a book of verses underneath a bough where we may let the world pass.

But perhaps it is this worry, this restlessness, that keeps us in our necessary path of effort and endeavour. Most of us who look back from old age have at least a comfortable feeling that we have "got away with it." At least we kept out of jail, out of the asylum and out of the poor house. Yet one still needs to be careful. Even "grand old men" get fooled sometimes. But at my rate we don't want to start over; no, thank you, it's too hard. When I look back at long evenings of study in boarding-house bedrooms, night after night, one's head sinking at times over the dictionary — I wonder how I did it.

And school days — at Upper Canada College anno Domini 1882 — could I stand that now? If some one asked me to eat "supper" at six and then go and study next day's lessons, in silence in the long study from seven to nine-thirty — how would that be? A school waiter brought round glasses of water on a tray at half-past eight, and if I asked for a whisky and soda could I have had it? I could not. Yet I admit there was the fun of putting a bent pin — you know how, two turns in it — on the seat where the study master sat. And if I were to try that now at convocation they wouldn't understand it. Youth is youth, and age is age.

So many things, I say, that one went through seem hopelessly difficult now. Yet other things, over which youth boggles and hesitates and palpitates, seem so easy and so simple to old age. Take the case of women, I mean girls. Young men in love go snooping around, hoping, fearing, wondering, lifted up at a word, cast down by an eyebrow. But if he only knew enough, any young man — as old men see it — could have any girl he wanted. All he need do is to step up to her and say, "Miss Smith, I don't know you, but your overwhelming beauty forces me to speak; can you marry me at, say, three-thirty this afternoon?"

I mean that kind of thing in that province of life would save years of trepidation. It's just as well, though, that they don't know it or away goes all the pretty world of feathers and flounces, of flowers and dances that love throws like a gossamer tissue across the path of life.

On such a world of youth, old age can only gaze with admiration. As people grow old all youth looks beautiful to them. The plainest girls are pretty with nature's charms. The dullest duds are at least young. But age cannot share it. Age must sit alone.

The very respect that young people feel for the old — or at least for the established, the respectable, by reason of those illusions of which I spoke — makes social unity impossible. An old man may think himself a "hell of a feller" inside, but his outside won't justify it. He must keep to his corner or go "ga-ga," despised of youth and age alike....

In any case, to put it mildly, old men are tiresome company. They can't listen. I notice this around my club. We founded it thirty years ago and the survivors are all there, thirty years older than they were thirty years ago, and some even more, much more. Can they listen? No, not even to me. And when they start to tell a story they ramble on and on, and you know the story anyway because it's the one you told them yesterday. Young people when they talk have to be snappy and must butt in and out of conversation as they get a chance. But once old men are given rope, you have to pay it out to them like a cable. To my mind the only tolerable old men are the ones — you notice lots of them when you look for them — who have had a stroke — not a tragic one;

that would sound cruel — but just one good flap of warning. If I want to tell a story, I look round for one of these.

The path through life I have outlined from youth to age, you may trace for yourself by the varying way in which strangers address you. You begin as "little man" and then "little boy," because a little man is littler than a little boy; then "sonny" and then "my boy" and after that "young man" and presently the interlocutor is younger than yourself and says, "Say, mister." I can still recall the thrill of pride I felt when a Pullman porter first called me "doctor" and when another one raised me up to "judge," and the terrible shock it was when a taxi man swung open his door and said, "Step right in, dad."

It was hard to bear when a newspaper reporter spoke of me as the "old gentleman," and said I was very simply dressed. He was a liar; those were my best things. It was a worse shock when a newspaper first called me a septuagenarian, another cowardly lie, as I was only sixty-nine and seven-twelfths. Presently I shall be introduced as "this venerable old gentleman" and the axe will fall when they raise me to the degree of "grand old man." That means on our continent any one with snow-white hair who has kept out of jail till eighty. That's the last and worst they can do to you.

Yet there is something to be said even here for the mentality of age. Old people grow kinder in their judgment of others. They are able to comprehend, even if not to pardon, the sins and faults of others. If I hear of a man robbing a cash register of the shop where he works, I think I get the idea. He wanted the cash. If I read of a man burning down his store to get the insurance, I see that what he wanted was the insurance. He had nothing against the store. Yet somehow just when I am reflecting on my own kindliness I find myself getting furious with a waiter for forgetting the Worcester sauce.

This is the summary of the matter that as for old age there's nothing to it, for the individual looked at by himself. It can only be reconciled with our view of life insofar as it has something to pass on, the new life of children and of grandchildren, or if not that, at least some recollection of good deeds, or of something done that may give one the hope to say, *non omnis moriar* (I shall not altogether die).

Give me my stick. I'm going out on to No Man's Land. I'll face it.

23

WAR-TIME SANTA CLAUS

I once asked a Christmas Eve group of children if they believed in Santa Claus. The very smallest ones answered without hesitation, "Why, of course!" The older ones shook their heads. The little girls smiled sadly but said nothing. One future scientist asserted boldly, "I know who it is"; and a little make-strong with his eye on gain said: "I believe in it all; I can believe anything." That boy, I realized, would one day be a bishop.

Thus does the bright illusion of Santa Claus fade away. The strange thing is that it could ever exist. It shows how different from ours are children's minds, as yet unformed and nebulous and all unbounded, still bright with the glory of the infinite. As yet physical science, calling itself the truth, has not overclouded them. There is no reason for them why a bean should not grow into a beanstalk that reaches the sky in one night; no reason why a dog should not have eyes as big as the round tower of Copenhagen; no reason why a white cat should not, at one brave stroke of a sword, turn into a princess. Are not all these things known by children to be in books, read aloud to them in the firelight just when their heads begin to nod toward bed-time and the land of dreams more wonderful still?

We have to realize that the child's world is without economic purpose. A child doesn't understand — happy ignorance — that people are paid to do things. To a child the policeman rules the street for self-important majesty; the furnace man stokes the furnace because he loves the noise of falling coal and the fun of getting dirty; the grocer is held to his counter by the lure of aromatic spices and the joy of giving. And in this very ignorance there is a grain of truth. The child's economic world may be the one that we are reaching out in vain to find. Here is a bypath in the wood of economics that some day might be followed to new discovery. Meantime, the children know it well and gather beside it their flowers of beautiful illusion.

This Land of Enchantment of the child — with its Santa Claus and its Magic Grocer — breaks and dissolves slowly. But it has to break. There comes a time when children suspect, and then when they know, that Santa Claus is Father. Worse still, there comes a time when they get to know that Father, so to speak, is not Santa Claus — no longer the all-wonderful, all-powerful being that drew them in a little sleigh, and knew everything, and told them about it. Father seems different when children realize that the geography-class teacher knows more than he does, and that Father sometimes drinks a little too much, and quarrels with Mother. Pity we can't keep their world of illusion a little longer from shattering. It's not Santa Claus only that fades out. It's ourselves.

Then at last there comes to children the bitter fruit from the tree of economic knowledge. This shows them that the furnace man works for money, and that the postman doesn't carry letters just for the fun of giving them in at the door. If it were not that new ideas and interests come to children even in this dilapidation, their disillusionment might pass into an old age, broken-hearted for ever at its farewell to giants and fairies. One thinks of the overwise child of Gilbert's Bab Ballads: "Too precocious to thrive, he could not keep alive, and died an enfeebled old dotard at five."

Yet even after disillusionment, belief lingers. Belief is a survival instinct. We have to have it. Children growing older, and their mothers growing younger by living with them, cling to Santa Claus. If he is really not so, he has to be brought back again as a symbol, along with the Garden of Eden and Noah's Ark. No longer possible as a ruddy and rubicund old man with a snow-white corona of whiskers, he lives again as a sort of spirit of kindliness that rules the world, or at least once a year breaks into any house to show it what it might be.

But does he? Is there such a spirit in our world? Can we believe in Santa Claus?

All through life we carry this wondering question, these tattered beliefs, these fading visions seen through a crystal that grows dim. Yet, strangely enough, often at their dimmest, some passing breath of emergency, of life or death and sacrifice of self, clears the glass of the crystal and the vision is all there again. Thus does life present to all of us its alternations of faith and doubt, optimism and pessimism, belief and negation.

Is the world a good place or a bad? An accident or a purpose? Down through the ages in all our literatures echoes the cry of denunciation against the world. *Sunt lachrymae rerum*, mourned the Roman poet — the world is full of weeping; and Shakespeare added, "All our yesterdays have lighted fools the way to dusty death." Yet the greatest denunciation is not in the voice of those who cry most loudly. Strutting Hamlet in his velvet suit calls out, "The time is out of joint," and egotism echoes it on. But far more poignant is the impotent despair of those whose life has wearied to its end, disillusioned, and who die turning their faces to the wall, still silent.

Is that the whole truth of it? Can life really be like that? With no Santa Claus in it, no element of mystery and wonder, no righteousness to it? It can't be. I remember a perplexed curate of the Church of England telling me that he felt that "after all, there must be a kind of something." That's just exactly how I feel about it. There must be something to believe in, life must have its Santa Claus.

What's more, we never needed Santa Claus so badly as we do at this present Christmas. I'm going to hang up my stocking anyway. Put yours there beside it. And I am going to write down the things I want Santa Claus to bring, and pin it up beside the stocking. So are you? Well, you wait till I've written mine first! Can't you learn to be unselfish at Christmas time?

So, first I'll tell Santa Claus that I don't want any new presents, only just to have back some of the old ones that are broken — well, yes, perhaps I broke them myself. Give me back, will you, that pretty little framed certificate called Belief in Humanity; you remember — you gave them to ever so many of us as children to hang up beside our beds. Later on I took mine out to look what was on the back of it, and I couldn't get it back in the frame and lost it.

Well, I'd like that and — oh, can I have a new League of Nations? You know, all set up on a rack that opens in and out. I broke the old one because I didn't know how to work it, but I'd like to try again. And may I have a brand new Magna Carta, and a Declaration of Independence and a Rights of Man and a Sermon on the Mount? And I'd like, if you don't mind, though of course it's more in the way of a toy, a little Jack-in-the-Box, one with a little Adolf Hitler in it. No, honestly, I wouldn't hurt him; I'd just hook the lid and keep him for a curiosity. I can't have it? Never mind.

Here, listen, this is what I want, Santa Claus, and here I'm speaking for all of us, millions and millions of us.

Bring us back the World We Had, and didn't value at its worth — the Universal Peace, the Good Will Towards Men — all that we had and couldn't use and broke and threw away.

Give us that. This time we'll really try.

24

TO EVERY CHILD

Misery breeds war.

You can never have international peace as long as you have national poverty.

You may multiply the pomp of the parade grand as you will, but if behind it is the festering slum, war will come as certain as the spread of pestilence.

What I mean in a plain way is that we must enter on a vast, titanic struggle against poverty and want. What we United Nations did in war we must do in peace, the same union of hearts, the same purpose for all.

This must be the work of the Spirit, not of line and rule and document.

Each of us must stand appalled at the further existence, after the war of misery and poverty, of lives frustrated by want, of children underfed, of people sunk from their birth below a chance to live. We must decide that that must not be, just as we decided that savage conquest and brutality should not be.

To effect this we must unlearn our economics, scrap the whole of it. I have, personally, fifty years of it to throw away!

The fault with economics was the assumption that what *can only be done by the Spirit* could be done by material interest.... Business had done much for mankind; but society won't hold together on a business basis alone.... Nor on any basis which excludes the animating Spirit of the common man.

There is no fear that the world will not easily support us all. A family may be crowded, but a nation never. The old Malthusian doctrine of overpopulation as preventing social happiness, of the poor dying as the buffer to save the rich, is all gone. Did it ever convince any one?

Even Malthus married and was a father.

Especially with the children lies our chief chance. Older people are battered out of shape, or were never battered into it. Faces all wrinkled and furrowed with care cannot be altered now. But to every child we must give the chance to live, to learn, to love.

Nor does social regeneration mean the obliteration of individual life. The roots lie too deep. There are limits to the amalgamation of society to the common employment of everything by everybody. One's own is one's own. Many of us would rather have a house all our own in the bush than share a palace with a prince — especially with some of them.

We can have a League of Nations if we like. If we do it will be a consequence, not a cause. Thus will come International Harmony — by not looking for it. So it is with life. Try to buy happiness, by the quart or by the yard, and you never find it. Motion it away from you while you turn to Duty and you will find it waiting beside your chair. So with Good Will on Earth. Cannons frighten it. Treaties fetter it. *The Spirit brings it.*

ENDNOTES

1   "How Soon Can We Start the Next War?" *Here Are My Lectures and Stories* (New York: Dodd, Mead, 1937), 25–6.

2   Department of Culture and Heritage, Leacock Museum, National Historic Site, Orillia, (SLM), Leacock Collection, Leacock to W.T. Conder, 11 January 1936 [draft]; Leacock to Hugh Eayrs, 2 January 1931.

3   John H. Thompson with Allen Seager, *Canada 1922–1939: Decades of Discord* (Toronto: McClelland and Stewart, 1985), 221; Michiel Horn, *The Great Depression of the 1930s in Canada* (Canadian Historical Association Booklet No. 39, 1984), 3.

4   McGill University Archives, Presidents' Papers, RG2 Box 60, file 957, Currie to Leacock, 17 May 1930.

5   Clipping files in SLM contain reviews of his later books. The best source on the sales of each book, and a wealth of general information, is Carl Spadoni, *A Bibliography of Stephen Leacock* (Toronto: ECW Press, 1998).

6   SLM, Leacock to Frank Dodd, 2 January 1937. See Alan Bowker, "Stephen Leacock's Discovery of the West," *Zeitschrift für Kanada-Studien*, 2002, 22, Jahrgang Nr. 1-2, Band 41, 43–59.

7   Carl Spadoni, "The Book that Booze Bought," *Papers of the Bibliographical Society of Canada* 26 (1987), 88–105.

8   An excellent discussion of the "faces" of Leacock, and one of the best critical studies of Leacock or any other writer, which has perceptive comments on his serious "voices" is Donald Cameron, *Faces of Leacock* (Toronto: Ryerson Press, 1967), especially 68–76.

9   SLM, Leacock to Conder, 11 January 1936.

10 Carl Spadoni, "Introduction," Stephen Leacock, *Sunshine Sketches of a Little Town* (Peterborough: Broadview, 2002), xxvi–xxvii.

11 A number of these pieces have been collected in Alan Bowker, ed., *Stephen Leacock Social Criticism* (Toronto: University of Toronto Press,

1996). See also Ian Ross Robertson, "The Historical Leacock" in D. Staines, ed, *Stephen Leacock: A Reappraisal* (Ottawa, 1986), 42–47. The *University Magazine* had a remarkable circulation of 6,000 in a Canada of 6 million people with a small educated class — a figure no comparable Canadian quarterly has subsequently matched.

12 SLM, Macphail to Leacock, 29 May 1935, regarding *Humour: Its Theory and Technique.*

13 Robertson Davies, *Stephen Leacock* (Toronto, 1970), 47.

14 See Cameron, 37, 172; Peter MacArthur, "An Appreciation" in *Stephen Leacock* (Toronto: Ryerson Press, 1923), 127–134; Davies, *Leacock*, 47. See also Elizabeth Kimball, *The Man in the Panama Hat: Reminiscences of My Uncle, Stephen Leacock* (Toronto: McClelland and Stewart, 1970),110–18; James Doyle, *Stephen Leacock: The Sage of Orillia* (Toronto: ECW Press, 1992), 59.

15 Davies, *Leacock*, 8.

16 Elsie Tolson, *The captain, the Colonel and Me (Bedford, N.S. since 1503)* (Sackville, N.B.: Tribune Press, 1979), 210–214. In 1888 Peter Leacock's father died and left Peter the income from one-quarter of his considerable estate. SLM, Leacock to C. W. Vincent, 2 August 1941, 7 July 1941, June 1941; Leacock to the Bank of Canada 11 April 1942.

17 An undated clipping from a Winnipeg paper during Leacock's western tour in National Archives of Canada (NAC), Leacock Collection, Nimmo Collection, recalls E.P. and "Jimmy."

18 Wendy Owen, "Cashing in on the Boom: Stephen Leacock's Remark-able Uncle Made and Lost His Fortune On the Canadian Frontier," *The Beaver*, 66:6, (December 1986/January 1987), 5–11; Allan Anderson, *Remembering Leacock: An Oral History* (Ottawa: Deneau, 1983),15–16; SLM, 14 September 1943, H. Shave to Leacock (copy) — in 1943 the house was a school run by the St. Agnes Priory. On the Hudson's Bay Railway see pamphlet, *Hudson's Bay Route Interesting and Instructive Lecture by E. P. Leacock, Esq., M.P.P* (1884); Doug Owram, *Promise of Eden: The Canadian Expansionist Movement and the Ideas of the West* (Toronto: University of Toronto Press, 1980),180–191; and Gerald Friesen, *The Canadian Prairies: A*

History (Toronto: University of Toronto Press, 1987), 206 ff.

19 NAC, J.W. Dafoe Fonds, vol 2, E.P. Leacock to Dafoe, 19 June 1926.

20 Ralph Curry, *Stephen Leacock: Humorist and Humanist* (Garden City: Doubleday, 1959), 36. See also Kimball,100–148.

21 Carl Berger, *The Sense of Power: Studies in the Ideas of Canadian Imperialism, 1867–1914* (Toronto: University of Toronto Press, 1970), 639, says that when Leacock was asked whether George Parkin, the Principal of Upper Canada College, had any friends "below the rank of Viscount" he replied, "Plenty — back on the farm."

22 *Hellements of Hickonomics in Hiccoughs of Verse done in our Social Planning Mill* (New York: Dodd, Mead, 1936), 82.

23 *Hellements*, 81; see also several essays in *Too Much College or Education Eating Up Life With Kindred Essays in Education and Humour* (New York: Dodd, Mead, 1939).

24 "My Recollection of Chicago," in Carl Spadoni, ed., Stephen Leacock, *My Recollection of Chicago and The Doctrine of Laissez Faire* (Toronto: University of Toronto Press, 1998), 3–6.

25 McGill University Archives, Presidents' Papers, Peterson Fonds, RG2, box 15, file 9, Sir George Parkin to Principal Peterson, 19 January 1900.

26 "My Recollections of Chicago," 3.

27 *Humour and Humanity: An Introduction to the Study of Humour* (London: Thomas Butterworth, 1937), 232. Davies says that humour was "the only subject on which he was ever pompous or silly." ("Stephen Leacock," in Claude Bissell, ed. *Our Living Tradition, First Series* [Toronto: University of Toronto Press, 1957), 140.]" Silver Donald Cameron treats Leacock's theories at greater length and with more sympathy, but he also believes that "Leacock's weaknesses as a writer are more salient in his discussions of humour than anywhere else."(*Faces*, 54). The only critic who considers Leacock's ideas in depth and favourably is Gerald Lynch in *Stephen Leacock: Humour and Humanity* (Kingston and Montreal: McGill-Queen's University Press, 1988), 24–56, who argues that "Humanism served for Leacock's religion and humour was indeed its literary manifestation, its spirit made word."(56).

28 *Humour and Humanity*, 233.

29 McArthur, 161–2.

30 *Humour: Its Theory and Technique* (New York: Dodd. Mead, 1935), 237.

31 Harry Graham (1874–1936), forgotten now, caused a furore in 1899 with his *Ruthless Rhymes for Heartless Homes*. Some examples of his humour: "Billy, in one of his nice new sashes,/fell in the fire and was burned to ashes;/Now, although the nights grow chilly,/I haven't the heart to poke poor Billy." Or: "Making toast at the fireside,/Nurse fell in the grate and died;/And, what makes it ten times worse,/All the toast was burned with nurse." Etc.

32 *Humour and Humanity*, 233. See Steven Pinker, *How the Mind Works* (New York: Norton, 1997), 545–554. Pinker situates the discussion of humour between art and religion: compare with *Humour and Humanity*, 20–31.

33 *Humour and Humanity*, 9.

34 "Imaginary Persons," *Funny Pieces: A Book Of Random Sketches* (New York: Dodd, Mead, 1936), 91–3.

35 *The Unsolved Riddle of Social Justice*, in Bowker, ed., *Social Criticism*, 76.

36 Thorstein Veblen (1857–1929) became famous with the publication in 1899 of the *Theory of the Leisure Class*, which applied a type of Darwinism to the study of modern economic life. The industrial system regimented and disciplined ordinary people but those who controlled it were concerned with making money and displaying it in "conspicuous consumption" — the more useless the goods or lavish the display the more appropriate as a symbol of their power. Veblen greatly influenced contemporary economists and subsequent social thinkers in America. Leacock's analysis of the growth of the industrial system in *Unsolved Riddle* owes a debt to him, as does his picture of the greedy plutocrats in *Arcadian Adventures*. In his only published discussion of Veblen, Leacock suggests that Veblen was very like himself in being better able to analyze problems than propose solutions: "What did Veblen propose to do about it? Nothing, so far as I remember."(*My Discovery of the West* [Toronto: Thomas Allen, 1937] , 137).

37 "Democracy and Social Progress," in J.O. Miller, ed., *The New*

Era in Canada: Essays Dealing with the Upbuilding of the Canadian Commonwealth (London: J.M. Dent, 1917), 17.

38 "The Woman Question," in Bowker, ed, *Social Criticism*, 57.

39 *Unsolved Riddle* in Bowker, ed., *Social Criticism*, 75, 140.

40 "Democracy and Social Progress," 31–2. Leacock's social criticism before 1920 is discussed in detail in Alan Bowker, "An Introduction" and "Postscript" to *Stephen Leacock: Social Criticism*.

41 "The Economic Analysis of Industrial Depression," *Papers and Proceedings of the Canadian Political Science Association*, V (May 1933), 23

42 A.B. McKillop, *Matters of Mind: The University in Ontario, 1791–1955* (Toronto: University of Toronto Press, 1994), 513.

43 *My Discovery of the West*, 35–6.

44 *Ibid.*, 135.

45 "The Anatomy of Gloom: An Appeal to Bankers," *Model Memoirs*, 211.

46 Wilbur, J.R.H., "R. B. Bennett as a Reformer," *Canadian Historical Association Annual Report*, 1970, 103–41; Alvin Finkel, "Canadian Business and the 'Reform' Process in the 1930's," PhD thesis, University of Toronto, 1976; Larry A. Glassford, *Reaction and Reform: The Politics of the Conservative Party under R.B. Bennett, 1927–1938* (Toronto: University of Toronto Press, 1992). See Robert MacIntosh, *Different Drummers: Banking and Politics in Canada* (Toronto: Macmillan, 1991), 65–101, on the bankers' reaction to events and Social Credit, and Leacock's trip to the west.

47 Spadoni, *Bibliography*, 237.

48 Spadoni, *Bibliography*, 267, 296.

49 Donald Forster and Colin Read, "The Politics of Opportunism: The New Deal Broadcasts," *Canadian Historical Review*, LX, 3, 1979 324–349, especially 336. Leacock wrote the preface to the printed version of Bennett's first speech; see *The Premier Speaks to the People: The Prime Minister's January Radio Broadcasts issued in book form: The First Address Delivered from Ottawa on Wednesday, January 2nd, 1936 between 9:00 and 9:30.* (Ottawa: The Dominion Conservative Headquarters, 1935).

50 *Hellements*, vi.

51 "Rebuilding the Cities," *Last Leaves* (Toronto: McClelland and Stewart, 1945), 86.

52 His assistant and chosen successor, Dr. Hemmeon, was a social-ist. Though he deplored some of the utterances of a young colleague, Eugene Forsey, Leacock defended his right to say what he thought as long as he did not do so in the classroom. See McGill University Archives, Presidents' Papers, RG2, Box 42, file 302, Leacock to Currie, 13 May 1933. See Michiel Horn, *Academic Freedom in Canada: A History* (Toronto: University of Toronto Press, 1999), 128–144; Vishnu R.K. Chopra, "Stephen Leacock: An Edition of Selected Letters," PhD thesis, McGill, 1975, 32–35, 159–175; SLM, 1935 correspondence between Sir Edward Beatty and Leacock.

53 David Lewis, *The Good Fight: Political Memoirs, 1909–1958* (Toronto: Macmillan, 1981), 24.

54 F.H. Underhill, "The Importance of Being Earnest," *Canadian Forum*, XIV (November 1932), 74. See Michiel Horn, *The League for Social Reconstruction: The Intellectual Origins of the Democratic Left in Canada, 1930–1942* (Toronto: University of Toronto Press, 1980), esp. 3–35.

55 Underhill, "The Conception of a National Interest," *CJEPS*, I, 406–7.

56 Doug Owram, *The Government Generation: Canadian Intellectuals and the State, 1900–1945* (Toronto: University of Toronto Press, 1986), 135–317, and J.L. Granatstein, *The Ottawa Men: The Civil Service Mandarins, 1935–1957* (Toronto: Oxford University Press, 1982), 1–133.

57 The only recent discussion of Leacock's economic thinking is Myron Frankman, "Stephen Leacock, Economist: An Owl Among the Parrots," in Staines, ed., *Stephen Leacock: A Reappraisal*, 51–58. Judgements of contemporaries include: Harold Innis, "Stephen Butler Leacock," *CJEPS*, X, 216–30; Eugene Forsey, *A Life on the Fringe: The Memoirs of Eugene Forsey* (Toronto: Oxford University Press, 1990), 21–33. Later assessments include Carl Berger, *Honour and the Search for Influence: A History of the Royal Society of Canada* (Toronto: University of

Toronto Press, 1996), 73–4; A. B. McKillop, *Matters of Mind*, 512–520; Owram, *The Government Generation*, 192–220.

58 "Greater Canada: an appeal" (1907), in Bowker, ed., *Social Criticism*, 6–7.

59 "Sir Wilfrid Laurier's Victory," *National Review* (London), LII, 833.

60 *Canada: The Foundations of its Future* (Montreal, 1941), 246. See also *Economic Prosperity in the British Empire* (Toronto: privately published by the House of Seagrams, 1930), 118–28; 180–205, 246.

61 *Canada*, 250.

62 "The Revision of Democracy," *Papers and Proceedings of the Sixth Annual Meeting of the Canadian Political Science Association*, 6 (May 1934), 5–16.

63 *My Discovery of the West*, 239–241.

64 SLM, Leacock to Cudlipp (copy), 24 January 1937. See "Economic Separatism in the British Empire," *Quarterly Review* (London) #525 (July 1935).

65 *Economic Prosperity*, 196.

66 There is no evidence that Leacock supported any of the discriminatory measures against Asians once in Canada; he simply wanted them kept out. We must also assume that Leacock's views were not too repulsive to his readers or his publishers, including Bronfman, who wanted to ensure that Leacock did not say anything derogatory about immigrants in his history of Canada, but presumably had no objection to Leacock's characterizations of Native peoples or his views on oriental immigration. See Michael Marrus, *Mr. Sam: the Life and Times of Samuel Bronfman* (Toronto: Penguin, 1991), 304.

67 McGill University, Rare Books and Special Collections, Leacock Collection (QMMRB), Box 25, 12 April 1939, Leacock to Keddie.

68 Cameron, 2.

69 *My Discovery of the West*, 167.

70 "How Soon Can We Start the Next War?" *Here Are My Lectures*, 25.

71 "When Men Retire," *Too Much College*, 175.

72 David Staines in his "Afterword" to Stephen Leacock, *My Financial Career and Other Follies* (Toronto: McClelland and Stewart, 1993), quotes (202–3) from a letter from Leacock to his son in 1934 regarding religion: "Those who can believe these things are happy

in the comfort of them, and die happy in them [...] But those of us who cannot believe them must find our salvation elsewhere."

73 QMMRB, Box 25, Leacock to James Keddie, 28 September 1939, and [n.d.].

74 SLM, Leacock to "Dear Frank" (copy), 13 July 1941.

75 SLM, Leacock to Greenwood, 4 April 1940. The original draft of the final chapter also included bonds of union with France, which was presumably dropped when France fell. Several paragraphs on Canadian—U.S. history were lifted from "All Right, Mr. Roosevelt." See QMMRB, Box 6, file 12, MS for "Bonds of Union."

76 SLM, Leacock to Bardwell, 12 October 1941.

77 QMMRB, Box 25, Leacock to Keddie, 20 September 1939. SLM, Leacock to "Dear Frank," 13 July 1941: "I have worked all winter very hard, that is, as hard as one can at 71 and am getting into better health... but I can't travel any more and have to get to bed with the birds."

78 QMMRB, Box 26, Leacock to Cleveland Morgan, 27 January 1944. The "case against social catastrophe" was published posthumously as *While There is Time*. See also Box 29, file 9, Leacock to Morgan, 14 November 1943, 26 November 1943, [n.d.], 23 February 1944.

79 "'Buy and Buy and Buy', Says Leacock," Vancouver *News Herald*, 29 December 1936, clipping attached to "Report on the Trip of Dr. Stephen Leacock to Western Canada" by Cockfield, Brown, and Co. Ltd., 30 January 1937, Archives of the Canadian Bankers' Association, Toronto.

80 SLM, John Lane to Leacock, 18 June 1940.

81 SLM, Leacock to Bardwell (draft), 5 August 1941.

82 John Ralston Saul, *Memoirs of a Siamese Twin: Canada at the End of the Twentieth Century* (Toronto: Viking, 1997), 222.

83 *Hellements of Hickonomics in Hiccoughs of Verse done in our Social Planning Mill* (New York: Dodd, Mead, 1936).

84 "The Lake Simcoe Country," *Canadian Geographic Journal*, II (September 1935), 109–16.

85 *Adventurers of the Far North: A Chronicle of the Frozen Seas* (Toronto: Glasgow, Brook & Co., 1914), 2.

BIBLIOGRAPHICAL INFORMATION

"Life on the Old Farm" is Chapter 2 and "My Education and What I Think of It Now" is excerpted from Chapter 3 of Leacock's autobiography, written in 1943–4 and published posthumously as *The Boy I Left Behind Me* (Garden City: Doubleday, 1946).

"My Remarkable Uncle" was first published as "The Most Unforgettable Character I've Met," on *Reader's Digest*, 39, no 231 (July 1941), and in book form in *My Remarkable Uncle and Other Sketches* (New York: Dodd, Mead, 1942).

"The Struggle to Make Us Gentlemen" was first published in *Old Times*, a supplement to the Upper Canada *College Times*, in January 1941, and in book form in *My Remarkable Uncle*.

"Looking Back on College" was a lecture Leacock gave many times (with variations) during the 1930s. It was first published in McGill publications and magazine form in 1935. It was published in book form in *Funny Pieces: A Book of Random Sketches* (New York: Dodd, Mead, 1936).

"On the Need for a Quiet College" was first published under a different title in *Commentator* (February 1938), and in book form in *Model Memoirs and Other Sketches from Simple to Serious* (New York: Dodd, Mead, 1938).

"Andrew Macphail" was first published in *Queen's Quarterly* (1938–9), and in book form in the English edition of *The Boy I Left Behind Me* (London: The Bodley Head, 1947).

"How Much Does Language Change?" was first published in *Model Memoirs* (1938).

"From the Ridiculous to the Sublime" is Chapter XI of *Humour: Its Theory and Technique* (New York: Dodd, Mead, 1935).

"What Is Left of Adam Smith?"*Canadian Journal of Economics and Political Science*, I (February 1935).

"Through a Glass Darkly" was published in the *Atlantic Monthly* 158

(July 1936), and reprinted with additional matter in *Funny Pieces*. The *Atlantic Monthly* text is used here.

"So This Is Winnipeg" was first published as a newspaper article and then as Chapter III of *My Discovery of the West* (Toronto: Thomas Allen, 1937). "The Land of Dreams" was published for the first time as Chapter XV of the same book.

"I'll Stay in Canada" was first published in *London Evening News* (February 1936), and widely republished; then in book form in *Funny Pieces*.

"This International Stuff" was first published in *The Rotarian* (July 1936), and in book form in *Funny Pieces*.

"Canada and the Monarchy" was published in the *Atlantic Monthly* 163 (June 1939).

"Bonds of Union" is Chapter VII of *Our British Empire* (London: John Lane, 1940).

"Paradise Lost" is "Leacock's Retirement Speech" quoted in *Montreal Star*, 5 May 1936.

"Looking Back from Retirement" was first published in *Here Are My Lectures and Stories* (New York: Dodd, Mead, 1937).

"Bass Fishing on Lake Simcoe with Jake Gaudaur" was first published in *Too Much College: With Kindred Essays in Education and Humour* (New York: Dodd, Mead, 1939).

"Common Sense and the Universe" was first published in the *Atlantic Monthly* (May, 1942) and in book form in *Last Leaves* (Toronto: McClelland and Stewart, 1945).

"Three Score and Ten" was first published in *The Spectator* (January 1940), and in book form in *My Remarkable Uncle*.

"War-Time Santa Claus" was first published in *My Remarkable Uncle*.

"To Every Child," possibly published in 1944 by Pan American Airways, in book form in *Last Leaves*.